CONDUCTIVE EDUCATION

A System for Overcoming Motor Disorder

Edited by Philippa J. Cottam and Andrew Sutton

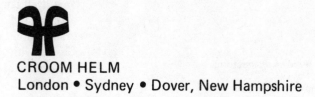

CROOM HELM
London • Sydney • Dover, New Hampshire

© 1986 Philippa J. Cottam and Andrew Sutton
Croom Helm Ltd, Provident House, Burrell Row,
Beckenham, Kent BR3 1AT

Croom Helm Australia Pty Ltd, Suite 4, 6th Floor,
64-76 Kippax Street, Surry Hills, NSW 2010, Australia

British Library Cataloguing in Publication Data

Conductive education: a system for overcoming
    motor disorder.
    1. Movement disorders—Patients—Rehabilitation
    I. Cottam, Philippa, J.   II. Sutton, Andrew
    616.7′06   RM735

    ISBN 0-7099-2290-6
    ISBN 0-7099-4201-X Pbk

Croom Helm, 51 Washington Street, Dover,
New Hampshire 03820, USA

Library of Congress Cataloging in Publication Data applied for:

ISBN 0-7099-2290-6
    0-7099-4201-X Pbk

Phototypeset by Words & Pictures Ltd,
Thornton Heath, Surrey
Printed and bound in Great Britain

CONTENTS

INTRODUCTION: A TIME TO DECIDE . . .

Once again conductive education is provoking excitement and interest in the English-speaking world. Just as in the late sixties and early seventies there is now widespread discussion, privately, professionally and in the news media. Inevitably – and most desirably – there is also controversy about the feasibility and effectiveness of this approach. Perhaps, now, however, there is also a more keenly felt need in our public services to be on the *qui vive* for new, effective (and cost-effective) means of providing for human welfare, along with a correspondingly sharper recognition that *all* provisions, new or old, have a duty to demonstrate that they do indeed deliver their promised benefits. Perhaps, too, further consideration of conductive education will be more fully informed of its nature and its implications.

For conductive education makes astonishing claims for what it can do to further the welfare of the motor-disordered. Developed in Hungary in the period following the Second World War, conductive education aims to establish 'orthofunction' in motor-disordered children and adults. Relevant conditions include cerebral palsy and spina bifida in children and Parkinson's disease and post-traumatic hemiplegia in adults. Conductive education is not a medical treatment and orthofunction implies no cure of the underlying condition, solely the ability to function in society without requiring special apparatus such as wheelchairs, ramps or other artificial aids. Conductive education is not a therapy but an education. Orthofunction is the product of teaching which, like all good teaching, involves the development of the whole personality, the emotional as well as the intellective. Orthofunction is reportedly achieved and maintained by around three-quarters of those who have received conductive education.

Initial enthusiasm for conductive education in Britain resulted in numerous attempts to emulate the achievements or at least the methods reported from Budapest, attempts which are continuing both in Britain and in several other countries across the world. This work is now sufficiently long established to have generated evaluative studies. Despite the enthusiasm and devotion of those attempting conductive education, these investigations have as yet been unable to document any benefit to those receiving this help of the dimensions reported from Budapest.

This book aims to provide interested parties, parents, patients, politicians and practitioners, with some basis to address this question and to come to their own conclusions. The first part of the book attempts a picture of conductive education on its home ground whilst the second offers an impression of the brave attempts outside of Hungary to emulate this approach. The third part is more speculative, touching on some of the puzzling questions that conductive education so often prompts, 'how does it work?', 'how should we approach it?', 'what should we do about it?'

The book has been written by members of the 'Birmingham Group' of researchers into conductive education who during 1980 and 1981 had been quite independently caught up by the renewed interest in conductive education in Britain. The efforts of this group united both practical experience of attempting conductive education in schools with theoretical research into possible bases of the approach. This, along with a rather different range of backgrounds and experience from those previously directed at this issue in the West, has led us along a somewhat different path from that followed by many in the conductive education movement outside of Hungary. From the common starting point of Ester Cotton's courses and the relatively small number of readily available written reports of Hungarian and English practice, we subjected our two programmes of practical work to critical evaluation and became very aware of two fundamental problems in the attempt to implement conductive education in Britain. Firstly, we just did not know how to do it: we had no real knowledge base sufficient to establish a viable educational practice. Secondly, even if we *had* known, we would have still been quite unable to inject what was a total educational system in its own right into already existing educational structures with their own altogether different goals, methods and organisation. Our quest for a knowledge base led us first in the direction of Soviet psychology but this proved rather a false trail. Petö's approach, despite remarkable contiguities with Vygotskian psychology and Makarenkoist pedagogy, does in fact seem original and indigenous both in its origins and its current practice. Nevertheless, this direction proved highly illuminative and confirmed our comparative approach, providing us with a novel perspective on the Hungarian work quite different from the western view – particularly apparent in the way in which we extended into the adult field and Parkinson's disease. At the same time we turned our attention increasingly to a practical solution of the organisational and institutional problems of establishing conductive education.

This book is one of the outcomes of our work over the last four years. All its authors have now made their pilgrimages to the Institute in Budapest and confirmed there the conclusion already suggested by our work in Britain. This is that the knowledge base of conductive education lies buried in the practice of the Institute and its conductors and that the only way to extract it would be with their active collaboration in setting up the same practice and investigating and evaluating how it works. We hope that this book provides enough background information on conductive education either to attract its readers to a similar conclusion or, at the very least, to ensure a more informed debate on possible alternative courses.

The book offers a state-of-the-art report on what we know about conductive education, valid at the end of 1984. Its bibliography provides as complete a record of what has been written on conductive education in English as we have been able to assemble by personal enquiries in Britain and abroad and through study in the Institute's own archives in Budapest, again valid up to the end of 1984. There can be no doubt, however, that both the book and its bibliography will be slipping out of date by the time of their publication, a matter for which we make no apology since it is a rare and exciting privilege to be involved in something in British education and psychology where knowledge goes out of date within a few months.

The year 1985, we feel, should see a watershed in the current interest in conductive education in Britain. We are approaching the limits of what can usefully be learned of conductive education in Hungary from outside – and there is already enough information about conductive education as practised in Britain and other western countries to urge fundamental reappraisal of the direction or directions that future work of this sort should take. Whatever the ultimate fate of conductive education outside Hungary, this book is the swan-song of the Birmingham Group. We consider that further work of the kind that we and many others have undertaken, has now served its purpose. The bold promise of conductive education, in a field that so desperately needs fresh initiatives and innovations, is such as to urge involvement of an altogether different order. It is to the establishment of that order that we dedicate this book.

P.C. and A.S.

ON WORDS, NAMES AND USAGES

In Hungarian the stress is always on the first syllable of words and the letter *s* is pronounced as English *sh*. Hence BOO′dapesht ['budapeʃt] for Budapest, AHN′drash ['andraʃ] for Andras. Petö is pronounced PEH′tuh ['petœ] almost rhyming with English better, and certainly *not* PEE-TOW, rhyming with veto, as is so often heard in this country. The surname Hári is already familiar to English ears in its correct punctuation; Mária is MAH′riuh [mariə] and not as in Spanish or Italian. Also generally familiar is the word *Magyar*. The letters *gy* in Hungarian are pronounced like the *d* in module and an unaccented *a* like our short *o*: *Magyar* [modʒəγnll] almost rhymes with dodger.

Hungarian names are stated surname first, the personal name following, thus Petö András and Hári Mária. Thus too the Petö András Intézet, i.e. the András Petö Institute.

Transliteration from Russian is according to British Standard BS2979-1958 (without diacritical marks) – thus, for example, Luriya – except in direct quotations from the other authors.

Though this book has tried to extend its consideration of non-Hungarian conductive education as widely as possible, it is still largely to the English-speaking world that it is addressed and inevitably we have viewed even this limited constituency through the prism of British education and experience. We ought therefore to explain briefly to our wider readership a couple of peculiarly British usages that have crept in. Firstly, in Britain the term 'physical handicap' (PH) refers both to orthopaedic and motor-control problems but not to sensory disorders. Secondly, the terms 'educationally subnormal (severe)' (ESN(S)) and educationally subnormal (moderate) (ESN(M)) were official and professional jargon between 1971 and 1983, referring to schools for the severely and moderately mentally retarded and, by extension, to the children attending them. Though none of those terms now has official currency, both remain in common use amongst educational, medical and welfare personnel.

LIST OF CONTRIBUTORS

Philippa Cottam Lecturer in Language Pathology and Therapeutics, Department of Linguistics, University of Sheffield, Sheffield S10 2TN.

Veronica Nanton Parkinson's Disease Society Research Fellow, University of Birmingham, PO Box 363, Birmingham B15 2TT

Andrew Sutton Honorary Research Fellow, Department of Psychology; Associate, Centre for Russian and East European Studies, University of Birmingham, PO Box 363, Birmingham B15 2TT.

Jayne Titchener Senior Lecturer, West Midlands College of Education, Walsall WS1 38D.

PART ONE:

DEVELOPMENTS IN HUNGARY

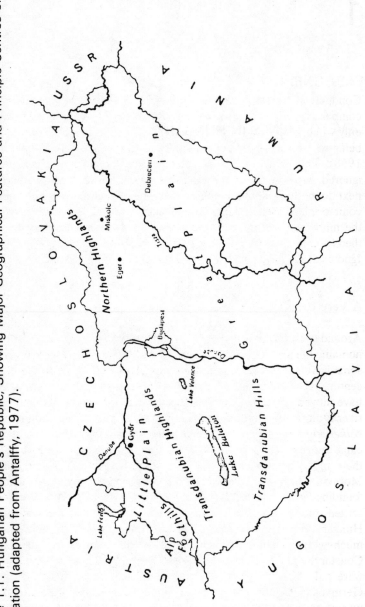

Figure 1.1: Hungarian People's Republic, Showing Major Geographical Features and Principle Centres of Population (adapted from Antalffy, 1977).

1 THE SOCIAL-HISTORICAL CONTEXT

Andrew Sutton

Conductive education is Hungarian. It is a basic principle of comparative education that an educational system is comprehensible only when related to the wider social context of which it is a part, this being so even when the education in question is 'special' (Goldberg, 1968). This principle is none the less valid for being so frequently ignored. Most people in the English-speaking world, however, know next to nothing about Hungary and the Hungarians, while their commonplace assumptions, if they have any at all, are often way off the mark. Any attempt to understand conductive education must, therefore, begin with an outline of its social-historical context (see Ignotus, 1972, for a far fuller and more satisfying account).

A Very Brief History of Hungary

Around two thousand years ago a group of tribal peoples was living a nomadic life in Asia, somewhere east of the Urals. They were not, as some have suggested, amongst Atilla's Huns and, when in the fifth century AD Attila was as far west as Orleans, these tribes appear to have moved no further towards Europe than the steppes around the river Don. In the ninth century, however, as part of the continuous *völkerwanderung* that marked the first millenium of our era, they came under powerful pressure to move further westwards and in 894 their mounted archers made their first authenticated raid into Moravia. They called themselves the 'Megyars' – perhaps after some founding father – or the 'Ten Arrows', the *On-ogur*. By 896 they had settled the then sparsely inhabited area which is present-day Hungary. Their impact upon Christendom was initially, however, much wider. Their horsemen raided as far south as the gates of Constantinople and westwards into Burgundy. Their depredations were only finally halted by a decisive defeat at the hands of the Germans in 955, by which time the nomadic horsemen were already turning to intensive stock-breeding and to agriculture. Christianity was also exerting an appeal and in 972 their duke opted to accept the Roman version rather than the Byzantine. At first only the ducal court

3

was affected, then, in the year 1000, the new Duke István (Stephen) received a royal crown from the Pope and the Kingdom of Hungary was born. Westernisation proceeded apace and the King's vigorous efforts in organising the church led ultimately to his canonisation. Over the next four centuries the medieval Kingdom of Hungary saw varying fortunes. It was geographically a considerable kingdom, reaching right to the Adriatic for much of this period, and at times part of extensive dynastic allegiances, but its varied peoples – not just Magyars but other Asians, and Slavs, Germans and Romance peoples too – did not yet begin the long process of assimilation that would only in our own century end in a nation state. In the thirteenth century the Mongols swept into the kingdom causing terrible devastation but withdrew almost at once (because of the death of their Khan, some say) and the Kingdom of Hungary survived: so, too, here and there within it, did the Magyar language. The next threat from the east, however, from the Ottoman Empire, proved less transitory. In 1528 the Ottomans defeated the Hungarians at the battle of Mohács and the King was slain. After a further generation of warfare the Kingdom of Hungary was no more, parcelled out between the Austrians, the Turks and the Prince of Transylvania. So things remained for a century and a half, during which time the area experienced both Reformation and Counter-Reformation. In 1687 the Austrians defeated the Turks at a second battle of Mohács, not to restore an independent kingdom but to incorporate a depopulated land into the Hapsburg domains.

The eighteenth century, following Prince Rákoczi's fruitless attempt to re-establish independence, saw a period of reconciliation and reconstruction. The law and constitution of the Hungarians was guaranteed, especially under Empress Maria Theresa, – the rights, that is, of the great landowners and the petty gentry who comprised about 5 per cent of the population. The process of Magyarising the diverse peoples of the great central plain began, binding the population of this area at least into a unified nation speaking a common language and attached to the same institutions. Despite occasional differences and upsets over this period, at its close the Magyar nobility and gentry stood by the Austrians through the revolutionary and Napoleonic periods.

The nineteenth century saw new forces for change, as a rising middle class pressed for language reform (Hungarian rather than Latin or German), social reform (the abolition of serfdom) and political reform. In 1848, the Year of Revolutions, under the leadership of Lajos Kossuth, Parliament abolished the feudal system and established a constitutional monarchy. The new Emperor, Franz-Joseph called the Tsar to his aid. The rebellion was crushed and a period of oppression followed till Austria's worsening international position forced a 'compromise' with the Hungarians, the *Ausgleich* of 1867, which established the dual monarchy of Austria-Hungary with Franz-Joseph as Emperor-King. Economic development now accelerated as capitalism brought new commerce and industries. Modernisation was rapid, at least in the capital: within a generation three small towns facing each other across the Danube – Buda and Obuda (old Buda) on the right bank, Pest on the left – had experienced a massive influx of immigrants from the polyglot lands of Central Europe and the Balkans, urbanised and Hungarianised them:

> ... the new uniform municipal administration united in 1873 three provincial-like towns. Most of the houses were single-storey ones; the roads were unpaved, the garbage was carted away, if it in fact was, by convicts, drinking water was delivered to the houses in carts and barrows with cries of '*Donauwasser!*' ... Yet, at the turn of the century here stood a large city of one million inhabitants, complete with public utilities, electric supply, five bridges, paved roads, lively traffic, developed industry – one of Europe's modern metropolises. (Mesterházi, 1984)

Bustling Budapest opened the first underground railway on Continental Europe (named Metro, after London's Metropolitan Railway), the numbers of industrial workers in the country doubled and the delayed industrial revolution gave birth to trades unionism. The millenium of 1896 celebrated at once the real industrial advances of capitalist society and the absurd romanticisations of a heroic Magyar past that had never existed. Yet there were growing tensions between the Magyar-speakers and the various non-Magyars subject to their rule, and neither the realities of Hungary's progress nor the myths of its past could make up for the inequalities, injustice and discontent of Hungarian society. Then, following the assassination of Franz-Ferdinand, the Austrian heir apparent, Hungary entered the war on the side of the central power, losing nearly 400,000 dead.

With the collapse of the central powers at the end of 1918 there was a liberal revolution, the declaration of a republic and the separation of Hungary from Austria. The victorious *Entente*, determined to solve the Baltic question that had precipitated the war, demanded that the new republic should cede vast outlying territories which included large numbers of Magyar inhabitants, and the liberal government resigned in March 1919. A Soviet republic was declared in its place, which survived only 133 days. In that time it nationalised the land and introduced wide-ranging social reforms. It was blockaded by the *Entente* and invaded by Romanian, Serbian and Czech forces, collapsing finally in October 1919 to be followed by White Terror and counter-revolution. In 1920 a new government formally dissolved the link with Austria and signed the Treaty of Trianon which reduced the area of Hungary by two-thirds. The territories ceded to Czechoslovakia, Romania and Yugoslavia were mainly inhabited by non-Magyars but considerable numbers of Magyars now found themselves minority-group citizens outside the boundaries of Hungary. Though the country was still technically a kingdom the decision about restoring the monarchy was put off *sine die*, with Admiral Horthy, one-time Commander-in-Chief of the Austro-Hungarian navy, acting as Regent.

Horthy's government was right-wing and reactionary. Attempts to work towards a liberal, constitutional regime were unsuccessful. The hostility of neighbouring states, nationalist desires for a revision of the borders established by the Treaty of Trianon and tensions attendant upon the world economic crisis, all contributed towards a general fascistisation of Hungarian life, drawing the country first towards Mussolini's Italy and then to Hitler's Germany. In 1938 and 1939 this association was rewarded by territorial gains and Parliament began to pass anti-Semitic laws. Even so, with the outbreak of the Second World War Hungary remained at first technically neutral. Further territorial gains were made at the expense of Romania but a price had to be paid. It proved impossible to maintain an independent foreign policy and Hungary entered the war for the Axis in 1941, first against the Soviet Union, then the western powers, subsequently losing the greater part of its army in the Don Bend. The government turned its attention to a *rapprochement* with the western allies but found them firmly committed to the goal of unconditional surrender. In March 1944 German troops occupied the country and power fell into the ruthless hands of the extreme Nazi Arrow Cross Party. The first Soviet troops were over the frontier by October but the country was not completely liberated until April 1945. The war had cost the country 40 per cent of its national wealth and 600,000 dead, about 400,000 of them Jews exterminated in the final year of the war.

A National Assembly, comprising representatives of democratic parties, had already met in the liberated eastern part of the country before the end of the war and in 1946 Hungary, now within the Soviet sphere of influence, was once more proclaimed a republic. The land had already been redistributed, the banks and industry were now nationalised. After the elections of 1947 the liberal parties were excluded from power and, in 1949, following the merger of the two workers' parties as the Hungarian Workers' Party, Hungary was declared a people's republic in which the Hungarian Workers' Party held the monopoly of power. Social and economic development proceeded apace, too fast and too insensitively to have been altogether well done. The ruling party acted unlawfully against many of its citizens, most spectacularly in the trumped-up show trial of one of its heroes, László Rajk, though many others shared the same fate and the population as a whole experienced fear, repression and privation. These errors are now laid at the door of Mátyás Rákosi, First Secretary of the party, and his governing clique who pursued a hyper-Stalinist line. Whatever one makes of the counter-revolution of 1956 and the Soviet intervention that ended it (and there is no simple black-and-white picture, from whatever political stance, e.g. Lomax, 1980), it marked the opening of a period of careful social construction and development, within Comecon and the Warsaw Pact but far from a slavish copy of Soviet models. From 1956 to date the First Secretary of the reconstituted Hungarian Socialist Workers' Party has been János Kádár who had been in turn the police chief and a political prisoner of Rákosi. In 1961 Kádár offered Hungary another compromise, 'Those who are not against us are with us', and has since built up the nearest thing to consensus politics in Eastern Europe.

Hungary Today

The 1981 census found there to be 10,713,000 Hungarians, making their country one of the most densely populated in Europe. Nearly 20 per cent of them live in the capital, Budapest, around a third in the large towns, leaving nearly half spread often sparsely in the villages and the countryside. Officially the economy is mixed, though not very, around three-quarters of the national income coming from the state-owned sector, a fifth from co-operatives, the remaining twentieth being divided between the produce of private farm-plots and the private sector. Around two-thirds of working-age women work, constituting nearly half the work force. Unofficially there is a vast secondary economy in which moonlighting and other forms of personal commercial activity contribute substantially to the incomes of large numbers of the population. The Hungarian People's Republic is near enough a nation state, with less than 4 per cent of its population speaking a mother tongue other than Hungarian. It does seem that the national minorities, Germans, Slovaks, Croats, Serbs, Slovenes and Romanians, are treated fairly in the new Hungary, with their own schools, cultural institutions, newspapers etc.

Correspondingly, there are Hungarian minorities scattered through all the bordering states, in Yugoslavia, Austria, Czechoslovakia, the USSR and Romania, perhaps three million people, two million of them in Transylvania which is now part of Romania. It is widely alleged that the Hungarian minority in Romania is subject to increasing pressure to Romanianise, this being a source of friction between the two countries. There is also a considerable Hungarian *diaspora*, particularly in North America. Some two million Magyars emigrated in the years between the two world wars in response to unemployment and other social stresses. As a result of this and other emigrations there are large concentrations of people of Hungarian descent, many of whom retain their Hungarian culture and maintain close links with the old country. Toronto, for example, has 25,000 'ethnic Hungarians' with a strong cultural identity. Thus, there are about fifteen million 'Hungarians' in the world today (i.e. people speaking Magyar as their native tongue), only about two-thirds of whom live in Hungary, a situation very different from that of both royal and imperial Hungary when the country was twice to three times its present size with only a third to a half of its inhabitants Magyar-speakers.

The geography of present-day Hungary is summarised in Figure 1.1. The country is now small and landlocked but has access to the Black Sea via the Danube and, if the Rhine–Danube Canal is ever completed, it will have access to the North Sea too. The country measures at most 528 km east to west and 268 km north to south, and comprises 1 per cent of the European land mass. Not only is it at the meeting point of central Europe along the ancient trade and migration routes, it lies at the confluence of Atlantic, Mediterranean and Asiatic air streams, resulting in a very variable climate. The terrain itself is also varied, including mountains and plains, prairies and marshland and Lake Balaton, Europe's largest freshwater lake. Budapest now has over two million inhabitants. There are 7 other cities with populations over 100,000, the largest of these, Miskolc, having just over 200,000. The last 40 or so years have seen the continuing growth of modern industry, especially in the capital. Budapest remains, however, a very beautiful city and the largest spa in the world, which along with its low prices, charm and hospitality make it a major tourist resort.

The language of the country is Hungarian (Magyar). This is not a member of the Indo-European language group which includes in the British Isles such superficially diverse tongues as English, Welsh and Punjabi, and on Continental Europe most of the languages from Portuguese to Russian. Hungarian stands outside, a member of the Finno-Ugric group. Its only, distant European relative is Finnish (with Estonian), though there are related tongues spoken by scattered tribes in Asiatic Russia. The original Finno-Ugrian peoples were separated from each other at least two thousand years ago, since when Hungarian has developed altogether independently from its cogenitors. It is, therefore, a language on its own. Though it has incorporated loan words and other influences from the various cultures that it has met and interacted with over the course of its existence, the bulk of its vocabulary is still Magyar in origin. Grammar and syntax, too, stand apart from those of the Indo-European languages. All this makes Hungarian a very difficult foreign language to learn and, correspondingly, learning foreign languages presents a considerable effort for the Hungarians. Social, cultural and historical forces, however, have meant that many Hungarians have had to face this effort. Since the war Russian has been the prime foreign language taught in the schools, though of late English has become quite common as a second language, at least amongst professional people. Many older people still speak German and many others have learned it in recent years to a degree, for the tourist trade. At the higher levels of academic and scientific life Hungarians are great internationalists and many speak excellent international English. Additionally, the state makes great efforts to publish scientific and cultural materials in English. Even so, whilst the foreigner in Hungary is rarely wholly stranded linguistically and Hungarians are almost invariably most generous and courteous in their efforts to make things understood, the visitor is frequently aware of an enormous linguistic divide across which the bridges feel sometimes a little shaky, especially with respect to specific points.

Hungarian Education

Education first came to Hungary under St Stephen (Zibolen, 1976; Bencédy, 1982) with the need to train clergy for the newly expanding church. Literate priests were also needed to build up and maintain the machinery of secular government. First Benedictine monasteries, then also cathedral schools, universities and urban schools brought education to the medieval Kingdom of Hungary but at the end of the period the Turkish occupation and the partition of the country into three wiped out much of the progress so far made, greatly reducing the cultural effects of the Reformation. Outstanding educators did emerge, however, at this time, such as Jan Komensky (Comenius), who tried in Transylvania to create a new school to meet the requirements of his age, but the most salient feature of education as a whole at the end of the Turkish suzerainty was sectarianism. Instruction continued to be in Latin, supplemented by German, the languages of scholarship, government and commerce (Magyar was just one of several languages spoken by the poor who comprised the overwhelming bulk of the population).

In 1777, under Maria Theresa, a plan was published, the *Ratio Educationalis*, which proposed a unified Hungarian school system, to include a three- to four-year grounding in the vernacular. In practice, however, education remained limited and largely under the control of the churches and in 1806 a 'Second Ratio' was published as part of a general attempt by the Hungarian magnates to restrict freedom of education.

Yet progress was already under way. By the beginning of the nineteenth century the nobility's quest for identity had led to championing of the Magyar language (though it did not replace Latin as the official language till 1844). In a growing atmosphere of reform the early part of the century saw educational developments advanced even by the standards of already industrialising western Europe. The first kindergarten was opened in 1827 and there were nearly one hundred such establishments by the time of the revolution of 1848. The 1848 revolution brought a call for a modern school system, freed from the churches and staffed by well-trained teachers teaching practical contemporary material. A Bill was proposed but never passed and the restoration of imperial power led at first to a reaffirmation of church authority over education and an active attempt to Germanise the education system. Then in 1868, directly following the Compromise, the Bill of 20 years before was reintroduced and passed with the help of capitalist interests which, free from the direct Austrian yoke, now demanded a basic education for workers and peasants.

The elementary school system so far created was far from ideal and came to be used as an oppressive tool in the attempt to Hungarianise non-Magyar minorities. Yet a left-wing teachers' trade union played a major role in the short-lived Soviet Republic of 1919 and laid down a detailed plan for a transformed, specialist education system to include state schooling for all from the ages of three to eighteen and school medical and dental services. The new school year of 1919, however, saw the successful counter-revolution. The Compulsory Education Act of 1921 abolished not only the plans and achievements of the Soviet Republic of 1919 but even some of those of the liberal reformers of 1868. Under Horthy's regime, 'the schools were caste schools and the education system was full of built in dead ends for the under-privileged' (Bencédy, 1982, p. 4). The bulk of the population could send their children only to impoverished elementary schools, secondary schooling was in the hands of the churches with generous state subsidies, while higher education fared well in some respects, though the numbers of students were restricted and reduced. The system had a stultifying effect on social mobility. Official figures from the time indicate that only 6 to 7 per cent of all the pupils who completed the fourth grade of elementary school gained admission to the secondary schools. The way in which this system took pupils from particular social origins and prepared them for particular destinations is indicated in Table 1.1. In 1938 only 78 per cent of the country's school-age children entered school at all and only 19 per cent achieved education comparable with today's eighth-graders.

Table 1.1: Social Class and Secondary Schools in the Hungary of the 1930s (from Ferenc Foldës, quoted by Zibolen, 1976).

	As a percentage of the population	As a percentage of the secondary-school population
Poor peasants	35.0	1.3
Workers	21.4	3.8
Landowners	16.8	12.2
Bourgeoisie	26.8	82.7

This system was swept aside after the war (Horváth, 1976). In August 1945 the Provisional National Government replaced the previous, divisive system with the establishment of an eight-year unitary, universal and compulsory elementary education, the 'general school' (*általános iskola*), to serve as the basis of a new educational system. In 1948 all non-state schools, kindergartens and hostels were taken over by the state, all buildings and property used for educational purposes became state property and all school employees became state employees. The rapid industrialisation of the country and its social and political transformation as a people's republic demanded a major effort by the education system, its teachers and pupils. This effort seems not to have been in vain:

> Despite the difficulties facing a relatively poor and undeveloped country, to say nothing of its trials and tribulations during the glacial period (1945-55) which followed the 'Liberation', the achievements of the People's Republic in the last decade must be reckoned quite outstanding. The establishment of a common 8-year school for all children, the widespread provision of preschool training, the provision of full-time secondary education for at least 45 per cent of the pupils up to the age of 15, and the rapid expansion of all forms of higher education are only some of the more striking features of the cultural revolution that is taking place. Magyars refer to it jocularly as 'the learning disease'. Indeed, the fact that this great little country has contrived to accomplish so much with its scant resources and in such a short space of time makes the oversophisticated doubts and questionings of educationalists who fight shy of the concept of total planning look a trifle ridiculous. (Richmond, 1966).

This great leap forward was not, of course, without its problems, particularly an initial emphasis upon quantity rather than quality at all levels, and to counter this the system has been made subject to careful government and party review. It should not be thought, however, that change comes only from the top (see Norman, 1980, for an account of the formal management of the system). A role in the process of adaption has been played by debates within the teaching profession, which have mobilised teachers and compelled education authorities to introduce changes. A recent such debate in the weekly magazine *Élet és Irodalom* (Life and Literature) seems to have not only influenced official policy but to have also substantially increased the magazine's circulation, by 25 per cent (see Zöldi, 1978), suggesting that the 'learning disease' continues to smite the

Magyars despite one reform introduced in 1978, to let pupils have every other Saturday free.

The General School

The eight-year, general-school system and its requirements serve as the basis for the Hungarian education system today and so provide the essential, immediate educational context for conductive education.

The constitution of the Hungarian People's Republic guarantees all citizens the right to education without distinction of race, sex or religion. The task of the general school is considerable:

> The function of the primary school is to provide a basic education for each new generation, to develop the pupils' fundamental skills and inclinations, especially their thinking ability, to lay the foundations for learning new knowledge, to create in them a need for learning and the ability to learn independently. The primary school must lay the foundations of the ideological and moral demands and customs and communal behaviour, of socialist patriotism and internationalism, of the respect for work and the working man. (Bencédy, 1982, pp. 13-14)

Children enter school in the September following their sixth birthdays. Every normal, healthy child then receives at least eight years general schooling. Ninety-seven to ninety-eight per cent of all six-year olds in Hungary enter general school. Education is compulsory until the age of 16: those who have not completed the eighth grade of general schooling (about 10 per cent of each group, mainly the children of unskilled workers) must stay on at the general school till they are 16. The remainder complete their compulsory schooling in various kinds of high schools.

The following account of a visit by an English educationalist offers a recent impression of one Hungarian general school.

> The general school visited is situated on the outskirts of Budapest in an area of new high-rise housing development. The head teacher suggested that both the area and the accommodation were unpopular and families were in general, reluctant to move there. Some blocks remain unoccupied – one has a large group of gypsies squatting in it whose children attend the school. Because of the new housing developments the school has recently been enlarged, now taking about a thousand pupils – a large school by Budapest standards.

The school buildings are functional and closely resemble UK post-war buildings for basic secondary schools. There are, however, some fundamental differences in the social provision offered – children up to ten-years-old may stay at the school for the extended day, being taught or supervised in the afternoons by a different group of teachers for less formal work and also spending some time on Pioneer activities – the national youth organisation.

The general impression from touring the school during the morning lessons was very positive. The school has undergone major changes, virtually doubling its size in the last two years. Many teachers moved to other schools when this occurred and large numbers of 'problem' families were housed in the school's catchment area. Consequently, over three quarters of the staff are teachers who completed their training in the last two years. Despite these problems, children were alert and interested, pupil–staff relationships seemed relaxed and humorous. Children moving to their next lesson greeted the Head with smiles but continued to chat together. The standard of work seemed very good – as far as one can judge without understanding the language of instruction! Two ex-pupils of the Institute of Conductive Education attended the school, a nine-year old in grade 4 (age appropriate) and a twelve-year old in grade 6 (one year behind). About 20% of pupils have to repeat a grade. . .

The Head herself appeared remarkably young for her senior post, perhaps in her early thirties, wearing Levi jeans and trainers. She seemed delighted to be visited and eager to answer any questions and she and senior colleagues asked a great many questions about English education. (Pearson, 1984a)

Preschool Education

In 1980, 88 per cent of preschool-age children attended kindergarten (*óvoda*). The object of kindergarten in Hungary is not solely to help parents by caring for their children but also actively to prepare for general school. Children who have been brought up entirely at home over the preschool years are provided with a one-year preparatory class to give them experience of community life and learning. In all, 98.5 per cent of first-graders had experienced some form of preschool provision as a planned preparation for school, one of the highest proportions of any country in the world, either capitalist or socialist. Family allowance is payable for the first three years of a child's life – for six years if the child is handicapped.

Music in Schools

The structure and achievements of the postwar Hungarian education have attracted little attention from educationalists in the West – with one exception, the teaching of music, acclaimed and emulated throughout the world. The nature and scope of Hungarian music teaching, though the fruit of an enormous collective effort, is very much due to the inspiration of one man, Zoltán Kodály, who, with an already established reputation as a musicologist and a composer, turned his creative energies increasingly to making musical education an integral part of the development and education of the whole child. Damned by his association with the 1919 republic and constrained by the limitations of the Horthy years, Kodály gained official acceptance only after 1945. Even by the early sixties, however, the effects upon the school system were enormous:

> To say that all Hungarian children can sing at sight and with perfect intonation is, no doubt, exaggeration; but that many can is an answer to those in England (and they are, unfortunately, numerous) who feel that efficient sight-reading is an educational *ultima Thule* to be gained only at some indefinite point of futurity. (Young, 1962-3)

Enormous, too, has been the national effort required to musicalise Hungarian education, to raise music to the status of a basic school subject. The students who train to teach at both kindergarten level and in the first four grades of general school are selected for their above-average musical ability and further musical training comprises an important feature of their professional preparation, especially for the future kindergarten teachers who receive weekly instruction in singing, *sol-fa*, ear training and an instrument, as well as having to sing in a choir. Given the extensive kindergarten provision in Hungary, therefore, most children's musical education is well under way before they reach compulsory school starting age:

> ... the youngest children, the three-year olds, are taught to sing eighteen to twenty songs and singing games, to chant nursery rhymes, to step and clap the beat to duple-meter songs or rhymes, to use hand drums and other simple rhythm instruments, to feel the beat, to learn to distinguish the sounds of drums, cymbals and triangle, and to hear and respond to soft and loud music. They are expected to recognise familiar tunes on xylophone and recorder.

The four-year-olds add another twenty-five or more songs, singing games and rhymes to their repertory and learn to clap and walk in $\frac{2}{4}$ and $\frac{4}{4}$, distinguishing between accented and unaccented beats. They are introduced to the concepts of high and low and fast and slow ... The steps to singing games are used to give emphasis to their rhythmic quality. Children are expected to recognise a familiar tune simply from hearing its clapped rhythm.

The five-year-olds ... add still another thirty or so songs to their singing repertory. They continue to develop the concepts of fast–slow, high–low and loud–soft. The familiar songs are repeated in a variety of tempi to which they must respond correctly with their tapping, clapping or stepping. They are expected to be able to clap the rhythm of a familiar song without singing it simply by inner-hearing, and to echo-clap simple duple-motor rhythm patterns both in groups and individually. All songs are taught by rote and no accompaniment is used with the singing other than occasional rhythm instruments.

... At the end of this three-year period the six-year-old in Hungary can usually step the beat and clap the rhythm correctly to any of the songs in his repertory. He can, as a rule, sing most of those songs in tune from memory. He understands the usual concepts of high–low, loud–soft and fast–slow, and can demonstrate his understanding behaviorally. (Choksy, 1974, pp. 37-8)

Whilst it is the quality of the music education itself that has attracted musicians and music teachers to Hungary in large numbers, it has to be remembered that Kodály's ultimate aim was of a higher order, to enhance the development of the child *as a whole*, to create a 'total adult' by means of an education that was indeed comprehensive, aesthetic as well as intellectual. Some perhaps unexpected empirical support for this approach, albeit at a rather low order, has been reported (Choksy, 1974, pp. 10-11) in the form of psychological research that has identified beneficial effects from regular music teaching upon achievement in other subject areas. It has to be remembered, too, that there is no single, straightforward 'Kodály method', available off-the-peg to be applied to pupils whether for musical or for other academic, aesthetic or educational goals. Kodály's broad concept of musical education cannot be successfully reduced to elements such as singing by score and perhaps the vital pedagogic process is *'the teaching of teachers singing and living for their mission'* (Mészáros, 1983, emphasis in original).

Special Education in Hungary

A school for the deaf was opened in Vác (near Budapest) in 1802, one of the earliest in Europe; the first Hungarian school for the blind was opened in 1829 and the first for the mentally handicapped in 1875 (Bachmann, Gordos-Szabó and Lányi-Engelmayer, 1977). As elsewhere in Europe and North America, the turn of the century saw major developments: all establishments for handicapped children were brought under the direction of the Ministry of Education; the numbers and variety of special schools increased; greater attention was paid to the curriculum; the Special Education Teachers' Training College opened; the journal *Gyógypedagógia* (Special Education) was founded, and Pál Ranschburg opened the Special Education Psychology Laboratory in Budapest. The First World War halted further progress, however, preventing the passing of a Bill to make education compulsory for all handicapped children, and the aspirations of 1918 and 1919 of course came to naught. Then in the years of the Horthy regime, despite noble efforts by individuals, special education found itself under increasingly difficult conditions. In 1938 there were less than 5,000 pupils in only 48 special schools and the training of special educators altogether ceased for three years.

As a national system to provide for all in need, therefore, special education in Hungary dates back only to the years following the Second World War. By 1980 (Kovács, 1981) there were over 37,000 pupils attending 167 special schools and 407 special classes attached to general schools. In addition there is a national logopaedic service (speech therapy, though as an educational not a 'health' provision) and there are children's homes and institutions for severely and profoundly mentally handicapped children. Special education is provided separately for the moderately and severely mentally handicapped, the blind, the partially sighted, the deaf, the partially hearing, the speech impaired and the motor-disabled. In rural areas the mildly mentally handicapped (by far the largest group of special pupils) are educated in special classes within the general schools, and in cities and more populous areas (where there are at least four special classes) they are brought together in day special schools. There are also residential schools for some of these children. All other handicaps are provided for residentially as a matter of course. Though the notion of integration in its western sense has evoked some interest and some experimental arrangements are in force to integrate certain handicapped children into the normal general school, the system as a whole is a 'segregated' one in both philosophy and practice. All children in Hungary are screened before reaching compulsory school-age, to see whether they are capable of taking part in the intensive general-school programme. Those whose fitness is questioned are referred to a special commission (*bizottság*). The commissions are headed by an experienced special educator and include a psychologist, a physician and other specialists as appropriate. The commissions aim to identify children for special education as early in their school careers as possible. Whilst special-school placements may be reviewed at any time it does seem that the majority of them last till the child completes general school. There are commissions for mental handicap in every county, with a single national committee, based in Budapest, for each of the other handicaps, visual, auditory, speech and motor.

The basic aim of the special-education system is to enable children who are handicapped to master the curriculum and syllabus of the general school (the first four grades only in the case of mild mental handicap). (Vincze, 1982) More severely mentally handicapped children are considered merely 'trainable' and educated accordingly, and the lowest grade, the profoundly mentally handicapped, are excluded altogether from the education system and provided for by the health service.

It is also worth noting that, despite the public health advances of the last 40 years, Hungary has a high and growing rate of prematurity, around a third of women smoke during pregnancy and there is a rising trend for alcohol consumption amongst pregnant women (Lányi-Engelmayer, Katona and Czeizel, 1983).

The college first founded in 1900 in Vác (moving to Budapest in 1904) is now the Gusztáv Barczi Teacher Training College (named after a noted Hungarian special educator) which trains the teachers and logopaeds for the special-education system and conducts relevant research, curriculum development etc. Even if the Hungarians' continuingly explicit reliance upon a segregated system of special education might appear somewhat retrograde to many in this country, the preparation of the teachers and the organisation of their work appears to be of the highest quality – and has been for some time (see Kelmer-Pringle, 1955).

Walking and the Educational System

To attend school in Hungary a child must be able to walk. This general requirement applies not only to the general schools and kindergartens but also to ALL the special education establishments already mentioned. To take part in the general school children must be able to take a full part in it. Those who cannot get about for themselves, at least within the confines of the school, who cannot take part in the lessons as they are taught, go upstairs, use normal furniture, lavatories etc., are unable to participate in the intensive general-school programme and cannot, therefore, attend. Use of a wheelchair provides no exception to this general principle. Children who cannot get about satisfactorily for themselves are excluded from the general-school *and* special-school systems and are entitled only to home tuition which must by law be provided for by the appropriate local school (i.e. by the general school, or by a relevant special school if the child has an additional problem). This entitlement amounts to only six hours per week of home tuition.

There are two residential special schools for motor-disabled children[1] serving the whole of Hungary: the one in Mexikói út in Budapest is for motor-disabled children capable of following the general-school curriculum; the other in the country town of Sály, for children who are mentally as well as physically handicapped. *Even in these two special schools for the motor-disordered, the same principle applies: children who cannot walk, cannot attend.* Thus, Mexikói út, an exceptionally well staffed school of over 150 pupils, has three wheelchairs, for use solely with children convalescing from operations or with some other temporary need (Sutton, 1984a, Suppl. IV).

The Institute for Motor Disorders

The prime role of the Institute in the education system is to produce orthofunction in children with motor disorders, i.e. to enable them to take their places and function as pupils of the Hungarian general- or special-school system. It does this by means of conductive education. In addition, the Institute also keeps the national register of children and young people with relevant disorders, reviews and follows up ex-pupils, provides conductive education for adult patients and trains the 'conductors' who do this work. Yet, whilst the Institute is under the Ministry of Education and clearly fulfils functions that are 'special', it stands somewhat outside of the rest of special-education provision in Hungary, on a number of counts. At a superficial level, this is apparent in the Ministry's annual statistical returns, in which the Institute's statistics are presented separately from those of all other special schools and classes. The Institute has its own national 'network' of services, separate from the rest of the special-educational system and separately managed, and its own system of professional training, outside of the Special Education Teacher Training College and quite differently structured. More fundamentally still, its function is not to provide for the *long-term* educational needs of children who would otherwise be considered unable to manage the ordinary school programme, but rather to remediate and then to discharge into the school system children who are now able to manage there. Moreover its motor-disordered pupils, though provided for separately from the rest of the educational system and, therefore, what we might call segregated, are within their particular context an integrated population that includes both children of normal mental potential and those who are for various reasons retarded in their mental development.

András Petö and the Development of Conductive Education

Conductive education was devised and developed by András Petö. The only published biographic sketch in English is enigmatic:

> *Petö, András, Dr* (1893-1967) – physician. He completed his studies in Austria and worked there as the leader of many institutions of rehabilitation until 1938. At this date he laid the groundwork for his system of conductive education later to be developed in Hungary. As professor at the Training College for Teachers of the Handicapped from 1945-1963 he had the opportunity to prove the efficiency of the education. This is how the National Institution for Kinesitherapy became established in 1950. The Institution ran under his direction, was turned into the Institute for Training of Educators of the Locomotor Handicapped and into the Educational Home for the Locomotor Handicapped in 1963. It was here that he began the training of conductors. His posthumous works contain many manuscripts and notes worthy of evaluation. (Bachmann, Gordos-Szabö and Lányi-Engelmayer, 1977, p. 94)

Indeed, Petö remains a mysterious and intriguing character. He was born into a Jewish family in Szombathely, in the west of Hungary close to the Austrian border, a very 'German' area in those days. His father ran a shop and his mother was a teacher. Money was short and, from his second year at gymnasium, the young András worked in his spare time to help the family finances and to pay for his two brothers' education, continuing this right through his university career in Vienna where he studied medicine from 1911 to 1916. For the next 22 years he worked as a physician in Vienna and its environs, working in a variety of clinics and hospitals, sometimes in physical medicine, sometimes in psychiatry, rising to become the director of two hospitals. At the same time he pursued a vigorous intellectual and literary life. He knew Freud and other founding fathers of psychoanalysis, as well as Jacobson the hypnotherapist and Moreno of sociogram and sociodrama fame. He was also drawn to Marxism and joined the Party in Vienna in 1919. Petö himself wrote poems, plays and philosophy (all in German), was interested in ancient and oriental religions, meditation and the occult, and edited a magazine or journal on natural healing. In 1938 he left Austria, presumably because of the *Anschluss* by the Third Reich, went briefly to Paris, apparently intending to go further west, but returned to Hungary and remained there throughout the years of the Second World War. He appears to have supported himself by commercial activities, running a factory for recycling waste paper and another producing *ersatz* coffee, following his medical interest in his spare time.

And then, in 1945, in the early days following the liberation, Petö requested facilities to work with motor-disordered children. He was given a couple of basement rooms in the building that then housed the College of Special Education, the barest necessities and 13 children. Additional resources came from a Swiss charity, two or three medical students volunteered to help out and other children soon swelled the numbers of his pupils. By 1947 or 1948 he had been made a professor at the Special Education College and in 1952 he opened what was then called the National Motor Therapy Institute, in Villány út. There followed a period of growth, consolidation – and struggle. Relationships with the Special Education College were strained, so too were they with the Ministry of Health that controlled the Institute. There were many who regarded Petö as a charlatan but, in 1963, his work achieved major recognition, the Institute was transferred to the Ministry of Education and its system of conductor training officially established. Petö, now of poor health, continued to work and died at his desk in 1967. Though the Institute at once lost its *föiskola* status (i.e. it was no longer a university-level institution), in 1968 a state decree made district physicians throughout Hungary responsible for notifying all motor-disordered children for registration at the Institute.

Petö's early published work from the interwar period is scattered and, because of his ready recourse to pseudonyms, perhaps not all ultimately traceable. Much of it appears to have been literary or philosophical rather than medical. There seem no known prewar pointers to the method that was to follow, nor does it seem known precisely where, when or how he derived the approach that he called 'conductive motor pedagogy (*konduktiv mozgaspedagogia*) and is now widely known as 'conductive education' (Konduktiv nevelés). Nor, once his Institute was in operation, did Petö devote much time to writing down the bases for his system. His attitude appears to have been that people read and took note of the written word not for the intrinsic value of what was written but only out of personal or political expedience: since, he felt, his work made no such immediate appeal, he would get on with the job of developing conductive education, leaving others to describe and research the system when the time was ripe. As a result his published work on conductive education amounts to a handful of articles and to a small book of lectures, now virtually unobtainable, edited under his supervision by Mária Hári.

Dr Mária Hári had been one of the medical students who had helped Petö in the earliest days of the Institute. She never left and, after a brief interregnum took over as director after Petö's death. She remains director and has retained his largely practice-oriented tradition. Many of the staff of the Institute have been there 25, even 35 years and, therefore, also knew and worked with Petö himself. During his lifetime he appears to have enjoyed a wide social circle of acquaintances and contacts and there are many Hungarians who, though they disagreed with him in certain respects and may indeed still disagree with aspects of the Institute's work, readily assert that he was a remarkable person: 'genius' is a word frequently used. During his lifetime his reputation spread abroad. He corresponded widely with others working in the field of motor disorder and by 1965 it seems that his work was known in England, at least in smart circles (Halász, 1965). A considerable store of his unpublished notes is treasured at the Institute, and over the last few years a number of these have been produced in bound and printed form for use by students on the conductor training course. Several ciné films were made of Petö at work with motor-disordered children and adults but these were unintentionally destroyed a few years ago. There is, therefore, very little to show directly of the thoughts and work of Petö apart from the living oral and practical tradition of the Institute which, though it has been developed and modified in specific respects in the years since his death, remains a vivid and material legacy from his life and work.

The Network

The Institute in Villányi út has been gradually expanded. In the Villányi út complex are situated the residential facilities for children, the library and archive, the administrative and clerical facilities. Nothing is ever intentionally discarded and records exist for all the children and adults ever known to the Institute. Work at Villányi út includes conductive education with the residential pupils (kindergarten and school-age) and with adult outpatients suffering from hemiplegia and multiple sclerosis, evaluation of new children and follow up of former pupils and patients, clinical sessions by visiting medical specialists (orthopaedist, neurologist, etc.), mother-and-baby sessions, training of student conductors, consultation, screening and guidance. Also at Villányi út is the day school for children from the Budapest area. Because of the shortage of space, however, classes for adults suffering from Parkinson's disease are held in the gym of a general school a mile or so away in Buda. There is also an overspill day school for children situated in Pest.

The arrangements described above are those in force at the time of writing. Back in Pető's time a new, larger Institute was proposed – though not by Pető who would have preferred greater decentralisation. The planning and building of this new Institute dragged on for years, outliving the original architect, but it was at last formally commissioned and occupied in April 1985. The scope of the Institute's activities, however, are now such that the old building at Villányi út is being maintained as part of the network.

The new Institute occupies a prestigious site in the Buda hills and has been named the András Pető Institute for Motor Disorders (*Mozgássérültek Pető András Intézete*). Overspill arrangements will cease when the new pattern of work of the expanded network is fully established.

There are several outside services provided in Budapest by conductors from the Institute that are not overspill. These include work in two 'social homes' for seriously mentally handicapped children, in a special school for mentally handicapped children and at a neurology clinic. Such arrangements appear to have been established through personal contact and good will.

Outside of Budapest conductors paid and supervised by the Institute operate in five local centres. There are also three other centres established by local effort and locally funded, that employ conductors trained at the Institute. There is little relationship as yet between the pattern of this network and the major concentrations of population. Indeed it seems that the location of the country wide network has depended more upon the vagaries of where conductors might have married and settled rather than upon a rational, national plan. Conductors may also occasionally be found working in neurology clinics, etc. but it remains the case that the overwhelming majority of conductors work directly for the Institute where the great bulk of conduction in Hungary is carried out.

Conflicts and Complements

Inevitably there are some anomalies and contradictions in the Institute's relations with its wider social context, some of the latter antagonistic. For example, the Institute is part of the Ministry of Education but has proved difficult to fit it into the existing framework. Initially it was put in the section that deals with destitute children then shifted to the universities section, neither really appropriate, but it has never been administratively a part of special education. In fact, its relationship with the special-education system is at best cool, for the Institute has genuine conflicts of orientation with the College of Special Education over such matters as professional training (which the Institute demands should be on the apprenticeship model), the genericisation of the conductor-role (which the College regards as impossible, at least at school-age) and the use of standardised tests (which the College embraces and the Institute deprecates). Critics point to the self-contained nature of the Institute's work and to its failure to have carried out evaluative research on conductive education. Whatever the rights and wrongs on either side, it has been the case that the Institute and its network have tended to remain rather isolated even from educational and medical specialists working in closely related fields in Hungary. Lack of research and research publications has meant that no one (except those trained as conductors) has much idea of how conductive education works – or even whether or not it does – and trained conductors apparently prove very hard to come by outside of the Institute's own network. Only very recently have some conductors begun to give papers describing their work, with the result that some Hungarian specialists are only now beginning to learn of conductive education.

Yet known it is, and treated with that uneasy respect accorded something which, for all the criticisms levelled against it, is acknowledged as being successful in its primary function, in this case to create 'orthofunction'. Perhaps an awareness of this achievement of

Petö and his Institute has in part contributed to a wider endeavour to improve the performance of the motor-disordered, for, though there is a long Hungarian spa tradition of treating rheumatic disorders and the like with healing baths, there is no obvious medical or educational tradition of combatting motor disorders that goes back beyond the start of Petö's work in 1945. Since 1963 Petö's Institute has provided the statutory service for all school children in Hungary suffering from relevant disorders but others have now developed work in adjacent areas.

At the Szabadsághegy Paediatric Institute, for example, Ferenc Katona has developed a hi-tec system for diagnosing brain damage in babies (Katona, 1983), along with a complex system of intervention which is largely carried out at home by the child's parents over the first year of life (Lányi-Engelmayer, Katona and Czeizel, 1983), he has now established an extensive national network through the paediatric departments of county hospitals, to identify and treat brain-damaged children, and claims excellent results. In the West his work has attracted both interest and controversy, the latter chiefly because of problems of agreeing the validity of his early diagnoses and it does not as yet appear to have attracted emulation or replication. In sharp distinction is the work of Anna Dévény a gifted and empathetic lady, trained both as a physiotherapist and an artistic gymnast, who runs classes in a small gym in a converted shop near the Parliament building, in the fifth arrondissement of Budapest. Her approach is that children with movement problems (not just motor disorders but a wide range of physical conditions) should learn not just to move but to move beautifully, which she seeks to bring about by a combination of her own brand of physiotherapy and by teaching them artistic gymnastics (Dévény, 1980). Neither Katona nor Dévény would see their own approaches as denying the work of the Institute (though both have their specific criticisms) – rather they would see what they are doing as complementary at different stages of the overall developmental and educational process.

It is now 40 years since the liberation of Hungary from fascism – and 40 years since the first appearance of what was to develop into conductive education. These years have seen both conflict and consensus and Hungary today is a paradoxical society, a socialist state with a pervasive regard for business. There are paradoxes too in the Institute's position within its wider society. It is sometimes asked in this country 'But why was it *in Hungary* that conductive education arose?' Such a question betokens ignorance of a vigorous and dynamic society. On better acquaintance, why should it not have been Hungary? Emerge there it did, apparently out of the inspiration and work of one man, and its development has been within the context of the demands and opportunities, the conflicts and constraints of the new Hungary.

Note

1. The term 'motor disabled' has been used here to distinguish these children from the children attending the Institute for Motor Disorders. They include children with orthopaedic conditions and some graduates from the Institute who have been able to attend normal school. Children at Mexicói út and Sály must be mobile and their schools cannot, therefore, be compared with English schools for the physically handicapped. (see Sutton, 1984a, Supplement IV)

2 THE PRACTICE

Andrew Sutton

Educational practice is hard to describe. An observer inevitably selects, directing attention to this feature or that according to what seems personally significant or interesting or expected. Moreover, the process has a temporal dimension. What is observed is one moment of a process which moves towards the attainment of long-term goals. Statistics can confirm the spoken or written word, still photographs can capture an image and documentary film or video provide a powerful impression. Combine all the available media, however, and one may still fail to capture the essence of an educational process. Perhaps the art of education is ultimately conveyed only by a work of imagination.

Unfortunately conductive education still awaits its Makarenko. Indeed, for us in the English-speaking world, it still awaits even a sufficient accumulation of factual description to offer more than an introductory impression of a complex pedagogic and developmental process.

Particularly, there is little that stems from Hungarian sources. The only English-language book on the work of the Institute for the Motor-Disordered (Akós, 1975) is a collection of analytic essays that require some prior knowledge of the practices discussed. So too does a more recent discussion of the principles of conductive education (Hári and Tillemans, 1984a, 1984b). In the late sixties and early seventies, the period of the Spastics Society's initial enthusiasm for conductive education, Dr Hári was invited to Britain and materials from her visits include some direct descriptions of the Institute's work (Hári, 1968, 1972) – but these materials have remained largely unpublished and have enjoyed only a limited readership. Two recent articles by Hungarian journalists (Eöry, 1984; Varnai, 1984), specifically commissioned to supplement the limited output from the Institute itself, have added only fleeting glimpses of the practice. Statistical data from the Institute records have been presented (e.g. Akós, 1975, pp. 70-8) but not in a form acceptable to western researchers. There have been a number of photographs of pupils at the Institute published but these tell us little of how the children *move*. Several English-language films have been made of the Institute's

27

work but few appear to be currently in circulation in Britain. Whilst this list of sources mentioned here may not be exhaustive, it is certainly the case that those of us outside Hungary who would like to know what the practice of conductive education is like (certainly those of us who speak and read only English) have to go to Budapest to see for ourselves, or rely upon the impressions or reports of those who have.

Travellers' Tales

Hard as it is to describe an educational practice the task is all the harder when it involves teachers and pupils who speak a wholly unintelligible foreign language, who act and behave according to unfamiliar cultural norms, who are members of a society with different traditions and values from our own, and who are working towards goals and utilising methods that are equally outside our expectations and experience.

Not all of us who have visited the Institute, of course, have committed our impressions to paper. Even so, a scattered body of descriptive materials written in English has accumulated over the last two decades. Much of what has been written has never been published (Parnwell, 1966; Seglow, 1966; Kearslake, 1970; Varty, 1970a; Wilson, 1970; Haskell, 1971; Carrington, 1973; Budd, 1975; Siddles, 1976; Jernqvist, 1980a; Barker, 1981; Tillemans, 1981; Cottam, 1984; Sutton, 1984a), existing only in the form of cyclostyled papers and reports. Whilst some of these materials have been quite widely photocopied for private circulation, others seem to have been largely forgotten and may be traced only by chance or with difficulty. One (not further quoted here) is even sternly marked 'FOR INTERNAL CIRCULATION ONLY. NOT FOR PUBLICATION'. There may, of course, be yet other unpublished accounts in English, still unidentified.

Considering the interest in conductive education expressed over the last two decades and many professionals' eagerness to emulate the Institute's work and accomplishments, there has been remarkably little actually *published* by English-speaking visitors to the Institute, to describe the practice observed there. The 'classic' account is that of Cotton (1965), following a study visit to the Institute on behalf of the Spastics Society. Far less well known has been a report by House (1968), an American professor of speech pathology. Two British visitors published short accounts in the seventies (Loring, 1971; Holt, 1975) and there were also two brief reports based upon earlier unpublished materials (Carrington, 1974; Haskell, 1977). None provided the detailed account of practice made by Cotton. Finally, Caspar (1984) has offered quite a different perspective, that of an English parent whose child is staying at the Institute. Again, this list might not be exhaustive – but even if twice as long it would still represent a fairly small body of direct observation of the practice of conductive education placed in the public domain.

There is also a film report on the Institute, made by the BBC and shown on *Newsnight* (BBC2, 5 May 1983). This does not appear to have been widely seen.

It can, therefore, be very hard for us in the English-speaking world to gain an impression of conductive education as practised in the Institute for the Motor-Disordered in Budapest. Relevant materials tend to be either few or unobtainable, and even basic bibliographic research into what is available seems only to have begun in the last two or three years. For the large part, what can be found comes from the hands of English-speaking visitors (mostly British and mostly people working with children suffering from cerebral palsy, often from a medical or para-medical background). As far as can be traced, no visitor who has reported on the Institute's work has been either a Hungarianist or even Hungarian-speaking. Further, conductive education in Hungary is proudly and self-consciously an educational process, yet its examination by English-speaking observers has not on the whole been in educational terms and barely at all as a question of comparative education. But of course, without reference to the nature of *ordinary* education in Hungary there is no way of judging what at the Institute is different or special.

The 'travellers' tales' of those of us who have visited the Institute, whether spoken or written, published or unpublished, must, therefore, be regarded with some caution. Such tales represent an important stage in the discovery and investigation of any foreign practice but, it is to be emphasised, this is only a preliminary stage, one which arouses interest, sparks off hypotheses, provokes discussion. It is a stage prone to profound misunderstandings and, with respect to the discovery of conductive education by the English-speaking world (and by other westerners too), it is a stage which has gone on now for two decades. Its balance has been overwhelmingly in favour of conductive education for, though some visitors have had specific qualms about what they have seen, no report has yet been traced that denies the remarkable results claimed by the Institute. This stage of investigation, therefore, seems to have justified a transition to a much more substantial examination of the practice.

Unfortunately, such work has yet to be done. For the moment, travellers' tales are all that we have. A selection from these accounts is presented here, picked to represent some of the most vivid, relevant or concrete accounts of what was actually seen, so that interested readers might draw their own conclusions from as wide a sample as possible of impressions of conductive education in practice, as a base for further discussion.

Villányi út

All available accounts of conductive education in Hungary describe work at the main Institute in Villányi út (Villany Road – Villány being a wine-growing area to the south-west). Although nothing funda-mental in the practice of conductive education will change with the opening of the Petö András Intézet, there will in future be much more space and aspects of the work will certainly look different.

The main building on the Villányi út site is single-storied, with a more recent two-storey wing. A separate building behind houses the day school. There are no ramps, children move from one level to another by using the stairs which are also in frequent use as a teaching aid. The bulk of the main building consists of the 'group rooms' in which the residential children live and learn. Two hall-like areas are divided off by curtains for most of the day, to provide extra tuition space for adult outpatients and for the class-teaching of the school-age spina bifida children. There are toilets and washrooms, a kitchen and a library/archive that spills out into bookcases in the adjacent circulation area. A side wing contains administration, medical rooms and a sick bay, its corridors stacked to the ceiling with the case records of former pupils and patients. There is a workshop for making the particular orthopaedic apparatus that the Institute requires, where the cobbler in charge is an ex-conductor and where all student-conductors learn to cobble the Institute's own support footwear out of basic materials.

The recent television report (*Newsnight*, BBC2, 5th May 1983) described the Institute as being 'situated in a drab suburb of Budapest'. This is a little unfair. Though it stands on a major throughfare in Buda, facing some rather old blocks of flats with small local shops at street level, the Institute is just along the road from the attractive campus of the Agricultural University and backs on to a leafy hillside of suburban villas running down behind the well-known Gellért Hill. The buildings of the Institute certainly show the signs of their extensive and unremitting use over the years and could do with a redecoration (as they could when Kearslake visited in 1970!). But it is this unremitting utilisation, not the building itself, which provides the overwhelming impression: throughout the day every corridor and circulation space, every nook and cranny – and, weather permitting, the gardens and grounds too – are in constant use for conduction and the other activities of the Institute.

The new Petö András Intézet also stands in Buda. It is an impressive six storied structure on a wooded hillside in a select neighbourhood, next door to the Party Hospital.

The facilities for the children comprise a peculiar blend of normality and specialisation. Many of the Institute's facilities are determinedly normal, making no concessions to the children's motor disorders. Much is, therefore, just as it would be anywhere else, with stairs, lavatories, eating implements, furniture that would be found in an ordinary house or school. On the other hand, there is the strikingly unusual social world of the Institute, with its intense concentration on achieving orthofunction and the centrality of the group.

The group (*czoport*) is the basic teaching unit in conductive education. The group rooms for residential pupils in Villányi út have been the place where the children sleep, eat, learn to master their motor disorders and receive their education. These rooms therefore have had to be in a constant state of flux. Their use, their layout and furnishing have to be adaptable, robust and sparse. Although efforts are made to brighten and decorate the group rooms, the demands of conduction are primary and the facilities inevitably appear somewhat bleak compared with those of British residential placements – and with living and learning facilities seen elsewhere in Budapest.

The pervasive multipurpose furnishings that for many observers have come to epitomise 'the Peto method' are the ladder-back chairs and the 'plinths' (the wooden-slatted beds) used in many, though by no means all of the motor-training activities with children and adults. It has to be emphasised, however, that much of the children's seated time (and a lot of walking too, in certain cases) involves the use of normal nursery-size chairs, and that much of their work is undertaken seated at normal school tables. The determined and total absence of the archetypal symbol of physical handicap, the wheelchair, has been a frequent subject of remark by visitors to the Institute. For example:

> There are no wheelchairs in the Institute, although there are a number of heavily handicapped children. Those who require support in walking usually hold on to a chair which they push in front of them. Some children have very light plastic splints as an aid to walking, but these are usually temporary measures. (Loring, 1971)

> The furniture and equipment is of the simplest possible and a good deal of ingenuity is required to provide what is needed at the right moment. The basic furniture consists of the plinth in which the children do their exercises. This is covered by a plastic top at meal times and serves as a table and at bed time it is made into a bed with the addition of blankets, sheets and pillows. Bowls are brought in when the children have to wash, each child has his own bowl, his own pot and his own toothbrush, flannel, towel, soap, etc. He keeps his possessions in a bag hanging behind his chair. The children also have satchels with their school books and writing equipment in them. Similarly, the equipment for the physical activities is of the simplest. When necessary, leg supports, sticks, boots and crutches are used, but these come into play as little as possible. (Wilson, 1970)

> No wheelchair is in evidence anywhere; children were ambulant, using chairs as walking aids and they did the maximum towards dressing and undressing and eating, washing and toileting, with time provided as necessary for their efficiency. They negotiated doorways and congested places, and sometimes long sections of the central corridor on their way to the bathrooms, but they all went under their own 'steam' . . .
>
> At breakfast times children were expected to spread their own pieces of bread with the paste (or other filling) provided and even very badly handicapped children managed this. Most of the children managed to drink out of one handled china mugs, but for newcomers or the bad athetoids, large plastic two handled beakers were used filled only half full.
>
> At lunchtime most children again fed themselves, using big spoons, and although some obviously found it difficult nearly all finished the whole meal . . .
>
> Very little dribbling was present and children with wet clothing

from dribbling were changed immediately. (Kearslake, 1970)

The lack of specialised equipment is not a result of shortage of resources; it is a fundamental principle of conductive education: '. . . We have no special toys made especially for handicapped children, neither are there any wheelchairs' (Hári, reported by Varnai, 1984).

All staff at the Institute wear white coats. Why, some English visitors enquire, do they wear white coats? All Hungarian school-teachers and medical personnel wear white coats and, anyway, one will be told, think of helping an athetoid group with its tomato soup. The coats bear no distinguishing marks, other than the Institute's initials MSI stitched in small red letters on the left breast, and the visitor can only guess who is a senior conductor, who a junior and who a student. Similarly, there are no visible distinctions between conducting and non-conducting staff.

The conductors are the only people who work on the development of the mental-motor skills of the Institute's clients (adults and children) within the group rooms and other free spaces at Villányi út. Other white-coated figures include domestic, technical, administrative and library staff, as well as sessional medical specialists. The visitor's problem in identifying roles is compounded by the seemingly universal attitude of friendly enthusiasm that pervades the Institute.

The conductors work a complex shift system to ensure that their own work periods (presently set at five hours) should fit together and overlap to make for the optimal co-ordination of the pupils' day. These five-hour shifts involve a continuous period of work, the conductors within a group exchanging roles and tasks in a never-ending cycle of activities for the children. *All* the children's requirements, physical, emotional, cognitive and academic, are the conductors' responsibility – the physical demands of which are evidenced by the variety of support footwear that many conductors wear. The five-hour shift does not exhaust the formal requirements of the conductors' time. They must also prepare the next day's lessons, plan ahead, record and analyse pupils' progress, etc., though they are free to do such things at home should they wish (indeed, it is hard to conceive of where at Villányi út there would be room). Student conductors, on top of this, have their academic studies.

Additional cleaning staff come on in the evenings as the residential children prepare for bed. During the night the Institute is under the care of three nursing staff and all is calm. Then from the early start of the Hungarian working day the Institute in Villányi út is hard at work:

> When the residential pupils got up from breakfast to walk to their
> rooms it all had to be seen to be believed. There was a bustle which
> our children *never* experience. The children themselves and their
> methods of walking was enough, but conductors washed down
> table tops and moved plinths at top speed and the cleaners attacked
> the hall like vultures with their brooms and mops (they had done
> the children's rooms during breakfast). Nobody made allowance
> for tottering children and the 'totterers' got on their way regardless.
> (Varty, 1970a, emphasis in original)

For the rest of the day, pupils spill out of their group rooms into the
circulation spaces. In the mornings, mothers and babies attend their
two-hour groups and, both mornings and afternoons, adult hemiplegics and multiple sclerosis sufferers attend for groups in the larger
curtained-off hall. Throughout the day streams of adults and children
arrive for assessment, guidance, follow up, review and other outpatient
appointments; the dentist, the orthopaedist, the opthalmologist and the
neurologist hold their respective clinics; student conductors pursue their
studies where they can and, almost every week, visitors arrive from all
over the world to 'make the round', being whisked round the Institute by
Dr Hári to gain a first, fleeting impression of conductive education.
Whatever happens, however, the process of conduction goes unremit-
tingly on. The mark of a good conductor and a well-running group is that
no one, teacher or taught, will find the brief intrusion of a strange
observer anything like so interesting or absorbing as the task in hand.

Pupils and Patients

There are important distinctions to be made in identifying the
children and adults who benefit from conductive education. The
Institute serves children and adults suffering from motor disorders
(*mozgássérültek*). These are separated out from the wider population
whom we refer to as the physically handicapped, this distinction
having been recognised officially by the Hungarian state (Figure 2.1).
Motor disorders are problems of motor control, due to failure in the
mechanism of control in the brain or the nervous system. People
suffering from motor disorders, initially at least, have normal limbs
and bodies; it is their ability to control these that is affected.
Conductive education approaches these problems of control
primarily as learning difficulties that require teaching, rather than as

primarily medical conditions that require treatment. This is not, of course, to deny the possible relevance of medical help in certain aspects of management, but to place it within a wider developmental context in which orthopaedic malformations are regarded as arising largely from the failure to provide proper teaching at the appropriate stage. Motor disorders are, therefore, developmentally distinct from conditions in which it is the limbs themselves that are the primary problem. A child who is paraplegic is motor-disordered: a child with defective legs (as a result of, say, a congenital condition) is dysfunctional in another way and is not a candidate for conductive education.

Figure 2.1: Opening Paragraph of the Decree Establishing the Institute as Part of the Education System (translated from no. 15 of the Official Record of Decrees and Resolutions)

Resolution no. 2031 (1963 XII 30) of the Hungarian Revolutionary Worker-Peasant Government on certain questions connected with the establishment of the National Institute for the Conductive Education of the Motor-Disordered.

1. Through the development of the Institute established by government decree no. 36 (1963 XII 21) the special (conductive) education of the motor-disordered should be made possible regardless of age. In the course of this, accommodation must be made for infants and children of school age, minors of school age and adults. Provisions for motor dysfunctions other than of neurological origin (i.e. traumatological cases) will also be made in future, in health institutions or in institutions of special education.

Age also provides distinctions. Firstly, the relevant population may be conveniently divided between those who suffer a motor disorder from birth or early childhood and those who fall victim to an accident or degenerative condition later in life (not a hard-and-fast division since the Institute accepts the occasional pupil damaged by some trauma or disease in middle childhood). Relevant childhood disorders include cerebral palsy (spasticity, athetosis and ataxia) and spina bifida. Children with muscular dystrophy used to be accepted but are no longer. Relevant adult conditions include hemiplegia (and aphasia) following stroke or road traffic accident, Parkinson's disease and multiple sclerosis. Secondly, in children, age of commencing conductive education is an important factor in their prognosis. As a general rule, the younger the children begin conductive education the better the likely outcome and the shorter the intervention required to achieve it. Children who grow up without help in overcoming their disordered movements suffer increasing orthopaedic deformities. If a child remains unhelped till after the age of five or six, then it becomes very hard to control secondary, physical effects. Ultimately it has to be recognised that the child's problem is no longer solely or even primarily a motor disorder as defined here and the effects of conductive education will be correspondingly limited. With adult conditions, however, it seems to be much less critical for motor outcome if conductive education is not begun soon after the onset or recognition of the condition.

Distinction has to be made too between the notions of, on the one hand, a 'disorder' and, on the other, a 'disability' or 'handicap'. Conductive education distinguishes between these on a developmental plane, one in which development is seen as closely dependent upon educational input. Children or adult patients may suffer from a physiological condition that has a deleterious effect upon the control of movement. This effect is the motor disorder. If the children or adults receive no help – or an inappropriate intervention – then the developmental effects of this disorder will be a disability or handicap. They will become dysfunctional, unable to fend for themselves without special apparatus or allowances or help. If, however, they are taught how to master their disorders, they will not become disabled or handicapped. They will not of course be *cured* of their underlying condition but they will be able to function independently, not dysfunctionally but orthofunctionally.

An analogous distinction has to be made with respect to the mental potential of the Institute's pupils. Many children suffering from conditions resulting in motor disorders also have problems of mental development. In certain cases this is certainly the outcome of further cerebral damage that directly affects the development of the children's mental functions. In all cases, the limitations of experience that result from lessened or distorted motor activity, along with other factors affecting the children's experience of their world (especially their social world), have varying degrees of effect upon mental development. At the Institute the preference is to regard cases of mental retardation in motor-disordered children as being due primarily to the second mechanism rather than the first, unless there is a striking indication to the contrary. Many of the children admitted to the Institute, therefore, are not only motor-disordered but also retarded in their mental development, sometimes to a considerable degree.

A quantitative definition of the Institute's clients is harder to provide. The Institute maintains descriptive statistics aplenty. Extensive and freely available as these are, they appear more in the nature of official returns than what would be regarded in the West as research data. They often tend to pose more questions than they answer and their tantalising running together of categories can be downright infuriating. Further, only Pearson (1984b), one of the many visitors to the Institute over the years, seems to have attempted a systematic collection of such returns. Table 2.1 and Table 2.2 offer a sense of these data and give some indication of the scope of the Institute's work.

Table 2.1: Numbers of Pupils on End-of-year Roll at the Institute and its Network, 1979-83 (from Pearson, 1984b)

Year	Residential pupils			Day pupils	Outpatients (children)	Network
	Age in years		Total			
	2-5	6-15				
1979	63	136	199	80	499	265
1980	72	116	188	80	487	329
1981	95	90	185	75	574	365
1982	86	100	186	74	205	615
1983	80	119	199	81	706	807

Identification

The decree of 1963 required the Institute to establish and maintain a register of all children in Hungary identified as suffering from motor disorders and provide them with conductive education. Five years later a further decree provided for the automatic referral of appropriate cases to the Institute and its network by district physicians, though in practice this seems to have been poorly observed. Only about a quarter or so of the Institute's children are in fact picked up through this channel, the remainder having come through parental referral, screening and other means. (There is no automatic referral required for adult patients, who tend to come by way of certain doctors and clinics with a close association with the Institute.)

How effective, then, is the Institute in catering for Hungary's motor-disordered child population? Some indication may be gained from reworking some of the figures that Pearson collected at the Institute.

Table 2.2: Conductive Education in Hungary, 1983: Numbers of Cases (from Pearson, 1984b)

Budapest	
Main Institute	
Residential pupils	199
Day pupils (at Villányi út)	40
Day pupils (in overspill arrangement, in Pest)	41
Babies at mother-and-baby sessions	124
Children attending once monthly (from surrounding countryside)	378
Children in normal schools, attending for exercises after school hours	55
Other children attending on an occasional basis	149
Adult outpatients	202
Budapest network	
Adults with Parkinson's disease	102
Patients at neurological clinic	10
Children in two special-care institutions (60 and 61)	121
Children at a special school	16
Physical handicapped at a health institution	10
Provincial network	
Towns with residential conductors Nagykan	45
Veszprem	90
Kaposvár	60
Towns visited by conductors Debrecen	74
Nyíregyháza	40
Out-of-netword provincial services	
Three towns, with conductors paid for by the counties	239
Advice	
Via consultation at the Institute, in hospital and rural clinics in 1983	4062

In 1983 there were 8,774 names on the register, children, young people and adults aged 30 years or under. (This list may include some newly disabled young adults but the bulk of cases recorded will have been afflicted from birth.) There is no way, of course, of knowing how completely this national register actually records the Hungarian motor-disordered population. It would not be surprising if some cases had been missed and it is possible that some selective factor or factors might operate to avoid registration. Be that as it may, of the 8,774 cases registered:

    8 had no information available;

1,316 had either died or were suffering from muscular dystrophy (which the Institute no longer treats);

  620 could not be accommodated by the Institute or its network because of lack of facilities;

   88 had slipped through the net for other reasons.

There remained, therefore, 6,734 cases, out of whom 1,007 were considered inappropriate for conductive education.

The figure of 1,007 represents 15 per cent of those remaining 6,734 cases (or 12½ per cent of the original 8,774 cases on the register), suggesting that whilst conductive education is provided for *most* of the children identified as suffering from motor disorders in Hungary, it is definitely not provided for *all*. Very late identification (and, therefore, serious orthopaedic problems) or the presence of further, complicating conditions probably account for some of the 1,007 cases turned away, but it seems likely that the main reason for considering conductive education inappropriate from the outset is the complication of profound mental handicap. How this is decided and by whom (and how valid such decision may be) must await further investigation.

Severity

The severity of children's motor disorders has no bearing upon their eligibility for admission to the Institute. The figures calculated above support this, so do the impressions of visitors to Villányi út. The most considered impression by a British visitor has taken careful account to separate out the severity of the underlying disorder and the level of function achieved despite it (her comparison is with the children with whom she works in England, in the Petö Unit at Ingfield Manor school).

To make an accurate assessment of these aspects (i.e. severity of motor disorder and mental potential) during such a short visit is impossible. However, one is able to form an impression based on one's experience of working with similar children. A first impression was formed after assessing apparent functional activities of the children and then a second opinion after observing more detail of movement and approach to specific tasks . . .

FIRST IMPRESSION

Friday evening. The children we observed before tea were

involved in various activities sitting at the tables. Some were playing with cars or drawing, the older ones were doing their homework. One very athetoid boy, approx. 10 years of age, was doing his homework – this was writing. The quality of his writing along lines approximately ½″ width spaces was quite remarkable. His athetoid tremor although apparent in his condition did not reflect in his writing. During tea it was impressive to observe the independence of the children. All of them were able to feed some if not all types of food without assistance. The relaxed freedom of the meal time was also impressive. The conductors were around eating their meal at the same time as the children but were not directly watching every move they made. The children chose when to pour their drink and when to drink it. There was conversation between them. It was all very un-institutional. After tea, all the children walked either to the bathroom or to their group room to wash and get ready for bed. The atmosphere of the Institute was comfortable, caring and very relaxed. There was no feeling of tension or rush, the time belonged to the children.

Saturday morning. Such a friendly, busy kindergarten atmosphere. The sound of children talking, laughing and teasing each other. Most of the children were gathered together ready to be entertained by some people from Budapest who were to perform a puppet show. After the entertainment the mobility of the children was incredible, the majority of them independently ambulant using a variety of walking aids – sticks, chairs, quoits and some without aids. A few other children were assisted to walk, again in a variety of ways. All the children appeared lively, alert and interested and were remarkably vocal. Could these children be as handicapped as ours? I thought not and made a broad estimate that the majority of the children had a mild to moderate degree of physical handicap and that all were fairly bright.

IMPRESSION after observing for six days.

After observing the children more closely than the first impression allowed the problems the children had and were finding they could control became more apparent. These children were all cerebral palsied with athetoid and/or spastic symptoms. Yet a majority of these children were achieving an incredibly high degree of functional abilities. We saw children at varying stages of progress/independence. The children in the Institute had begun and were continuing to learn how to cope with their problems and to have a more independent life. One group of children were almost ready to leave the Institute and to attend normal school. The aim of the Institute is not to keep the children but to move them back into normal society as orthofunctional people. Most of the children at the time of our observations appeared to be less handicapped than the children at Ingfield, although in reality I do not think this to be so. In my opinion many of these children had begun their lives with a severe physical handicap with associated learning problems, comparable in severity to the children in our schools. Thus the functional abilities appeared to me even more remarkable and difficult to appreciate and understand. How could such control be possible? The progress they had achieved in a few early years was quite fantastic and a glimpse into the possibilities to be attained by children affected by this cruel disability given the right start at an early age and the consequent opportunity, teaching and follow-up. (Barker, 1981)

Orthofunction

The goal towards which the Institute works for its pupils and patients is orthofunction, that is the abilitiy to function as members of society, to participate in the normal social settings appropriate to their age, kindergarten, school, college or work, without need for wheelchairs, ramps, special furniture, toileting arrangements, etc. The criterion of orthofunction is not, therefore, an attribute of the pupils alone: it depends in part upon the tolerance or support of an individual's particular social context and thus cannot be indexed by measures of the pupil's motor skills or other personal features or attainments. Nor is orthofunction a once-and-for-all matter: it has to be not only attained but also maintained over the years out in the world that follow a successful course of conductive education. It is a concept that is both social and developmental.

Figures are available from the Institute to indicate the immediate destination of children leaving residential placement there (Figure 2.2). These do not distinguish between ages or conditions. The concept of orthofunction is not the same as the current western notion of integration. It is in one sense much more, in that the children who attain orthofunction have to attend normal schools or kindergartens without any physical allowances:

The object of Conductive Education is not to accommodate the severe dysfunctional patients in an institute, or to send them to a special school, but to accomplish a basic task to render possible a normal education, travelling in the streets, self-supporting and work. In order to bring about an equilibrium between child and environment, we do not change the environment, but the adaptation of the child's constitution. (Hári, 1968)

Figure 2.2: Immediate Placements of Children Leaving Residential Education at the Institute, 1978 to 1983 (from Pearson 1984b)

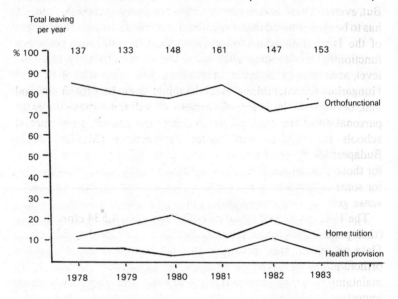

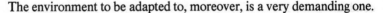

The environment to be adapted to, moreover, is a very demanding one.

Underlying everything is the demand that no child shall attend school – even a special school for motor-disabled children – unless able to walk and get about independently, at least within the confines of the school.

To make 'orthofunction' children and adults have to make not just normal standards but high ones at that. They will have to attend for the normal length of lesson, using the normal furniture and materials of the school. They will have to proceed through the extensive general-school curriculum, excused only PE and perhaps craft, through a school syllabus considerably more advanced than that offered to many children in our own state schools. They will have to write their school work like the others do, even if they can type. If they have a continence problem they will have to eat the same 'loose' Hungarian food. They will have to travel on the same hurtling public transport as does everyone else.

The lot of the physically disabled in Hungary has not been an easy one, even by our own far from ideal standards. The achievement and maintenance of 'orthofunction' may therefore be all the more remarkable in this context. (Sutton, 1984a, Suppl. IV)

But, even if orthofunction implies much more than mere integration, it has to be remembered that it is defined and indexed within the context of the Hungarian education system. Thus a child may be orthofunctional, but attending a special school at 'auxiliary' or 'training' level, according to the criteria for mental development applied to all Hungarian schoolchildren. A child might even be orthofunctional and, because the local school cannot – or will not – make the extra personal effort required, placed in one of the country's two special schools for children with motor dysfunctions (Mexikói út in Budapest for those of normal mental potential, Sály in the country for those with a mental handicap). In one sense, then, orthofunction for some children may amount to rather less than integration in the sense generally current in the West.

The 1983 register of motor disorders recorded 4,534 *closed* cases (their present ages running from early childhood through to 30 years). Data on these cases' present status offers some idea of how the orthofunction achieved at the end of conductive education is maintained over the years that follow. The figures are mute over such important questions as the children's conditions and their ages during conductive education. From the 4,534 cases discharged from the Institute there was no follow-up information on 162 and a further 485 had been closed without receiving a complete course of conductive education (shortage of facilities within the network appears to have been a significant factor), leaving 3,887 cases closed after a full course of conductive education and with current information available:

  3,250 of these were orthofunctional;
  278 were being educated or were working at home;
  359 had proved unsuitable for conductive education.

It is again a matter of judgement what one takes as the appropriate reference population when calculating the proportion of cases to be still orthofunctional following conductive education:

71½ per cent of the total 4,535 cases;
81½ per cent of the 3,887 cases who had received conductive
education and on whom current information was
available.

And those who do not attain or maintain orthofunction? The 358 cases from the 1983 register that had proved unsuitable for conductive education (8 per cent of the 4,534 closed cases, 9 per cent of the 3,887 followed up) probably transferred to health institutions because of profound mental handicap. The 278 cases 'at home' (6 per cent of all closed cases, 7 per cent of those followed up) would, if still of school-age, be receiving six hours per week home tuition, provided by the appropriate local school: if over school-age, 'working' in many or most cases may amount to no more than housework.

The Hungarian figures are indeed tantalising. Figure 2.3 offers another example, indicating the numbers of cases known to be orthofunctional from the total 4,534 on the 1983 register, broken down by year of birth. Such global long-term information, whilst indicating something of the Institute's overall performance, still obscures important points. In general, such figures reassure one not only that conductive education is successful in achieving its goal of orthofunction in the majority of cases but also that orthofunction once achieved tends to be maintained. Many questions, however, remain unanswered. For example: was the population that received conductive education about 20 years ago substantailly the same as now?; how much do the standards required for orthofunction vary according to the characteristics of receiving institutions?; how far do variables such as age of starting conductive education, duration of treatment, specific diagnosis and mental characteristics interact with each other and with school factors to produce the final outcome?; and how far do the features of the provision itself (especially, perhaps, day *versus* residential placement) affect the outcome? Pearson's figures, like the subjective impressions of other visitors, pose as many questions as they offer answers.

Assessment

In general terms it is a child's *mental* potential that is regarded as the most important pointer to the long-term outcome of conductive education, not the degree of *motor* difficulty. This is consistent with the approach's educational nature.

New pupils are given a thorough examination by a most

Figure 2.3: Present Status (Orthofunctional/Dysfunctional) of All Cases on the Institute's 1983 Register According to Year of Birth (from Pearson, 1984b).

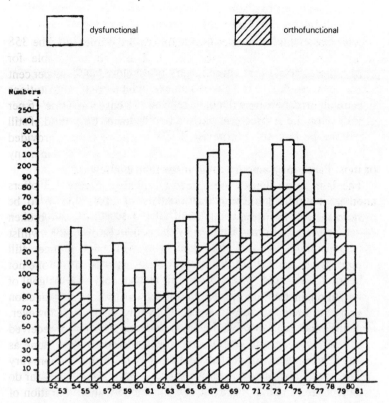

experienced conductor, the purpose of which appears to be largely to lay down baseline data. Information on previous diagnosis and treatment at other centres is also collated (a very different task from what this would be in Britain, since in Hungary children's medical records are held by their parents). The most important immediate decision is to fit the new pupil into a group. The child's age and physical condition are factors to be taken into account – it is vital, however, to test out a group in which the child might happily settle. Thereafter, a detailed personal file will be maintained by the senior conductor of the group, to provide a continuous record of progress, including photographs and examples of work. All children now also have video records.

Many young children on admission are mentally backward as well as motor-disordered. No attempt is made by the Institute to prognosticate future mental development on the basis of such early backwardness, nor to distinguish differential 'needs' for conduction. These will emerge out of the pupil's response to the process itself. The degree of mental retardation accepted by the Institute is considerable:

> My impression is that only the very profoundly handicapped will not be referred. Dr Hári gave as an example: a three year old who is totally irresponsive will not be refused as such a child is still able to develop (i.e. a three year old functioning below a six month level will not be refused). (Jernqvist, 1980a)

Above all the assessment is part of the pedagogic process:

> A new child fits into the system slowly over a period of time, the child's progress rate being itself, the assessment. Initially a detailed family history is taken by the conductor who has overall responsibility for the child and who will refer him to the appropriate consultant for treatment of specific problems of hearing, vision etc., as and when this is necessary. Assessment is only doctor orientated if the child is actually ill. A paediatrician visits the Institute daily to see children who are ill, a dentist and neurologist visit weekly, the latter looking after the control of epilepsy and an orthopaedic consultant, urologist, eye specialist and hearing specialist visit fortnightly. There are no psychologists. The conductor fills in a form to record what the child can and cannot do which is used later to assess the rate of progress. Children in a residential group are given approximately two months in which to show their learning capacity when those who fail to improve are cared for elsewhere. Apparently only 10% of new children fall into this category. Children in the residential groups are sorted out broadly speaking by disability and by age though not entirely, the main factor being whether the new child's personality blends harmoniously with those of the other children and whether he can succeed with the tasks set within the group. I was told that many of the children were in the I.Q. range of 60 or below, although formal testing was obviously frowned upon, which was seen as a challenge to conductive education and was not a reason for restricting one's efforts. (Carrington, 1973)

Once a child approaches school-age, however, a wider national procedure makes its demands. All Hungarian children have to be reviewed at this age to assess their suitability for general school. Children who might require special schooling are directed to a special commission (bizottság) which rules on their eligibility. Some children, who had attended the Institute from an early age and had already achieved orthofunction by this time and left, presumably have to take their chances with their local bizottság. Children who are pupils at the Institute when they are 5 years old have to be presented to the Commission on Motor Disorders which meets at the special school at Mexikói út. The bizottság then determines the level of school education that the child will now receive.

> Although 'committee' sounds daunting – rather akin to what happens to suspended pupils in the UK – their role is to offer help and advice and sometimes parents themselves approach committees for help.
> The psychological input appears fairly traditional by Western standards – certainly the psychologist I met at the bizottság for the motor-disabled, talked proudly of the 'Budapesti Binet Teszt' and the current progress in standardising the 'Budapesti WISC Teszt'!
> Although there is an emphasis on IQ measures, the results are interpreted fairly flexibly with other factors also being considered. The system for children with learning difficulties is similar to that operating in the UK under the 1944 Education Act. Children with IQs roughly in the 50–70 range are educated in special schools offering a limited version of the normal curriculum, emphasising literacy and numeracy skills, children in the 25–50 IQ range are also educated in special schools, but with an emphasis on self-help skills, language development, socialisation. Children whose IQ is below 25 are housed and educated in institutions run by the Health Department. (Pearson, 1984a)

It seems unlikely that there will be any of the lowest grade still at the Institute at school-age. For the rest, three levels of schooling are provided within the Institute, general syllabus, auxiliary syllabus and training. The children continue to live and work in their established groups but are meant to attend lessons for formal school work according to the findings of the bizottság. These findings are treated with some discretion by the Institute, both in its own internal arrangements and when preparing for the pupils' subsequent placements, for conductive education provides not just for the motoric but also the mental transformation of many children and this process is often only partially complete when the bizottság holds its school-starting-age deliberations. Whilst the child remains a pupil at the Institute, however, assessment and teaching are not separate activities:

> How does the conductor know how to guide the child to success? The conductor teaches and educates, and takes care of the most elementary functions to be done. She arouses interest, creates attention, informs the children about tasks, controls whether these are understood, guides the children to appropriate solutions and evaluates the solution, and – on the basis of her constant observation – makes the plan for further lessons.
>
> The most important aspect of behaviour of the conductor is the habit of observing and watching the minds, movements and states of children . . . She relates testing with teaching. She is planning the solution of task-performances on the basis of continuous evaluation – making use of every possibility, all manifestations of spontaneity in guiding the children. (Hári, 1970)

The Course of Conduction

Ideally, from the Institute's point of view, all Hungarian children suffering from motor disorders would be notified upon identification to a national network. This would provide parents' schools, mother-and-baby groups and perhaps day kindergarten facilities within the locality, with more intensive residential help from three years of age for those requiring it, the bulk of children attaining orthofunction before school-age or shortly afterwards. In practice the network is less well developed and many children come to the Institute late, in default of provisions near to their homes. Then once orthofunction seems attainable, the ideal outcome would be a co-ordinated introduction into a local school, with close supervision of the placement. In practice, things seem much as first observed by Cotton 20 years ago:

> Generally they stay as residential patients for 2 or 3 years, transfer to normal schools and return home to their parents. After leaving the Institute the children are completely independent; the parents are told what they are able to do, and are expected to watch that

deterioration does not take place. They must supervise their exercises but not help the children more than is absolutely necessary. Schools are advised of the children's academic standard and warned that if the child slips back they will be to blame, since at the Institute the child could manage the work with less tuition than in a normal school. Each year the children return to the Institute for a check up. (Cotton, 1965)

Pearson's (1984b) figures permit some idea of the duration of one stage in this process, residential placement (see Table 2.2), though there appear to be numbers of children who achieve orthofunction without recourse to this stage. The figures for duration of conductive education appear to vary from year to year.

Whatever the particular course of an individual child's identification and conductive education, the process is a lengthy one. Only those who know the child, as parents or as conductors, are able to describe such a long dynamic process. A rare account is available from the commentary given by Dr Hári to a film record of one child's progress, presented at a conference in Dublin.

[The child] is now 12 years old; he was born at the end of the thirty second week of gestation his birth weight was 1,75 Kgs. As far as his case history is concerned, he was born with Rh incompatibility, a congenital heart defect and hyperchromic anaemia. At the age of three years it was considered desirable to transfer him to a home for those children considered incapable of development. He was unable to sit, stand or walk. He could not drink alone, was bottle-fed with pulped food, wore diapers. He uttered sounds.

He was, however, not admitted to such a home but to our Institute at the age of four years. His diagnosis included choreic athetosis with a torticollis rotatoricus, divergent strabismus, medium hypocusis and microcephalus ... there were choreic and athetoid movements of a fluctuating character and amplitude in all his extremities as well as the trunk and almost a permanent swinging movement of the head. He could not hold himself with his hands and could not grab things because of the athetoid movements of his arms and fingers. He could not stand and walk alone. The question was: even if he ever learns to walk, how would he be able to speak or use his hands? Would he ever be capable of feeding himself since he was unable to influence the rotating movements of his head?

We decided not to exclude writing and speech education from his programme.

His mental and motor development was slow at the beginning. When he was six years old he was still unable to button things, to lace shoes or tie a knot.

Thanks to systematic group-education this developmental process speeded up. During the course of Conductive Education he learned to walk alone at normal speed and over long distances on varying terrain. He became able to use the communication facilities.

At seven, the rotating movements are there but are less explicit and he can bring the hands together. He can walk in the road without being supported. At nine years he became much more co-ordinated.

Now his graphic activities. First the paper had to be fixed and he led the pencil with interruptions. Parallel to his mental and motor development his graphic activity and sense of phrasing showed progress. He began to fix his head. His drawing could be recognised. The drawing of a man revealed proportions as did the drawing of the house. Fixing the paper became unnecessary. At first he wrote using a 2.5 cm line spacing, then the line spacing was reduced to 7 mm and writing became one of his means of expression.

To enable social integration it was necessary to make him continue his studies in an ordinary school. Although the rotating movement of his head has not quite disappeared yet and his speech can be understood but is not normal, the school accepted him because he can care for himself and he can eat normally. At present he is in the fifth grade. The film shows him in his school environment.

This child can improve further. The transition to school was successful. There are still articulatory faults and slowness in writing but the school has treated this flexibly. He will continue to improve after his final examination. He will develop his speech and writing and become a personality capable of working and fitting in society. (adapted from Hári, 1981a)

This boy arrived at the Institute 'late'. One such arrival has been described by an English visitor:

When a newcomer comes to the group great care is taken to make the newcomer feel welcome. I observed the arrival of one new child to a group. She was brought in by a conductor who introduced her to the children. All the children looked and smiled at her and obviously tried to make her welcome. The child was in a very distressed condition, unable to sit and whining miserably, but the conductor sat holding her hand with great patience and kindness for half an hour, at the end of which time the child was smiling and quite willing to join in the work of the group. (Wilson, 1970)

Those who arrive very late, however, can receive only limited attention: 'A fifteen year old seen for the first time will be given two months intensive education, or two hours a day during a period, but cannot be admitted'. (Jernqvist, 1980a)

Foreign visitors to the Institute can observe or note such specific events. They cannot, of course, experience the essential, long-term dimension of the conductive process. They can merely form cross-sectional impressions of moments along its way.

School for Parents

In the school for parents the prime goal is not directly motoric but the establishment of the interactional, affective process held fundamental to all development, the establishment of what Dr Hári refers to as 'the contact'.

In the parents' school the mother is taught how to manage at home, feeding, dressing, etc. The goal is to activate the child. The mother learns what tasks to set the child in order to make it cooperate with her. The mother comes back at varying times for check-ups and according to progress the tasks are changed. The mother should learn not to bother with the child's movements but should make an effort to activate the child. The child should learn to activate when called. The child should become more and more interested, turn towards impulses, become active, show pleasure when the mother approaches, learn to play and to go on playing, build up its endurance.

In the course of five to six months, the child matures so it can participate in group work within the frame of 'the school for mothers'. (Hári, as reported by Cotton, 1975)

Mother-and-baby Group

Every weekday, three times a morning, mothers arrive at the Institute with their young children, mostly in the second year of life, to work together in a mother-and-baby group. We have an account of this work from Dr Hári, dating from the early seventies:

All occupations are kindergarten activities and lead to education. The goal is to attempt by visual and auditory stimulations to make the child react to verbal demands and consequently to learn activities leading to definite goals. These goals should be reached by play. One should not use abstract movements but always set a goal. The group occupation is structured so that each game prepares for the development of self-help. In the beginning the children may feel insecure on the pot because it is a new situation. To minimise the insecurity they must grasp a ladderback and the pot may be of a larger size.

How precisely does the group work in the parents' school? First, activation by roll-call or song then potting, handwash and eating. It is important that the children become noisy, lively and interested while they are eating. When they eat they sit on small chairs in front of the plinth which is used as a table. The soles should be flat on the floor (or stool). The children eat the food they have brought. The mother is taught how she can make the child himself put the spoon, bread or mug to his mouth. One teaches the child to swallow when he drinks and not to dribble. Slowly one proceeds to solid foods, the child learning to chew. Swallowing and chewing prepare for speech. The mother must understand that a bottle may delay speech. After the meal come standing, walking and movement. There must be a motivated traffic, the movement having an aim. The play finishes with going home. . .

At the first attendances children should have their interest aroused. Children only cry if an occupation is forced upon them. The common work of the group affects not only the child but also the mother whose educating activity is the condition for success. She is instructed how to carry on in a practical way. It is an advantage that the mothers can compare their children to other children in the group and not only compare them with normal children. They can then better learn to judge progress and be more optimistic and conscious of their goals . . .

Continuity is essential in the Conductive Education of the parents. It must be carried on at home during the day in different situations, never abstract but fitted into the complex tasks of daily living and should continue until they have become a habit.

All this is explained to the parents with practical examples. It may be expected that a child should learn to drink out of a mug in two weeks, or hold a spoon or walk with support or get up without help or pronounce a word or recognise an object, etc.

The parents must continue the education consistently. A mother may tell you that she always turns her child at night because it needs affection. You can explain to her that it would be an advantage if she were to use the technique she has learnt in the school which will lead to self-help and still make the child feel she loves it. . .

The school for parents prepares the dysfunctioning child on the baby level for a more intense education. The earlier Conductive Education begins the better the result. It happens not infrequently that a child becomes orthofunctioning in the parents' school or as an Out-Patient. (Hári, 1972, as reported by Cotton, 1975)

Kindergarten

Some children, then, go on to residential kindergarten. Others, because they live a long way away or through late identification or other reasons, only begin their conductive education at this stage. The following account of part of the residential kindergarten day refers to the younger-age spina bifida children in Villányi út.

The younger class was following a kindergarten regime. Initially the children, aged from about three to six, were divided into three groups. One group were clustered around a low table at which one of the conductors sat. Some were sitting on chairs, some standing leaning on the table. They were engaged in learning a little number or counting song, singing it as a group and then taking turns to sing a verse individually. One child's performance was greeted with enthusiastic applause by the other children round the table and by the conductor. It seemed that he had previously been unable to master this song, now he had.

Round a second table, behind where the conductor was seated, five further children were standing, leaning against the edge of the table, and working unsupervised with some Lego-style materials made in East Germany. They were busy making individual models, all of which were taken away by one of the other conductors at the end of this activity and placed in general view on the top of a cupboard. When I sat close to this group one of the boys, aged about four, looked round to me and asked the question frequently put by the younger children at the Institute '*Bacsi?*'

(Uncle?), otherwise little attention was paid to me and the children worked on at what they were doing with no supervision from any of the conductors. No apparent problem of attention, distractibility or fatigue were observed in any of the younger spina bifida children throughout my time in this classroom.

Of the remaining three children, two were standing together at one of the cupboards, busy sorting something or other, while a third had her leg supports removed and was having an individual walking exercise with another conductor (assisted for part of the time by the third), in which she was learning to walk backwards without her leg irons, pulling a large chair behind her as a support. Some of the children were wearing support apparatus up to the hips, some up to the thighs, some up to the knees and some no apparatus at all. It was subsequently explained to me that the children characteristically have support if needed and that this is gradually reduced over the course of Conductive Education, the goal (not always achieved) being no support at all. The pattern varies, of course, according both to the severity of defect and to the age of commencing Conductive Education. Whilst this session was in progress a sturdy little fellow marched steadily in from the maths class next door, through the kindergarten class, on his way to the lavatory. He was wearing no leg supports.

There was the usual team of three conductors, though, (as was commonly the case in the Institute) it was not possible to tell from observing a single session which was the senior and which one the student. Whilst one conductor led the group in the counting song and another continued to conduct the individual standing exercise alone, the third busied herself noiselessly in preparing the unoccupied part of the room for the next activity. She cleared furniture well back and drew a large chalk circle on the floor, with wavy lines in it to represent water. Again, as was typical in the Institute, the actions of each conductor fitted precisely into those of the others, without any need for commands or other verbal communication, ensuring that the next activity would be ready for the children the moment that it was required.

The counting lesson having finished with the success of everyone in the group, and the Lego-type constructions having been collected up and put on display, one of the conductors announced the next activity, to take place around the chalk circle. All the children now moved away from the tables and set off for the circle. None of the children was helped, they all walked there according to the particular means accessible to them at their present stage of motor development. Some walked independently and with leg supports, some independently but without them. Those yet unable to maintain their balance pushed their chairs, whilst one did it by walking along holding a chair at either side. The whole was achieved in the children's own time and at their own pace, with occasional words of instruction or encouragement from the conductor and the children's own occasional, spontaneous comments. Those who arrived first spaced themselves out round the outside of the circle and stood there patiently and attentively awaiting the arrival of the slower ones. They stood by various means, some independently, three independently but holding each-other's outstretched hands in a rickety, tottering chain, some holding their chair backs and the one supported between his two chairs. The little girl who had been having the individual walking exercise, still without her leg supports, made her way to the circle very slowly pushing a chair, a conductor encouraging every step.

The conductor who had prepared the circle quickly chalked large symbols around its rim, a duck, a flower etc. The children being assembled in a ring, each child to a symbol, all three conductors stood around them and began a complex, dramatic singing and speaking game, the children joining in at once in unison. This involved the whole group's singing a chorus, during which a child was selected to walk into the middle of the circle. The child then sang or spoke a verse which selected another child (identified by the chalked symbol, as had been the first one) to take a turn in the circle ... and so on. As they sang the children continued to stand independently or together, according to whatever means of support they had started the game with – and as their turn was called they made their own way independently to the centre of the circle, again using their individual means of support. One child fell over but, as always, no adult help was given and he got himself cheerfully back on his feet and continued unabashed into the circle. As observed throughout the Institute (and elsewhere, in a normal Budapest kindergarten) the children knew the songs well and sang out in bold and practised voices. The conductors joined in wholeheartedly, in both the children's song and their enjoyment of the game, and each child's individual attainment was collectively achieved by the joint efforts and encouragement of both children and conductors. (Sutton, 1984a, Suppl. II)

At the recent International Seminar, held at Villányi út in September 1984, a kindergarten group of spastic children 'performed' for a large group of visiting seminarists:

> The group was made up of 15 children suffering from spastic diplegia, spastic quadraplegia and spastic hemiplegia, and ranged in age from 4½ years to 6½ years. They had worked together, on average, for one and a half years; the longest time any child had been in the group was 2 years, the shortest time 1½ months. When the children were admitted to the group 12 were unable to walk independently, 9 were unable to dress, feed themselves, cater for their toilet needs etc. Now, 11 can walk independently. The aim of the group is orthofunction appropriate to their age, i.e. kindergarten level.
>
> Within the session observed, the conductors were trying to show the level of the children in terms of posture, changing position, social ability, language, speech and play. Most of the children appeared to have intelligible speech and readily joined in with the rhythmic counting as they completed the task. With this group, repetition of the command did not always appear to be necessary. In the sitting programme the main conductor used a lot more gesture, demonstrating the required movement as well as giving the command. Perhaps this programme was less familiar to the children.
>
> Four conductors worked with the group. The main conductor who led the session, appeared to deal with the individual needs of the more able children. The sub-conductors worked on a one-to-one basis with the less able in the group. One of the most striking things about the session was the quietness and tranquility. There was no conversation between the conductors, they were aware of what needed doing and got on with it. The children were so interested in their work that they did not moan, cry or talk pointlessly to each other. Speech and language were used for the sole purpose of motor facilitation, there was little extraneous noise. This is a far cry from the classroom environment frequently found in British schools for the physically handicapped. Despite the fact that 30 people were watching the session the children gave their undivided attention to the conductor. (Cottam, 1984)

School-age

Many children achieve orthofunction at kindergarten age, others coninue at the Institute into school-age, while some only arrive at this stage. There is no strict age demarcation of groups at the Institute between kindergarten and school-age. Some school-age children work in groups that are chiefly composed of kindergarten children and vice versa. The following account refers to a spastics' group, comprising mainly school-age pupils.

Group 8 – Spastic, a systematic room. This was another very interesting room to observe. The conductors were excellent and the children worked very precisely. The symptoms of spasticity were evident but were seen to be mastered by the children and staff. We observed the lying and standing programmes as well as the children walking. Once again we were able to see that the problems the children faced were the same as our severe spastic children. In lying the children wore no splints, the complexity and precision of the movements was remarkable. The children had been shown how to initiate and complete movements in extension, flexion and combining both. All were able to actively abduct their legs and indeed this was a position which had become natural to them. The conductors constantly observed the precision and a child who sat up correctly was asked to lie down and repeat the task. During one lying programme, Dr Hári asked us to compare the conductors working in this group with those of another not so good room. The difference was apparent once she had pointed out a few inaccuracies in the poorer room. (It was only poor by comparison.) The difference being in the precision the children achieved, but the lack of precision was due to the conducting and not the ability of the children. This was demonstrated to us after Dr Hári had spoken to the poorer conductors and asked them to repeat a task. Most of the children in Room 8 wore splints on their legs or feet or both when not working in the lying programme. All were able to stand using various aids, e.g. large ladderback chair, two sticks, one stick and one ring, stick and chair, two chairs. Two children needing conductor facilitation in order to walk were able to stand without conductor assistance using an aid, the others were all able to walk with their aids independently. We observed a walking programme. This was developed as a game which the children enjoyed but it also involved the physical skills needed to become more independent. The game involved walking, bending down to pick up an object, and carrying the object back to the next child. This progressed to picking up two objects. The objects had to be carried in the hands as well as the hands holding the walking aids. During the game one child fell down, he was given a chair to hold on to in order to get up. Walking from breakfast to their group room was used as a teaching walking time. The children were constantly supervised by a conductor to see that the same precision was maintained. The children walked in various ways using their own particular aids. It became clear to us that teaching walking is useless unless one teaches the child to stand and let go of his aid. This was done in various ways according to the individual child's needs, but was observed during all teaching walking times. While the lying programme was in process a couple of children were taken by one conductor to work at walking in the corridors. This appeared to be a time when new progressions could be attempted. Dr Hári told us that these walking times were used for the children no longer needing the lying programme, although we saw different children walking one day and those previously walking partici-pating in the lying programme. We also observed the use of warm pads on the ankle and knee joints of some of these children. After wearing the pads for approximately ten minutes the conductors manipulated the joints. (Barker, 1981)

In comparison, here is a similarly aged group of athetoid children.

Group II – severe athetoid. All learning to speak and with feeding problems. We also have many feeding problems and observing this room was helpful to us. It was encouraging to see that the content of this programme was similar to the one we were using for our speech and feeding group. There was more holding of cheeks and heads while making sounds than we have used. However, the outstanding observations were made during activity times, e.g. bubble tub. These children, with the exception of one, were undoubtedly severe athetoid yet they held on to the bubble tubs, opened them, dipped in the little wands and attempted to blow. Some were successful with the blowing. (We had taken the bubbles for the children, unfortunately they turned out not to be very good bubbles.) Very few spilt. The interest, motivation and control was unbelievable. We saw these children eating biscuits. The biscuits were given out and left in front of the children while the conductors were 'busy'. All the children including a new child attempted to reach their biscuit and again most were successful. Had the conductors been hovering over the children I doubt the success rate would have been so high. More manipulative tasks were observed in this group when the children painted their hand prints previously made in plaster of paris. One particular athetoid boy dipping into his pot of paint knocked the paint over. He was obviously pleased to be able to easily dip his brush into the paint on the table. However, a conductor came over, mopped up the paint from the table and spoke to him. He then continued to use paint from the paint pot. He was learning to cope with the normal. (Barker, 1981)

Afterwards

Preparation for life outside the Institute is an integral part of the course.

... We start preparing the children for an independent life 8 months prior to their discharge from the Institute; this is when they start taking trams, go to the theatre and on excursions, in short this is the time when they are exposed to increasing burdens. The children get acquainted with the world surrounding them, the phenomena held to be almost natural to healthy people. (Hári, reported by Varnai, 1984)

For some, the burden of transition can be eased by an arrangement with the general school near the Institute.

The aim of the Institute is to send all the children back to ordinary schools if possible. As an intermediate step, children who have sufficient mobility are sent to an ordinary school in the neighbourhood, very near to the Institute, while still continuing to live in the Institute itself. At the time of my visit there were four children attending this neighbourhood school as a step towards returning to their homes and going to ordinary schools. They are not allowed to go out to this school unless they can walk there on their own, and are unaccompanied except in bad weather. Three of these children were in the third class of the primary school, average age 8 to 9 years. The Institute children were rather older than this, the eldest being about 11. A grade system operates in Hungary so that normally children from the Institute, when going to an ordinary school, would be admitted to a lower [grade] than their normal age group. When the children visit this ordinary school in the neighbourhood, they use exactly the same text books as they had been using in the Institute and can do their revision in the evening when they return. This kind of arrangement obviously facilitates the transfer from one school to another, so that when they go back to their own homes and attend ordinary school they will continue at the same stage where they were. It is important to remember that a grade system operates in Hungary. I am told that it is not the practice to accelerate children above their normal grade for their age, but children can be retarded up to as much as three years. (Wilson, 1970)

This transfer can, however, be quite hard:

Normal school is the goal of the Institute. We had the opportunity of visiting two normal schools to see two pupils known to the Institute. Both pupils were mildly handicapped – spastic diplegic, fully ambulant, normal hands, speech and, no doubt, of normal intelligence. We had a brief conversation with the children via an interpreter. The teachers did not speak English, nor German, which made detailed questioning difficult. The teachers were, however, pleased with the performance of their handicapped pupils – 'She learns well' but it was clear that they regarded C.P. as a question of feet, legs and walking.

The school was bare and ill equipped compared with the average English school. Staff wore white coats – pupils blue overalls. Class teaching was used – the children were sitting in neat rows, raising their hands and reading a piece each.

It is not as easy as is thought, for a child to graduate from the Institute to a normal school. The Headmasters and teachers apparently need a lot of persuasion from Dr Hári. She is not getting the support of the Government in this matter, that I expected her to get. Dr Hári mentioned, for example, that more than half the children should be in special schools according to the State Commission. One of the schools we visited had altogether six handicapped. (Jernqvist, 1980a)

The Institute treats the rulings of the bizottság on such matters with some discretion. Even so, life can still be a struggle:

Mária is 24 and works in a clerical post at a technical-translation institute. She is diplegic and years ago she attended the Institute. We had been taken to meet her as an example of an orthofunctional ex-pupil. We met Mária at the institute where she works. She came down the lift to meet us in the entrance hall, walking rather stiffly with the aid of a stick, and took us up back to the office in which she works. We found the circumstances of our meeting rather embarrassing. There were three other young women working in the room who were friendly enough and who, after finding us chairs to put around Mária's desk, got on discreetly with their own work. The man who seemed to run the office, however, looked distinctly put out at our intrusion and did not attempt to hide it.

We would have preferred to end this interview as soon as possible, to cut short our own and, we would have imagined, Mária's embarrassment. She, however, was not in the least put out. She explained her work, how she had learned to walk at the Institute and how she had left for normal school able to walk quite independently. Then, she explained, an orthopaedic surgeon had operated to straighten her knees. Now she had straight knees and walked with a stick. She would very much like to be able to attend the Institute again, to improve her locomotion. She cannot, however, because of her work.

Yet it was not herself that she wanted to talk about – not directly, anyway. Unabashed by the presence of her colleagues and the patently unwelcoming attitude of her supervisor, she detained us for a long time in order to question us closely about the conditions of life, social services, financial provision etc. of young disabled people in Britain. She was interested in the quality and availability of aids (including wheelchairs), access, employment prospects and leisure activities. She expressed the same blank, polite incredulity as did everyone in Hungary at hearing that it was not social policy to try to teach the motor-disordered how to walk as the prime priority. Most of all, however, she wanted to ask about accommodation, about the facilities available for disabled adults who do not live at home, about hostels, sheltered housing, grants for adaptions and especially about restrictions upon cohabitation and marriage.

Only when she felt that she could learn no more from us by this questioning did Mária show us out of the building. As she did she explained, perhaps by now unnecessarily, that she had a young man, confined to a wheelchair by an orthopaedic condition, and that they want to set up home together.

Mária is an attractive and shrewd young woman, appreciative of the start in life that the Institute gave her. She wants a lot more, however. She has joined the Budapest Association for the Motor Disordered and sees herself as part of the international struggle of the disabled to put their own case for a better life and to fight for it. (Sutton, 1984a, Suppl. V)

The Regime

It is the residential day that has presented the world with the canonical image of conductive education (though the day-school day, from 8 a.m. to 5 p.m. is also prolonged by British special-school standards). A mother of a residential school-age pupil at the Institute has described the children's day:

> Their days were one of intensive learning. From the moment they woke up they were actively involved in the learning process – from the time they pushed off their slatted beds (plinths) on to a pot and began dressing, through breakfast, to their morning lying tasks. They were not carried or moved, but walked collectively in and out of rooms. All movements were accompanied by speech. The day continued with morning break and school work until lunchtime. Again, all the children fed themselves or participated in their feeding by holding the spoon aided by a conductor.
>
> The afternoon included another task series, usually sitting to standing and some work with the hands. There was another school work session and then activities involving music and singing, painting and handwork.
>
> Supper time and showers and an early bedtime finished off a completely active day. They were tired but happy, and reacted as do all primary school age children – sleeping well (Caspar, 1984)

From start to finish of this day the children strive to manage themselves independently:

> We arrived at 6.30 one morning to see the children get up and also stayed one evening to watch the bedtime routines.
>
> On rising the children dressed themselves in socks, vests and pants using the particular techniques of thumb and forefinger, which are especially taught in this method. Since the children sleep on their plinths in the classroom, the large windows were then all thrown open and breathing exercises were done before washing and dressing, all of which must be done with the maximum of

independence. All children then pushed their chairs into the central narrow hall for breakfast during which time the classrooms were thoroughly cleansed and freshened for the day's efforts . . .

At bedtime children traverse the rather long distance of corridor to the showers, still moving without aid, leaning on either one or two chairs and returning again to their rooms for bed. Every child looked clean and comfortable when settled down for the night and after such Herculean efforts by day, must undoubtedly be more than ready to sleep. (Kearslake, 1970)

Dr Hári has described how individual activities are linked together to form the daily programme:

The daily programme is formulated by the observation of the conductor. The advantage of conductive education is that the child is not bound to one person, but to the conductor system: within this system the conductors are equal to each other, but at the same time completely informed and able to direct the development of a child and everything concerning his education. She is able to follow and help the child's active learning process all day long, the development and refining of his intellectual function, observational capacity and resourcefulness. The close relationship between the conductor and children enables her to fulfil their desire for play and joy. The conductors do not take into consideration crying as a means of communication within the group (anyway, this manifest-ation of feelings is most rare in the Institute). But on the contrary, she pays great attention to the smallest movement or change of mimicry because this may indicate that the child's self-respect has suffered because he did not attain the expected results. In such a case, instead of offering the psychopedagogically harmful consola-tion and affection she displays a friendly attitude and helps the child to overcome his difficulties. (Hári, 1968)

The regime that governs this programme is certainly gruelling – it is neither regimented nor harsh.

The atmosphere in the rooms was extremely pleasant at all times, and very permissive although the ability of conductors to restore a noisy, chaotic group of children to order in a split second and with the utmost of good humour was very marked.

Children if left alone for any length of time would break into spontaneous singing or beating of hands, or some other pleasurable bit of nonsense, to return quickly to effort again as required.

Generally there were two or three conductors to a group, with one trained main conductor (very experienced), in charge of the programme, one assistant and perhaps one trainee conductor to an average group of about fourteen to fifteen children.

Other conductors quite frequently came into the rooms to gather apparatus, or ask a question, and this was received with tolerance and did not appear to affect the degree of concentration expected from children.

Although once or twice in the twelve days I saw a child appear tired or fretful and be withdrawn from the group, for the main part the children appeared to be none the worse for their alarmingly long day's efforts (which started at 6.30 a.m. and ended with bed at approximately 8 p.m.)

Although this reflects a waking to sleeping plan of training, there were many long breaks of fifteen to twenty minutes during the day when children were not asked to do anything at all and which obviously were used as rest breaks by them, although not officially recorded as such. The attitude of conductors towards non-conforming children was interesting. Generally the child was talked to in a coaxing 'tirade' (unfortunately not understood by us) with obvious affection – but correction attitudes. If this proved unproductive, the child was left totally alone until such time as he chose to become part of the group again.

I noticed children who had resisted the group method at the beginning of our visit who were well on the way to conforming by the end.

To see a whole roomful of young children of similar handicap, all performing extremely well on plinths, and vocalising at the same time, and all being simultaneously guided and encouraged by two or three conductors was a remarkable experience.

The particular full-throated voices of the conductors, whether speaking or singing, certainly seemed an integral part of the system and by their very loudness I should think the children would find it hard to miss the message of the moment, but also by the pleasantness also would be encouraged to comply ... The onlooker obviously could become bored and naturally look for signs of boredom in the children, but little sign of this was actually present; the children seemed as interested as their conductors in achieving personal independence. (Kearslake, 1970)

The children's regime is devoted to the ultimate goal of orthofunction.

A good deal of the child's day is spent on movement education, since the achievement of independence of movement is one of the fundamental aims of the Institute. The aims are that the child should, if possible, be taught to sit without support, to walk unaided and to use tools as in hand-writing and other practical work. In each of these aspects of training there is a very carefully graded series of exercises. For example, training to walk begins with the children lying prone on the plinth and first practising their legs – crossing their legs or moving their feet apart, turning over and so on. Eventually the children, from a prone position on the plinth, pull themselves to a standing position where they remain supported by the plinth. Later they practise standing with the support of a chair, standing between two chairs and eventually reach the stage when they can release their hands, clap them in the air so that they have the experience of standing unsupported even for quite a short time. This leads to the first step, putting the heels down with support from the chair and later movement with the support of the conductor. In all the physical exercises they undertake, the children first of all express their intention in words, for example saying altogether 'I stand on my heels'. After they have said the words they then count up to 5, which gives the children time to reach the desired goal. By the time the word 'five' is uttered, the child's heels should be firmly in contact with the ground. In all the exercises a very important feature is the child's independence. He is expected to find his own way of achieving the desired result. The conductor will never move a child's limbs except in the initial stages to demonstrate what the aim is. When a child trying to walk falls down, it is noticeable that no-one comes forward to support him, to raise him again and the child does not look for anyone to help him. Nevertheless, a conductor will give inconspicuous help – for example by sliding the chair in his direction so that he can reach it and pull himself to his feet. Another conductor may place her foot alongside the feet of the child trying to raise himself to a standing position to prevent him slipping and to make the task a little easier. However, the child is always left with the impression he has achieved the goal himself. Sometimes the other children will help in a situation like this. They will stop what they are doing and watch the child, sometimes saying all together 'I stand up' and counting to give him a time limit for achieving the standing position.

The methods used in developing the use of the hands and particularly leading up to hand-writing are interesting. First of all the children, still on the plinth, begin by clasping their hands together and later grasping other objects, such as the edge of the plinth, to bring themselves up to a standing position, or the arms or sides of the chair. The next stage is to grasp a smaller object, such as a thick stick. This they do with both hands and begin making movements with the stick, for example crossing them over or pointing to a particular place on the table or plinth. A later stage is painting with the fingers, dipping the finger into the paint and making movements with it. This is not the free-style finger painting, such as is seen in nursery schools in this country. It is very much directed towards an end and is strictly controlled. For example, in one lesson I saw the children reproducing traffic lights with a red, yellow and green dot. This called for varying grades of control and precise placement of the fingers. (Wilson, 1970)

Despite the obvious emphasis on motor-education, the regime incorporates the normal, formal experiences of Hungarian school-children.

Whilst we were there, the whole group of 210 were assembled in the main hall for the annual April 4th celebrations to mark the end of Nazi domination in 1945. All children assembled gradually in their own pattern, using chairs, or walking as taught with counting and clapping of hands as they went. It was the largest group of young cerebrally palsied children amassed together that I had ever seen, and their great poise and physical control throughout the very formal ceremony which ensued was again very impressive. (Kearslake, 1970)

Yet even on such a formal occasion the children's spontaneous feelings are free to break through, sometimes quite surprisingly. For example, a ceremony to mark national teachers' day began very formally with a performance by the children's choir:

The children's choir was a mixed-age, mixed-diagnosis group, aged from around four to around nine years, who had practised together in the late afternoons. They stood up by whatever means were open to them, some independently, some with the help of chair-backs, a few with the help of sticks. One child at the side of the group was being facilitated in his standing by a junior conductor. Perhaps because they looked so frail, some of them in the front row visibly wobbling and tottering, the strength and tunefulness of their voices came as a shock. Perhaps, however, this was just a question of their age, since the quality of their singing would be envied by any choir of British school children of their age who suffered no disability at all. They sang part song with descant. They watched the lady directing them with great attentiveness, their faces showing enormous pleasure in their accomplishment. (Sutton, 1984a, Suppl. V)

Then the conductors' choir performed, there were speeches by staff and the presentation of long service awards, after which student conductors were presented with certificates:

The children's choir sat watching all this attentively. Sometimes a particular conductor would get a special excited acknowledgement from some of the children, an especial round of applause. The last part of the presentation, however, brought a break in their highly disciplined manner. This involved giving certificates to student conductors, amongst whom were the three young men with whose performance as conductors Dr Hári had expressed herself to us so pleased. Their appearance brought forth shouts of joy from the children, which rose to a scream in the case of one young man (more akin to English teeny-boppers than to what we had come to expect from pupils at the Institute). (Sutton, 1984a, Suppl. V)

After this the children filed out back to tea, in the same serious and deliberate function as Kearslake had observed children arrive 14 years previously.

Conduction

Visitors to the Institute have identified a variety of features of the work that have struck them as particularly important to the practice and process of conductive education. These may or may not, of course, be cardinal features of the approach in the minds of the conductors.

The Affective

The emotional interaction between conductor and child (the

'contact'), the children's enthusiasm and delight in achievement, their determination to achieve orthofunction, such factors seem primary requirements for the success of conductive education.

The children's indefatigable motivation in the face of the enormous task of achieving orthofunction is inextricably linked with the activities of the conductors.

> The programme throughout the day is intensive. Both children and conductors work hard. It appears surprising at first that the children are capable of working so continuously – but they are, and it fosters their concentration. Whatever the task, it is expected to be done as well as the children are able to do it with as much precision as possible. This involves a great deal of mental concentration and physical effort. For a timid, stiff or athetoid child to make the attempt to walk across the room actively, perhaps pushing a chair moving inches at a time, is a feat of physical endurance as well as patience and concentration for the child and the conductor together . . . If the tasks do not motivate him, then it is the conductor's job to alter the tasks, the presentation or the programme so that they do. When the children manage to perform a task successfully they immediately receive praise from conductors. Even the smallest bit of progress is noticed and praised, this stimulates both the successful child and the others to greater effort. (Budd, 1975)

One of the most striking features of the Institute to a visitor from Great Britain is how very hard the children work . . . There may be several factors contributing to the success with which the staff of the Institute can make these demands on the children. First, it is recognised that work is a thing to be done and everybody is doing it. Secondly, the programme for the day is devised as much as possible so that each session has something new, however small. Thirdly, it is contrived that each child always has an experience of success in relation to any task. For example, on one occasion I was observing the task for the children was to raise themselves from a prone position to a sitting position by pulling themselves up using both hands and grasping the slats of the plinth. One child was unable to grasp the plinth with her right hand, but the conductor gave her a block of wood to raise it slightly and was alllowed to grasp this instead. Thus she had the same experience of success as the rest, even though her task was not quite the same. Fourthly, the conductors try as much as possible to make the exercises more like a game and to introduce fun into them. Naturally some are more successful than others and, as a general rule, I would think that the younger conductors erred on the side of seriousness rather than frivolity. (Wilson, 1970)

Not, of course, that the conductors do things for the children. The pupil's role is an active one; the conductors' to ensure that it is. As a Hungarian observer has remarked:

The conductors show indescribable patience in the help that they give the children. Yet they modestly claim 'only to help'. The child will recognise what we want to teach him and he must learn to want to do these things. Everybody can be taught something. (Eöry, 1984)

House (1968) felt that he had never met happier children anywhere – even normal children: 'They are like children at a birthday party when it's everyone's birthday':

At the Institute they never push a child beyond what he is ready for, but they devise short-term goals for him, to keep his interest going on the way to the long-term aims. They never force him beyond his ability, but in group exercises the whole group waits with wonderful patience until each child performs what they know him to be capable of; sometimes this can mean waiting quite a long time in certain cases. On these occasions the conductor does not hold to a rigid timetable, but keeps it flexible to meet the need as it arises. Time is not allowed to be a limiting factor. The great thing is that there should be achievement and progress each day, and this is regarded as natural – to unfold as and when it can.

When after much encouragement not only from the conductor but also from the others in the group, whose chanting reaches an enthusiastic and joyous crescendo, a child manages at last to make some movement to the best of his ability, perhaps long after everyone else has succeeded, a tremendous fuss is made of him and there is clapping and rejoicing . . . They don't work on the child. What they do is to help the child to realise above all that everything emanates from within *himself*. He has the seed within himself of all that is normal and right for him. . .

When these conductors come to the end of their shifts with the children, they go off to live their own lives. They don't agonize over the cases or go over them, as one is apt to do in this field. They know that the potential is in the children as an inner principle and will still be there without them. (House, 1968)

The Group

It is not just the conductor who is responsible for the individual pupils' motivation and feelings of well being – it is also the group as a whole, the children's collective.

> ... It is essential ... that the children are not forced to solve any kind of problems or act in any particular way. The conductors put them on the right track to want to achieve a set objective. This is greatly facilitated by the children's active and disciplined, but also cheerful little communities. (Hári, as reported by Varnai, 1984)

Group upbringing is commonplace in Eastern Europe and the use of the group as a pedagogic tool has been developed in ways generally unfamiliar to teachers in the West.

> Both at the Institute and elsewhere this means of pedagogic organisation stood out in sharp contrast to the English way of running a class. The children worked together, often physically very close, in an orderly and disciplined way, without squabbling. When an individual child overstepped the mark, expressing himself, his involvement or enjoyment a little too loudly, then it was the other children round, not the conductor, who said 'hush'. When a single child struggled to achieve some individual accomplishment the others looked on attentively, urging and learning, sharing their pleasure and satisfaction at what their fellow was doing. Activities learned together were then performed singly, activities learned singly were then performed in the group. (Sutton, 1984a, Suppl. V)

This unfamiliar educational method produces child behaviour which western observers often find remarkably different to that produced by their own familiar methods. The following account concerns a group of kindergarten-age spastics.

> The children were asked who would like to say a poem to the class. Several hands went up and a little girl was chosen. She could just

about walk, partly holding on, partly staggering along unaided. She fell down and with great difficulty managed to get on her feet again. The whole group watched intensely and participated by counting for her, one, two, three, four, five, which helped her to get up and to achieve the end of her walk. There she stood, faced the class and recited a poem of several verses. This little girl, as I found out later, had only come to the Institute a month ago. When she finished the other children all clapped, and with their rhythmic counting helped to get her back to her seat.

This child was no exception. I soon found out they were all able to learn a poem. It was as if their learning ability had been stimulated and trained. It made no difference whether the task was to lie on their back or learn to bend a knee, whether it was to clap in rhythm or put on a sock; the approach was the same. 'The brain cannot be influenced from the periphery but only by fulfilling a task' (Prof. Petö).

The most important thing to enable the child to fulfil a task is the atmosphere in his surroundings. All stimuli are cut out and everything is directed towards the one thing to be accomplished. The children say what they are going to do before doing it, then each fulfils the task according to his ability. The group with its rhythmic counting helps each individual, and it is precisely this group that is the most important factor in this process of learning. As I see it, it relieves the individual child from the pressure of being watched and coaxed and expected to perform. In a way it leaves him alone, but not lonely, as he is a member of a group who all have the same aim in mind. It is in fact the group that develops the child's personality and individuality because he does not depend on the guiding adult. As Petö says, we respect the child's personality.

The strength of this was often shown to me when I saw a group of children working on their own. There were the young hemiplegics who walked in crocodile along the corridor, practising their walking exercises. They counted in rhythm and stayed in line, and everybody did as well as they could. There was the day when the Conductor had to leave the room suddenly, and one of the children started a song and the whole group joined in. On another occasion one child started a hand exercise and again everybody joined in. Every child, however young, has a feeling of responsibility to the group and to himself. It is up to him to learn, and there is no dependence on an adult, whether it is the mother or the teacher or the therapist. This approach is in complete contrast to anything I had experienced hitherto with Cerebral Palsy children. (Seglow, 1966)

Groups at the Institute are being continuously reconstructed for, as children move out into orthofunction, so new children are introduced. It is reckoned that if they had to start a group from scratch it would take around six months to establish the feeling of collectivity required. The fully functioning group, however, is a powerful tool in the hands of the conductors:

> The attitude of the Conductors towards the children who do not conform is one of affection, and coaxing is used rather than correction and coercion. If this proves unsuccessful the child is left entirely alone until he or she chooses to take part in the work of the Group. I was told that the children who had disliked the Group work conformed after a few days.
>
> It was very interesting to see the handicapped children working together as a Group and being encouraged by the Conductor and the trainee Conductors. Apart from the permissive atmosphere one was struck by the degree of independence expected of the children, all of whom were in some degree disabled, using chairs as walking aids and being encouraged to dress, undress, eat, wash and toilet on their own. Everywhere they went under their own steam and at their own speed, the pressure to hurry coming from the other children rather than from authority. (Loring, 1971)

Group upbringing quite reverses the current western ideal of individualised teaching, the much sought one-to-one relationship.

> Groups varied in size. Dr Hári prefers them to be at least 20 and says the best had 34 in it. Certainly the bigger groups seemed to work much better and if for some reason a group was reduced it was obviously not achieving so much (e.g. the outpatient clinics I watched were both reduced considerably because of transport difficulties and it was much more difficult for the conductor to keep the group going). With a bigger group the child had less attention and so found his own ways of being independent. (Varty, 1970a)

Play

Although conductive education is directed towards establishing adequate motor function it does not achieve its ends through specific training of children's motorics. The primary emphasis is directed towards establishing the appropriate function – and appropriate functions are then implemented through practical activity. 'The child doesn't do walking exercises or hand exercises: the child is doing an action or going somewhere to play, or making something' (Hári, speaking on film report, *Newsnight*, BBC2, 5 May 1983).

Many of the children at the Institute are of preschool-age, many of the school-age children are at a corresponding mental level. For such children play is the most suitable means to establish mental-motor development. 'Here they have turned the struggle for achievement into a game, not an exercise. They're not being taught to walk but to play, and the walking comes by itself' (Commentary to *Newsnight*, BBC2, 5 May 1983).

Play too, therefore, is a pedagogic tool, conceived of somewhat differently than is often the case in the West:

> The Budapest day is a long one for small children by our standards, but there is no allocation of time for rest periods, and very little for the free play that is so popular in our programming. The children showed no need for the play equipment that crowds the cupboards and floor of our Centres; each new achievement became an immediate plaything, being brought into use in ways that entertained them with spontaneous enjoyment. This spontaneous play arising directly out of the learning situation had real meaning for the children; instead of playing with a ready-made material or object placed before them, they were learning how to use themselves, and implementing their new abilities for play, through simple imagination and sense of fun. (Parnwell, 1966)

Task Series

Whilst the general tendency of conductive education is to work from the gross to specific, it must not be thought that the training and correction of component motor acts is ignored. Series of tasks (or 'task series') in which movements are built up and corrected, have been developed at the Institute over the years in enormous numbers and, tailored to individual requirements, contribute an important feature of each pupil's daily programme.

I should like to mention one or two examples of the task series, and by doing so refer to their characteristics. For example, one of the task series in lying position for contract athetoids leads every one of them to grasp in all positions, to turn prone and supine and reverse, to sit up and relax themselves to such an extent as to be able to lift the arms high up and then put them down to their sides again. The result of this task series is to achieve the lifting of the arms to head level. This final aim is broken down into parts. At first the children, while turning on their sides, stretch their arms to shoulder level. When they have achieved this position, they turn on to their backs, keeping arms in position. Thus they are lying on their backs, holding their stretched arms up vertically, then they roll over to their sides and stomachs, but now the arms are stretched beside the head. Finally, they turn back, keeping their arms beside the head. Eventually they can stretch their arms high in a sitting position beside the head and lie down on their backs. When the aim is achieved without transitional tasks, they can be left out. Thus the series become shorter and shorter.

Some of the elements in the task series are repeated in different situations. For example, sitting up and lying down with a stick in the hand is followed by letting go of the stick and raising the arms with open hands. After repeated sitting up and lying down with a stick in the hand comes the turning sideways and backwards with stick in hand. Then further sitting up and lying down follow so that the child's head is where his feet were previously. Finally rolling over onto the sides and prone position, then again sitting up and lying down completes the series, but in such a way as *prescribed by us as the final goal*.

It is fascinating for the children to accomplish the different elements of the series, and as *every partial result prepares the success of the following one, the success becomes always greater*. As a result of the positive satisfaction of the child's emotions increases more and more. His interest towards the tasks and the intensity of participation increases crescendo-like to the last task, which is at the same time an evidence of the concrete result attained through the series for the child. (Hári, 1968, emphasis in original)

Rhythmic Intention

Both in the task series and in the other activities of daily life into which what has been learned is integrated, the children's conscious intention is often made explicit, either in the words of the conductor or the children's own or in song. Speech or singing also serve as a rhythmic bridge between the intention and its accomplishment.

> The children are lying supine on their plinths. The Conductor says slowly and loudly 'I lift my arms above my head'; the Conductor and the children start to count slowly and loudly from one to five, and while doing so they raise their arms above their heads. The Conductor counts with them to keep the rhythm steady and slow. In this example counting is the *rhythm* and 'above the head' the *intention*.
>
> Not all children succeed in placing their arms above their head at the same time. The exercises are done rhythmically to achieve an aim or fulfil a task, and the counting continues until all the children have reached the aim. The child is placed in a group where the general aim is within his reach and he is expected to fulfil the task within his capacity. By repetition the movement becomes automatic, like riding a bicycle, and it is then possible to perform it correctly without counting. The child thus learns that counting is a means by which he can put himself right.
>
> The child works in the group unaided; occasionally the Conductor may put a finger on his knee to remind him to extend the knee more, or the helper may fix a foot to make it possible for the child to move the other leg alone. None of the exercises are built on analysis of muscle work, they are functional movements or follow the sequence of normal child development. (Cotton, 1965, emphasis in original)

It should not be thought that the rhythmic intentions are merely a mechanical drill:

> The children spoke the rhythmic intentions well and all attempted it in the group. Individually they often chanted and counted to themselves. Quite often a conductor asked a child to take over directing a task series and in fact 'What comes next, Johnny?' seemed a deliberate way of bringing the child out of a mechanical kind of chanting into the realm of conscious thought. The children and conductors sang very often – many times a day. (Varty, 1970a)

The Whole

Conduction is not, however, a bundle of pre-set or prescribed methods. Rather, it is an adaptive amalgam, a synthesis of the affective, the collective, the imaginative, the motoric, the intellective, blended and orchestrated to suit and engender individual pupils' development. No more, surely, than good pedagogy anywhere, directed albeit here to an unfamiliar purpose:

You would ask me now how we realise the programme we set? One would think we must have a specific method.

To show how we realise the programme I will give the course of one lesson. At the beginning of every lesson the first and most important [thing] is to establish the preconditions of success. Every lesson has an introductory section. To this part belongs [the need] to create a pleasant atmosphere, the feeling that the work is fun. This is provided by the collective dynamic of a well organised group. The aesthetic milieu, absolute order in the room, a good general state, the right grouping and positioning of the necessary aids are also important.

Having obtained the cooperative attitude of the children, the conductor establishes a self-conscious learning situation. She sets up an always clearly understandable goal. However simple it may be the children know that it is necessary to approach the goal because reaching it is connected with their daily activities in which they are greatly interested.

After this the child intends the fulfilling of the task. Why intending? In automatically occurring everyday functions the sequence of coordinated, purposeful behaviour occurs automatically, irrespective of whether there is any self-instruction – either a taught or a verbal one. A dysfunctioning person's part of functions do not follow one another in a coordinated way or sequence. In breaking up a task according to the children's ability and by intending [this] from these separate details, bound to a certain rhythmic, anticipation and proper timing is promoted, thus coordination. . .

There I must mention that every performance of a task means, in addition to the specific goal and effect, also the practice of successfully surmounting difficulties. The success reached after intention is immediately brought to the child's consciousness and, of course, the conductor gets the children to make another use as well of the new function. Under a variety of conditions the newly performed models or functions are to be applied in our daily programme. And for this it is ideal if such surroundings occur such as are animating, cheerful, loud and involve [a variety of] problems (not empty and abstract). (adapted from Hári, 1970)

Formal Education

Children of kindergarten-age at the Institute follow the national kindergarten syllabus; school-age children there follow the national curriculum for general school – or the level of special schooling (auxiliary or training) determined by the bizottság at school-starting age. Both kindergarten- and school-age children at the Institute receive the same musical education as do all children in Hungary.

School education is an integral part of the conductive processes for children. For example, specific motor skills introduced in a task series at the beginning of a morning session will be tested out, encouraged, practised, observed, analysed etc. in the kindergarten or school activity that follows, then what has been learned by child and conductor will be built on and developed by a task series in the afternoon . . . and so on. The child learns motor acts not as skills in themselves but as means of achieving the normal activities of everyday living. The activities of kindergarten or school, therefore, make an essential contribution to the processes of conductive education.

Education is important to the establishment of orthofunction in another way. If children are to be placed satisfactorily in school when they leave the Institute then they must have learned the normal routines and demands of the school system and have followed its curriculum. The use of grades in the Hungarian education system makes it possible for the pupils at the Institute to do this at a level below their chronological ages. Many of the Institute's children (especially those who began their conductive education relatively late) have experienced a delayed start to their mental development because of experiential deprivations stemming from their motor disorders. Further, the paramount importance accorded the children's motor development at the Institute means that formal school work may often have to take second place in children's programmes. As a result, pupil's may find themselves following a somewhat abbreviated daily school timetable. It is to this latter factor, rather than recourse to 'learning difficulties', that the Institute looks to explain the reason why many of its school-age children are doing school work at a grade level below normal age expectations.

For formal education the children work not in their group (*czoport*) but in a class (*ostály*). There is little homogeneity of educational level within the groups, which are formed on the primary considerations of common motoric needs and social-emotional compatibility.

The teaching is in the hands of the conductors, whose training qualifies them to teach up to lower general-school level (first four grades).

The children of primary-school age, that is roughly from 6 to 11, spend most of their school hours on the three subjects of hand-writing, arithmetic and reading. Hand-writing takes up a very fair proportion of the time. The arithmetic is taught in exactly the same method as in ordinary schools. On the whole, the teaching is in small groups of up to ten but the children are taught as a class. The arithmetic books which they use are well illustrated and the teaching methods are good. There is frequent use of colour and of rhythm and sound in counting. The reading book is the official book used in other primary schools in Hungary and the teaching is strictly by phonic method and hand writing is practised at the same time. Since Hungarian is a completely phonic language, this method is fairly successful. The children do, in fact, begin with isolated sounds and combine them in exercises before they move on to words but are very quick to suggest words that have this sound in them so that the matter becomes meaningful. Whatever the children do in school is displayed and discussed immediately after the end of the lesson. The children freely criticise one another and use is made of this group feeling in everything they do. In addition to the three basic subjects, there are other activities such as painting and music. In music the children sing unaccompanied with great pleasure and their singing is better than I have usually heard with cerebral palsied children. They are taught in music the time names for rhythm also. Most of the children are educationally retarded, which is common with cerebral palsied children. Nevertheless, some of the older children have reached the stage of classes 4, 5 and 6. Class 4 is the equivalent of a top primary school and classes 5 and 6 are the lower forms of a secondary school or a high school. In these groups there were at the time of my visit ten or twelve children in these three separate classes. They were covering the normal school subjects, including maths, physics, chemistry, history, geography, Russian and Hungarian literature and grammar. They were working in small groups of two, three or four children. (Wilson, 1970)

Indeed, the distinction between conduction in the school class and conduction in the group is an artificial one.

Since achievement in hand-writing is very closely connected with a good sitting position, the exercises in hand movements and in sitting are very closely connected. It is important that the children should sit on their chairs with their feet very firmly planted on the ground and begin with their hands flat on the edge of the table. After the practice with thick sticks, the children move to thinner sticks of pencil size and first of all make movements and directions with the blunt end of the pencil, still working by grasping the pencil with both hands. Eventually, it emerges that the child has a preferred hand and moves over to working with only one. After some efficiency is achieved with movement of the pencil in the total grasp, the grasp is changed so that the usual three fingers are used in holding the pencil. There is great stress on the achievement of a good hand-writing style and a considerable amount of time is spent on this. A universal style of hand-writing is common, I gather, in all Hungarian schools. This resembles the Civil Service style of hand-writing, which used to be common in this country before the Marian Richardson italic movement. In forming the letters the children use words to describe the movements, but this is not a device adopted specially in the Petö Institute but is the common method used in all Hungarian schools. Typewriters are never used by children who have hand-writing difficulties. The results achieved in hand-writing seem to be particularly good, except in the cases of some severe athetoids and quadraplegic children. In some of these case I have doubt about the wisdom of persisting in the aim to achieve good hand-writing, but the staff of the Institute have very good faith that eventually all the children will be able to write. (Wilson, 1970)

The film report by the BBC stated that at the Institute: 'Seven-year old brain-damaged children can write as legibly as any other children of the same age in a British school' (commentary to film report, *Newsnight* BBC2, 5 May 1983).

A brief sample of copy-writing (the word Budapest) taken from all the school-age pupils at the Institute at the end of the 1983-4 school year (Aubrey and Sutton, 1985) indicates that most spina bifida and spastic children following the general-school curriculum do indeed appear to write well by any standards (see Figure 2.3). It should be remembered in judging the hand-writing of pupils at the Institute – indeed in considering any aspects of their development – that the school-age children there may not be representative of children receiving conductive education as a whole. Many of the children attending the Institute at six years or above will be those who for some reason are learning very slowly or those who have started conductive education late – or both.

Figure 2.4: Examples of Copy-writing of School-age Children at the Institute: (1) girl aged 7 years, bilateral hemiplegia, preparatory class; (2) boy aged 8 years, spastic tetraplegia, general-school curriculum; (3) boy aged 9 years, athetosis, general-school curriculum; (4) boy aged 9 years, spina bifida, general-school curriculum; (5) girl aged 10 years, bilateral hemiplegia, general-school curriculum (from Aubrey and Sutton, 1985).

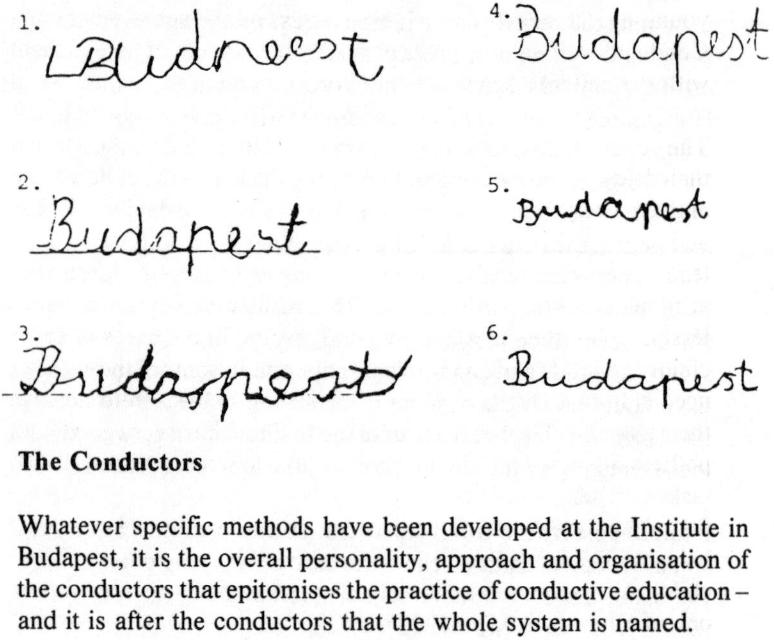

The Conductors

Whatever specific methods have been developed at the Institute in Budapest, it is the overall personality, approach and organisation of the conductors that epitomises the practice of conductive education – and it is after the conductors that the whole system is named.

> If one were to describe the essence of conductive education in one sentence one could say that rehabilitational purposes are achieved in a pedagogical way through a specifically trained person, namely the conductor. The personality and training of the conductor is the key factor in conductive education. The conductor integrates on a pedagogical level all the professional activities that are necessary for rehabilitation. In this way therapy and teaching fuse together in conductive education. We suppose rehabilitation to be a unified

learning-adapting process, which can be sufficiently realised only by the unity of pedagogical action. (Hári, 1972)

Certainly, their work has made powerful impressions upon visitors to the Institute. For example:

The Institute not only trains the children but also Conductors. These are young women of good educational qualifications. Only 5 per cent of all applicants are selected – and all seem to be able to establish a special rapport with the children. Indeed one of the notable things compared with schools in England was the completely natural and unaffected relationships between the young girl Conductors and the children. One suspects that the Conductors are selected in part at least, because they are 'naturals' with the children. (Loring, 1971)

The conductors waken the children at 6.15 a.m. and leave them on their beds at 9 p.m. Between these times they supervise, control and carry out their dressing and undressing, their potting, washing and bathing, their feeding, all their movements and activities, and teach them their elementary lessons of reading, writing and arithmetic. They take the children's temperatures, prepare their lessons and the necessary teaching material, and make the children's splints. They seek guidance and advice when these are needed from a variety of specialists, most of whom contributed to their training. There are no assistants. The conductors empty the potties and serve out the meals as well as their more specialized tasks of teaching lessons and stimulating motor activities. This all fits in with their role of helping the children as children and not being concerned solely with treating or training some part of the child. My first impression on observing the conductors at work was one of naturalness. They were fulfilling a mothering role in that they were solely responsible for all aspects of their charges' care. After all most mothers are familiar with the situation of keeping an eye on the cooking supper as they bath the baby, and listen to junior's reading homework. The second impression was one of professionalism as one admired the skill with which they encouraged the children to perform movements the way they wished, and the way they taught them. Each child is strongly motivated by the conductor and by the group environment to do all that he can. The conductor is motivated to create this stimulating environment because she knows that this is the way to achieve progress. Both child and conductor want to achieve more. These two initial impressions combine in the statement which was quoted to me: 'I ask you to do this because I love you'. (Holt, 1975)

Conductors usually work three to a group: characteristically, one (not necessarily the senior conductor) will be leading, another will be giving specific attention to an individual child or sub-group and the third will be preparing for the next activity. There is little apparent communication between the three as they work at their different tasks with great concentration and intensity. Nevertheless, what they are doing is highly planned and co-ordinated and the way in which they shift from one activity to the next, changing roles as they do, is extraordinarily smooth.

The conductors' job seems often construed in the West as some sort of combination of teacher, physiotherapist, speech therapist etc. Historically this is almost certainly unfounded, since it seems more than likely that there were conductors under Petö long before the other professions became established in Hungary. It is also said over here, using a very English idiom, that conductors work 'as a team'. But is this not also similarly a misperception? The conductors present a remarkable spectacle in many ways. Much of what one sees, however, the drive, the determination and optimism, the tone of their voices etc. seems common to Hungarian pedagogy generally. What stands out particularly is that they work together, usually three at a time, combining, coordinating, collaborating with a smooth, practised and, to the outsider, seemingly effortless efficiency that leaves no break or slack in the teaching day. They do indeed appear in every way (in the words of the BBC) 'the ultimate teaching machine' – as long as one realises that this 'machine' is warm, responsive and delighting in its pupils' success.

This is more than a combination or unification of disciplines. It is certainly far more than what is implied in the by now very weak notion of a 'team', whether as a 'multi-disciplinary team' or in 'team teaching'. This too is a collective, in both the class and the Institute as a whole (very Makerenkoist) and any attempt to replicate the Institute's work will have to capture this essence. (Sutton, 1984a, Suppl. V)

As in the case of the children, the group principle of working should not be construed as denying individual attention or effort. Indeed, the contrary is intended: 'The work of the team and the work that is individual and individualised do not oppose one another. It is in the team that individuation is the easiest to realise' (Hári, 1981b, translated from the French). At the same time, again as with the children, perhaps it is the collective nature of the work that carries the conductors through what can be a very hard day: 'The work is undoubtedly very demanding physically (the frequent furniture shifting is no mean feat!), intellectually and emotionally, and the hours are irregular' (Holt, 1975).

It is often asked why the word conductor is used for these teachers of the motor-disordered. The answer lies in the delicate dialectic between the individual and the group.

Like the Conductor of an orchestra, the Conductor regulates the activities of her group; occasionally practising individually with one child to bring his performance into tune with the rest of the group but normally leading the group which works collectively as a social unit in which one child's progress assists the performance of the others.

The Conductor directs the community and builds up the conditions of activity. She always takes care to hold the children's attention and maintain a cheerful atmosphere, which makes it possible to establish close contact with each individual child. The Conductor is acquainted with each child's capacity of performances, watches its development, and accordingly modifies the programmes. *The pre-condition of conductive education is the continuous experimental observation concentrated in one person: the Conductor.* (Hári, as reported by Cotton, 1975, emphasis in original)

The conductors work to a tight practical programme and within an articulate framework of educational principles – yet enjoy considerable professional autonomy and personal discretion. This demands a high level of training, supervision and morale. What they and their institution do represents a highly advanced pedagogy. However styled, the conductor is, above all else, a *teacher*.

Conductor Training

The training of conductors is governed by strict principles of personal suitability and the necessity to unify training with practice.

All conductors are trained at the Institute itself (its full title, *Mozgássérültek Nevelökepzö és Nevelöintézete* means that it is both a boarding school and a training institution). Recruitment is from high-school graduates who have to fill not only the normal state requirements for aspiring kindergarten and early general-school teachers (musical ability, for example) but, above all, convince that they can make the 'contact'.

The students are accepted at the age of roughly 18 or 19 on the basis of academic attainment, personality and physical health. The students are expected to have the baccalaureat examination in four or five subjects, which they take at the end of their secondary course in either a gymnasium or technical school. The students are more likely to come from the gymnasium which stresses arts subjects rather than from the technical schools where the stress is on sciences and technology.

Qualities of personality looked for are patience and the ability to make good rapport with children. Physical strength is considered to be important because the students require a good deal of stamina in this work. Students have to accept a job in the Institute on a six months' trial. If at the end of this period they prove unsuitable for the work, their engagement is terminated but this happens only rarely. During their period of inservice training, the student conductors do a full six-hour stretch of duty each day and have to do their study, group discussion lectures etc. in the other half of the day, that is in their spare time. An examination is held each semester and this is both practical and theoretical. Throughout their course, student conductors have to give demonstration lessons frequently. In their final year each conductor gives a demonstration lesson fortnightly in the presence of other students and the staff. These are criticised very thoroughly afterwards. The curriculum for the student conductors includes, very naturally, the subjects which are compulsory in the education of all students, that is the social sciences, including political economy, socialism and philosophy, Russian and Home Defence. The pedagogic subjects include general psychology, child psychology and the psychology of learning, didactics and the theory of education. Logic is included. Method is thoroughly studied, including the method for teaching of all school subjects except gymnastics. As their main subject, all students take conductive education, taught by Dr Hári, and biology, which includes anatomy and physiology and particularly the study of the eye and the ear. Phonetics and a study of deafness and visual defects have recently been included in the curriculum. The students also have the opportunity to practise craft work (polytechnics). Since last year, student conductors have had to take a State exam with an external examiner as head of the examining committee. The subjects included in this State exam are philosophy, didactics, the theory of education and conductive education. Dr Hári is the examiner for conductive education, being the only person qualified to do this work. (Wilson, 1970)

Much of the training is carried out by senior members of the Institute's own conducting staff, with visiting lecturers for specialist topics. The training course, involving both a full-time job and academic learning, is clearly a demanding task for young people straight out of high school. Nevertheless, the course seems to be of high status and there appears no shortage of applicants. Most of these applicants are young women but men are beginning now to apply in rather greater numbers than before. Recently a Japanese man from the Institute in Osaka successfully completed the four-year course, another Japanese man is halfway through it and a third has just started. The course awards a college-level diploma and conductors also take the state teachers' qualification. Whereas a few years ago conductors' salaries were higher than teachers', they have now slipped below par (a result of the Institute's being administered alongside universities, where lecturers are currently more poorly paid than school teachers).

To the visitor from abroad there is much that is unfamiliar in this system of training.

An important feature of this training system for conductors is that they go straight into it without previous training in the education of normal children and usually straight from school. Dr Hári is very firmly convinced of the value of inservice training on the grounds that all theory is immediately meaningful to the student since it is related to what they are doing every day. She also firmly believes in the principle of training special educators from scratch. She feels that those who train in other methods will be insufficiently flexible to adopt the new ideas. Particularly she is afraid that trained teachers from ordinary training high schools would not be prepared to undertake the more menial tasks in the care of the children. (Wilson, 1970)

To the Hungarians, however, the notion of training special educators as such from the very start of their professional preparation will not be unexpected, for this is the Hungarian tradition (see Kelmer-Pringle, 1955). Indeed it is the common East European way. But combining training with work so completely, as is done at the Institute, is at variance with general practice in the Hungarian education system and provides a source of tension for the Institute in some of its external relations.

The practice of conductive education has doubtless changed in certain specific aspects over the 20 years that English visitors have been bringing back their reports of the Institute. Over the same period Dr Hári's accounts of her work may have been directed to emphasise different features. Perhaps by now sufficient material has been produced in English to reveal major continuities. Even collected together, however, this material does not constitute a sufficient basis to copy what the Institute is doing and, it must be remembered, many of those who have wanted to emulate the Institute's work have had access to no more than a proportion of this work.

PART TWO:

DEVELOPMENTS OUTSIDE HUNGARY

3 THE PRACTICE OUTSIDE HUNGARY

Philippa Cottam

Attempts at conductive education have been reported from many countries outside Hungary. Often only as isolated instances, the method is being used in Western Europe, North and South America, Australasia, the Far East and India. Published material on this work is limited and, as a consequence, much of what is reported in this chapter was communicated personally to the author in response to direct enquiry.

Conductive Education in Britain

The main force in the development of British conductive education has been a physiotherapist working for the Spastics Society, Mrs Ester Cotton. She has developed her own philosophy of treatment based on certain principles of the approach and has organised lecture courses both in Britain and abroad. Since her first account of the work at the Institute in Budapest (Cotton, 1965) there have been a steady trickle of accounts of English practice both in trade magazines and journals (Cotton and Parnwell, 1967, 1968; Cotton, 1970; Miller, 1972; Varty, 1973; Cotton, 1974; Cotton, 1975; Budd and Evans, 1977; Hare, 1979; Cotton and Kinsman, 1983; Rooke and Opel, 1983; Titchener, 1983; Wilson, 1983; Cottam, 1985a in press). These have all described work that is Cotton-based and for the most part provide only vague descriptions of actual practice. Nevertheless, this body of work now represents the chief image of conductive education to the English-speaking world.

Even the most detailed published account of Hungarian practice (Cotton, 1965) falls far short of providing a sound basis of how to implement the method for those wishing to introduce conductive education into their schools. Unpublished accounts have often outlined the method in similar detail but have tended to show repetition of information rather than a developing understanding from visit to visit. It is, however, doubtful whether these materials have been seen by many, or even most of those who have taken up conductive education in this country. The lack of practical information

89

in the literature has been compounded by the fact that very little has been published in English by the Hungarians themselves. With the paucity of readily available written information the regular courses run by Ester Cotton have been the main source of information on the practice of conductive education.

Up until the late 1970s conductive education was being attempted primarily within the Spastics Society. The first reported group consisted of eight athetoid children and worked from 1966 to 1968 on a non-residential basis at the Lady Zia Werhner Centre for severely mentally and physically handicapped children, in Luton. Cotton and Parnwell (1968) in outlining their work stated that:

> The children attend the centre daily for six hours during which time they work through a set timetable without a pause, and without need for a rest. This can only be described as a modified system, since the working time in Luton amounts to 6 hours a day, five days a week as against 12 hours a day, seven days a week in Budapest. . . Our aim in training is symmetry leading to mastery of basic positions and patterns permitting movement.

Assessment of these children revealed only 'slight improvements' but as Gardner and Price (1967) pointed out, 'no adequate assessment of the progress of the children treated by the Petö method can be made after only seven months and it will be important to follow their long-term progress'.

Following its introduction at the Lady Zia Werhner Centre the method was taken up by a number of Spastics Society establishments.

It was only after several years of Ester Cotton's courses on conductive education that the method began to spread to local education authority schools. The introduction into the state system has not been evenly distributed across the country. Pockets of interest have developed as the method has been passed on, largely it seems, by word of mouth from teachers and therapists who had attended Mrs Cotton's courses. The spread and adaptation of conductive education in Britain appears to have been very much a grassroots affair, with teachers and therapists taking aspects of the method and applying them to their particular contexts, with little or no direct knowledge of its origins.

Unlike the Spastics Society schools where conductive education has been introduced, the state schools function on a day rather than a residential basis, and conductors are often isolated within their local education authorities (LEAs), with no support from figures of authority. Interest has been shown not only in schools for the physically handicapped but also for the mentally handicapped. As a consequence, groups have been less 'selective' and include all types of mentally and physically handicapped children. A few publications have described this work (Rooke and Opel, 1983; Titchener, 1983; Wilson, 1983) and a course organised by Rooke was held in May 1984, at Sheffield University. (Note that Rooke was the maiden name of the present author, Philippa Cottam.) It is fair to say, however, that within the state system Ester Cotton has remained the primary influence.

From the various published accounts of British practice four common features emerge:

- treatment of the 'whole' child or adult is stressed and this is achieved by uniting the disciplines of, for example, physio-therapist, teacher, speech therapist, etc.
- rhythmic intention is used as the teaching method.
- programmes based on the philosophy of the 'basic motor pattern' (Cotton, 1980) provide the teaching format.
- specific equipment is used, i.e. plinths and ladder-back chairs, designed along similar lines to furniture in the Budapest Institute (these are illustrated in Figure 3.1).

Conductive education is now being practised in more than 25 units or classes in Britain, either full time or in classrooms, for a few hours a week (CEIG *Newsletter*, no. 5, June 1983). The work ranges from mother-and-baby groups to adult hemiplegics, and covers the entire academic range from normally developing, physically handicapped children to the profoundly mentally handicapped. This diversity led to the formation in 1982 of the Conductive Education Interest Group (CEIG). Initiated by workers in the Spastics Society, the association was set up to provide a unifying force for those professionals interested in conductive education both in Britain and abroad (i.e. other than Hungary). By January 1985, the total membership was reported to be around 150, and included teaching, therapy and ancillary staff involved in special education both in Spastics Society and state establishments. The aim of the CEIG is to 'promote the knowledge, practice and quality of Conductive Education', the emphasis on improving the 'quality' of existing practice being stressed by Cotton in a lecture given at the inaugural meeting of the group in

Figure 3.1: Furniture Used in Conductive Education

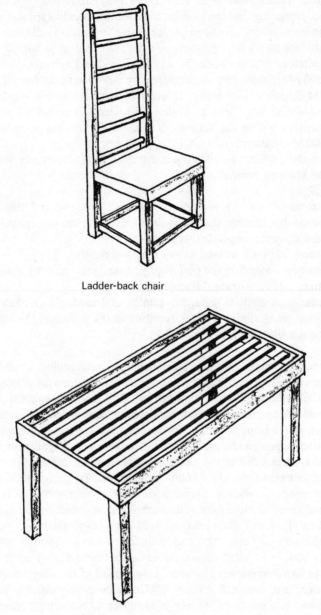

Ladder-back chair

Plinth

July 1982. Since its development the CEIG has prepared and circulated a list of members, a list of establishments practising the method, a bibliography and several newsletters including papers of current interest, as well as running basic and advanced courses in conductive education as it is practised in this country.

Despite this attempt to unify conductive education in Britain, a wide diversity of practice now exists. Accounts of practice in four different British settings are presented here to illustrate this diversity.

Ingfield Manor – a Residential Setting

Ingfield Manor is a residential Spastics Society school in Sussex for cerebral palsied children who are also ESN. The school has come to be the primary model, both in Britain and throughout the world, for those who want to learn about conductive education. In 1970, the method was introduced into the nursery at the school, on an 'experimental' basis. Using a group of ten children the following principles of conductive education were employed; group teaching, the conductor and a programme leading to movement, function and conceptual learning. The diverse group of children involved and the lack of a concrete Hungarian knowledge base brought about a significant departure in practice.

> All had cerebral palsy of different types, consisting of spastic quadraplegia, spastic diplegia, tension athetosis, choreoathetosis and bulbar palsy. This wide variety made programming difficult, so we looked for a common denominator among the children from which we could formulate the first programme. After analysing the children's very simplest (sic) functions and assessing their handicaps, *we found that all were lacking what we called the 'basic motor pattern'*. This pattern of movement is needed for all function and consists of sitting balance, full hip mobility with extension of the arms, and grasp, as well as the ability to fix one part while moving another. (Cotton, 1974, present author's emphasis)

The basic motor pattern has proved a particularly important British adaptation of the method. Cotton (1980) in the introduction to her later booklet, *The Basic Motor Pattern*, has acknowledged the separateness and originality of her contribution.

Figure 3.2: Using the Basic Motor Pattern to Develop Eating and Drinking Skills

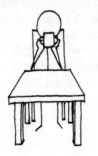

'When learning to drink the child can grasp a cup with two hands, bring the head into midline and fix himself by putting both elbows on the table lifting the cup to his mouth without falling backwards.'

'When drinking with one hand he may fix his free hand by grasping a vertical stick,

or a horizontal stick as on this picture of a child feeding himself.'

Source: Cotton (1980).

The book should not, however, be read as a description of Conductive Education which is a much wider subject dealing with all facets of pre-school training for the cerebral palsied child. The expression 'the basic motor pattern' was not used by Professor Petö. I have developed this concept during many years work and close co-operation with Dorothy Seglow (Senior Physiotherapist, Watford Spastics Centre).

The basic motor pattern has been used to develop a range of programmes which can be integrated into the current British special education system. As with conductive education, goals are functional: pottying, eating, washing, dressing, etc., are achieved by means of a task series incorporating the concept of the basic motor pattern. Figure 3.2 illustrates this general approach in the specific cases of eating and drinking.

The conductors working with the initial group at Ingfield Manor were drawn from a wide range of backgrounds, nursery nurses, houseparents, a speech therapist, a physiotherapist and a teacher, and worked in two shifts covering the whole residential day. Their training consisted of 'introductory talks and weekly inservice training', (Varty, 1973). In view of the twelve weeks per year school holiday, parent training was felt to be as important as staff training. Parents were intended to stay before a child was admitted to the school and for a week each year thereafter, in order to ensure a continuation of the child's progress during the holidays.

In the early 1970s conductive education was also introduced into two other Spastics Society establishments, the Cheyne Centre for Spastic Children (Chelsea) and Craig-y-Parc school (South Wales), although neither have continued it. Other Spastics Society schools which started using conductive education at that time and have continued to use the approach are the Claremont school (Bristol), Horton Lodge (Staffordshire) and the Springfield school (Liverpool). It has, however, been Ingfield Manor school (Sussex) which has been the flagship of the Spastics Society's efforts in this field. In 1976, the 'Peto Unit' was opened in the grounds of the main school for the specific purpose of using conductive education with preschool cerebral palsied children. In addition, the unit provided a study centre for those professionals wanting to learn about conductive education. Short courses are held at the school, consisting of lectures on the theoretical background, interspersed with observation sessions in the Peto Unit. In view of the paucity of published material on conductive education these courses have been of paramount importance in spreading information about the method both in Britain and abroad. Many foreign visitors, over the years, have attended the Ingfield Manor course and have used the knowledge gained to set up similar establishments in their own countries.

The Peto Unit (more recently referred to as the Conductive Education Unit) has twelve places for children aged from 3 to 7 who usually attend for two or more years. Some children are fully residential, others weekly boarders or day pupils. All the children have severe cerebral palsy and the educational level ranges from upper ESN(S) to upper ESN(M). Pepper (1981) has pointed out that as a result of opposition by social workers to residential placement for under-fives, the children admitted to the Peto Unit: 'Have mainly been children whose family backgrounds have been such that they would doubtless have been received into "care" anyway, thus in fact presenting a double handicap which has not always helped in evaluating the effectiveness of treatment.'

The Unit provides a preschool training (up to 8 years of age in some cases), intended as a preparation for integration into normal school or, placement in a special school. The children learn to participate actively in the skills of dressing, feeding, washing, and toileting, as well as in preschool activities which enable them to experiment and learn through play. The teaching and use of language is an integral part of the day and is included in all activities. Recommendations about further schooling are made by local education authorities before children leave the Unit.

The staff in the Unit, while being representative of the different backgrounds generally found working with physically handicapped children in this country, aim as far as possible to work together as conductors. By combining their knowledge and experience they attempt to provide an educational approach to the 'whole child'. There is still no formal training for conductors in Britain so their further professional preparation and development has consisted of a one-week training course at Ingfield Manor school, supplemented by short, observational visits to Budapest. Daily meetings for all members of the team are considered essential to provide consistency of approach to the children. Team members' specialised knowledge is used to advantage; the physiotherapist takes responsibility for chairs, splints, etc., the teacher looks at the educational needs of the Unit and oversees the work of the other conductors, and the speech therapist is responsible for the integration of alternative communication systems, such as blissymbolics.

The daily timetable in the Unit is divided between the physical task series and the activity times. In the task series movements are practised which will be required to achieve functional needs. The activity times – dressing, toileting, feeding, swimming, painting, etc. – provide an opportunity to use these learned movement patterns. The teaching method used is 'rhythmic intention'; the conductors state what they want the children to do and the children repeat the intention then count or use 'dynamic speech' as they carry out the movement. Figure 3.3 illustrates an extract from a lying programme observed at the Peto Unit. Some of the children have very little speech and rely on the direction of the conductors as the movement is attempted.

Figure 3.3: An Extract from a Lying Programme Used at the Peto Unit, Ingfield Manor School

I lie straight; one, two, three, four, five.
Hands down; down, down, down.
Chin to my chest; up, up, up.
Head down.
Arms above my head; one, two, three, four, five.
I look at the window; look, look, look.
I roll onto my tummy; over, over, over.
I stretch my elbows and fingers; stretch, stretch, stretch.
I look up; up, up, up.

Note: the child is lying in supine and rolling to prone.
Source: Personal observation by the author during conductive education course, June 1982.

In addition to providing full-time conductive education for twelve children, the unit also runs a school for mothers. This is an informal group developed for parents who live close enough to the school (Ingfield Manor school is in the heart of the Sussex countryside, quite some distance from any major towns). The main aim of the school for mothers is to teach parents how to handle their cerebral-palsied child. The mothers are taught how to encourage their child to sit better, to stand ready for the potty and to participate in dressing. It also serves as a meeting place for parents whose children have similar handicaps. Children who enter the school for mothers do not automatically enter the Conductive Education Unit when they are old enough for full-time schooling. Their entry depends on selection by the Spastics Society assessment panel and, presumably, the availability of alternative local authority provision in the neighbourhood.

Effectiveness of Conductive Education at Ingfield Manor School

According to the CEIG *Newsletter* no. 2, February 1983, 'it is fair to say that the "purest" form of Conductive Education outside Hungary can be found at the Conductive Education Unit at Ingfield'. One must, therefore, ask how many of the children who go through the unit achieve the goal of complete rehabilitation or orthofunction? How many children from the Ingfield Manor Unit go to normal schools?

An attempt at an evaluation of the Spastics Society's work in this field was made through a series of postgraduate dissertations at the University of London over the course of the 1970s (Clark, 1973; Cope, 1973; McCormack, 1974; Morley, 1979; Conochie, 1979). These were set up to evaluate the efficacy of conductive education as practised at Ingfield Manor, comparing it with more conventional approaches employed in other schools for the physically handicapped. The first of these, by Clark (1973), compared groups of children at Ingfield Manor and Irton Hall. It is worthy of note that this study predated the formation of the Peto Unit at Ingfield. Both schools are run by the Spastics Society and cater for cerebral palsied children with what are now called moderate learning difficulties. The children in Clark's study were matched for age, sex, length of time at school and severity of initial handicap. Information was obtained from 38 children at Ingfield Manor school (experimental group) and 58 children at Irton Hall school (control group).

Using an assessment procedure specially designed by Cope (1973), Clark attempted to measure change in eight areas: basic motor skills, fine finger control, gross motor control, eating skills, helping skills, grooming skills and social responsiveness. Statistical analysis of the results revealed that children at Irton Hall school performed better in the area of gross motor control. In all other areas of assessment Clark found no difference in scores from those of the Ingfield Manor children. No mention was made in the study of any child having achieved orthofunction. Clark felt that no definite conclusions as to the effectiveness of conductive education should be drawn from this study in view of the difficulties that he had experienced in the experimental design. Despite these difficulties he felt able to suggest: 'If Conductive Education does have advantages over conventional therapy they do not happen to be as dramatic as has been claimed, if they exist at all' (Clark, 1973). In 1974, McCormack followed up the same groups of children at Ingfield Manor and Irton Hall. She found that in the areas of basic motor skills and gross motor control, children at Irton Hall school still scored significantly higher. No significant differences emerged between the two groups on any other area of assessment. She concluded, that in broad terms, the results showed no difference between the effects of conductive education at Ingfield Manor and conventional teaching/therapy as practised by Irton Hall.

Jernqvist (1978a) evaluated the progress of 12 children, average age 4 years at the sart of the study, at the Peto Unit at Ingfield Manor. The children in Jernqvist's study were substantially younger than those in Clark's (1973) and McCormack's (1974) studies, who had been drawn from the main school, and had an average age of just over 12 years. After one year Jernqvist (1978a) reported that the children had improved on all areas of Cope's (1973) schedule (see Table 3.1). In a follow up report, Jernqvist (1980b), the progress of the same children after a two-year period in the Peto Unit was outlined. The results indicated that progress had been made in all areas of assessment, substantial improvement being noted in basic motor skills, grooming skills and dressing skills. Though there was no control group in her study, Jernqvist concluded that over a two-year period the children in the Peto Unit at Ingfield achieved a significant increase in scores, an improvement not found in either Clark's (1973) or McCormack's (1974) studies. Despite this, however, none of the children proved able to go to normal schools. As Jernqvist (1980b) pointed out, 'the two years have, in spite of statistically significant progress, meant little towards normality in terms of schooling'. Of the twelve children in the study, five were subsequently transferred to the main school at Ingfield Manor (for children within the educational level ESN(M)), three to Craig-y-Parc school (for physically handicapped children of average intellectual ability), one to Rutland House school (for children within the educational level ESN(S), all residential schools run by the Spastics Society, and one child was transferred to a residential school not run by the Spastics Society. In considering the reasons why the Peto Unit failed to achieve orthofunction, Jernqvist (1980b) argued as follows:

> We must differentiate between the ambitious goals of Conductive Education and the more realistic and specific aims of the unit. No one actually claims to be able to change a severely handicapped four year old cerebral palsied child into a normal child in a two-year period, but the ambition, the goal and the philosophy are there!

Table 3.1: Total Scores Obtained in Each Area of the Cope Schedule (1973) after One Year and Two Years of the Jernqvist Study

Area of assessment	Total baseline score	Total score after 1 year	Total score after 2 years
Basic motor skills	44	77	110
Fine finger control	26	34	52
Gross motor control	23	31	42
Eating skills	46	90	94
Grooming skills	29	87	176
Dressing skills	0	33	98
Social responsiveness	143	147	160

Source: Jernqvist (1978a and 1980b)

She also pointed out that in Britain, despite the Warnock report, the integration of handicapped children into normal schools remained particularly difficult.

British Conductive Education outside Ingfield Manor School

Almost every account of conductive education in Britain, both published and unpublished, has concerned the work at Ingfield Manor. In addition to those already referred to these include Rodker (1967), Varty (1970b), Wallace (1975), Jernqvist (1977, 1978b) and Laurance (1984). Very little written material is available to describe work elsewhere in this country.

Mother-and-baby Groups. As well as at Ingfield Manor, such groups are also held at the Lady Zia Werhner Centre (Luton), Horton Lodge school (Staffordshire) and the Watford Spastics Centre. The Watford group has, until recently, been run by a physiotherapist, Mrs Dorothy Seglow, who visited the Budapest Institute in 1966. Working closely with Ester Cotton, she has continued to develop her interest in conductive education with mothers and babies, and appears to have been an important influence in developing the concept of the basic motor pattern (Cotton, 1980).

The mother-and-baby group at the Watford Spastics Centre takes a maximum of six children and is held for one hour twice a week. The children are all under 2 years of age and vary substantially in terms of the degree of their mental and physical disability. At the Centre, homogeneity within the group is not felt to be particularly important in view of the age of the children involved. Within the group great demands are placed on the conductor who has not only to plan for the children and the group, but also for the mothers. Task series are devised based on the basic motor pattern and these are incorporated into play situations accompanied by nursery rhymes. Children in the group work on individual plinths, either supported or closely observed by their mothers. The aim of the group is to teach the mothers how to manage their children, and to heighten their awareness that every daily situation must provide a learning experience (Seglow, 1981).

Local Education Authority Schools. The most diverse adaptations of conductive education appear to have arisen in LEA day schools for mentally and physically handicapped children. Here, due to pressure of other commitments within the school, many conductors are only able to carry out conductive education programmes for a short time each week. In a survey carried out by Sutton in 1982 on attempts to use conductive education programmes in schools in the West Midlands (Sutton, 1984b), the amount of time devoted to the method ranged upward from as little as one hour per week.

From the few published accounts of British state school practice (Rooke and Opel, 1983; Titchener, 1983; and Wilson, 1983) certain common features emerge. Conductive education, in this setting, appears to be synonymous with a short, structured group programme aimed at simple functional goals, such as feeding and dressing. The 'conductor principle' involves teachers, therapists, nursery nurses, etc., sharing their knowledge and taking it in turns to lead the group. Group teaching is used but the groups are rarely homogeneous in any respect. The use of speech to regulate movement (rhythmic intention) is invariably used as the teaching method. Wilson (1983) has descibed the use of conductive education in an ESN(S) school in London. She stated that:

> 'Conductive Education' involves a constant 'swopping of roles' between teachers and therapists; which in turn, enhances the 'symbiotic union of community health and ILEA' . . . Therapists at the school integrate their work into the general classroom teaching and teachers attempt to use therapy to effect in the classroom. . . Primarily they encourage the child to be active, the responsibility is heaped more onto (sic) the child to succeed as much as possible.

The report made no mention of orthofunction, even as an objective.

The accounts of conductive education in LEA schools by Rooke and Opel (1983) and Titchener (1983) will not be outlined in detail here, as this work will be described and evaluated in Chapters 4 and 5.

Outpatient Hospital Clinic. Conductive education in Britain has been directed primarily towards working with cerebral-palsied children. Attention is now being drawn, however, to its applicability with adult patients (Kinsman, 1983a). As with all other groups considered in this chapter, the main influence has been Ester Cotton. In the recent publication *Conductive Education for Adult Hemiplegia* (Cotton and Kinsman, 1983) her philosophy of the basic motor pattern is much in evidence in the five task series presented as essential for the hemiplegic patient (i.e. sitting at a table, lying, free sitting, standing and walking). While no mention has been made of its use in Britain with multiple sclerosis patients, Kinsman is using the method with Parkinson's disease patients, although no report has yet been presented.

Conductive Education in Other Countries in Western Europe

At the 1984 International Seminar on Conductive Education held in Budapest, papers were presented outlining the use of the method in Austria, Italy and Belgium. This was the first time that information on this work had been made available in English and for the most part it provided only a scant overview of what is happening in these countries.

Austria

Despite the proximity of Austria to Hungary, only one institute in Vienna is known to be using the method. Mrs Keil, the director, was first introduced to Professor Petö in the 1960s and began using conductive education shortly afterwards with two small groups of cerebral palsied children in a private house. Her aim was to establish a conductive education institute in Vienna but this was blocked in the early stages by several financial and bureaucratic problems. Money from the National Health Insurance was only available for therapy, and as a result the method had to be referred to as 'pedagogical therapy'. There was also the problem of which professions should be employed in the institute, should they come from education or health?

Fortunately, Mrs Keil was trained both as a physiotherapist and as a preschool teacher.

The institute operates several conductive education groups as well as providing an introductory training course for conductors. The work of the institute has been greatly advanced since 1970 by the addition to the staff of a Hungarian who, despite not finishing her diploma, spent several years training at the Institute for the Motor-Disabled in Budapest. In addition, two physiotherapists have spent six months training at Ingfield Manor school, Sussex, and Mrs Cotton has given a course in Vienna.

The institute in Vienna caters for cerebral-palsied children of preschool- and school-age. Each group has a physiotherapist and a teacher working as conductors. There are two preschool groups that stay for half a day, from 7.30 a.m. to 1.00 p.m. Transfer to normal school is facilitated by the presence of a normal kindergarten adjacent to the institute. Children from the preschool groups who are able to walk spend the majority of their day in the kindergarten and attend the institute for only an hour and a half each day. For the school children there are several outpatient groups that come to the institute for two- to three-hour sessions, three to four times a week. In the last two years a group has been established for severely handicapped school leavers. They attend for the whole day and the aim has been to develop self-help skills.

For the last five years, the Spastics Society in Austria has held introductory courses in conductive education each year at the institute. One of the courses is a three-semester course with two lectures a week during each semester and the other is held for ten weeks in the summer. In addition to the lectures, 140 practical hours are also required. At the end of the course the participants have a theoretical and practical exam and every two years there is a finishing seminar at which questions concerning conductive education can be raised and discussed. Mrs Keil, however, feels that this training is inadequate and is anxious to organise an exchange of Hungarian and Austrian conductors with the help of Dr Hári and the Hungarian authorities.

Belgium

In Belgium, conductive education is being used at La Famille in Brussels, a centre for physically handicapped children. Inspired by a Polish neurologist working at the centre, the method was introduced into the kindergarten about five years ago following a visit to Budapest by three members of the staff. These included Ives Bawin, a physiotherapist, who has since become the main advocate of conductive education in Belgium. Initially, there was much opposition to the system and in an attempt to overcome this problem a course by Mrs Cotton was organised at the centre. In addition, a seminar on conductive education was held in Brussels in 1981, which included a paper by Dr Hári. While many of the initial difficulties have been overcome, with two more conductive education groups to be started at La Famille, the problem of conductor training remains. No instances of achieving orthofunction have been reported.

Italy

After a visit to Budapest in 1977 and a short course given by Mrs Cotton, conductive education was introduced at the Gaslini Institute, Genoa, by a paediatric neurologist, Professor Virginia Grillo. The children attend as outpatients for two hours each day, five days a week and follow a range of programmes designed to achieve orthofunction. For the rest of their time they go to normal kindergarten or school; there are no special schools for the handicapped in Genoa. The conductors from the Gaslini Institute give advice to the teachers on conductive education so that the skills learnt there can be reinforced throughout the school day. The groups run from October to June and during the summer the parents follow the conductive education programmes with their children at home.

Conductive Education in North America

In comparison with Britain, the role played by North America in the spread of conductive education outside Hungary has been minimal. Despite the fact that several individuals have been inspired by the method only limited interest has been generated from these isolated attempts.

United States

In most countries where conductive education has been introduced the method has spread, albeit gradually. In the United States, however, this has not been the case.

The method was introduced at the North Wisconsin Colony and Training School, in Chippewa Falls, Wisconsin, by Professor James House in 1968, after a long visit to Budapest. What most struck

House about conductive education was the 'quality and spirit of the love that is given to the children' (House, 1968). This emphasis on love as a key aspect of the method has surprisingly never been cited by any other western visitors. Encouraged by what he had seen in Budapest and backed by a grant from the Department of Health, Education and Welfare, the work developed into the Integrated Management of Cerebral Palsy (IMCP) project (Heal, 1972, 1974, 1976), designed to evaluate the effectiveness of procedures based on conductive education. The project was hampered in the initial stages by the resignation for personal reasons of the director, Professor House, and the death of his main collaborator. His replacement, Laird Heal, a psychologist, admitted 'substantial ignorance about cerebral palsy and its treatment' (Heal, 1972). The knowledge base of the American project was twofold, drawing both directly on the Institute in Budapest and upon the British Spastics Society.

The accumulated months of training and consultation by Dr Mária Hári and her staff at the Institute for Movement Therapy were an essential ingredient in the construction of the IMCP project. The consultation of Ester Cotton in London, England, was also extremely valuable. Finally, the three months sojourn of Margaret Parnwell gave the original staff daily contact with a consultant who had several years of first hand experience with Conductive Education. (Heal, 1972)

After two years of preliminary programme development the evaluation began with the selection of subjects in 1971. Follow up evaluations of the children's progress were made in April 1971, November 1971 and April 1972. Twenty-five subjects were involved in the study; ten assigned to the IMCP group and fifteen to the conventional treatment (CT) group. The IMCP children met the following criteria: they were cerebral palsied, non-ambulatory, age 5-13 years, able to understand simple instructions and admissible to the North Wisconsin Colony (admission requirements were a measured IQ under 70, permission of parents and Wisconsin residency). The CT subjects were matched as far as possible with the IMCP subjects in terms of diagnosis, age, mental age, motor ability, dressing ability and speech characteristics.

Heal (1974) described Integrated Management as a method by which 'motorically disabled children are trained in small, motivating groups of similarly handicapped peers. They are taught to pursue actively and voluntarily those movements that are both incompatible with reflexes and functional in their self-care applications.' The 13½-hours-per-day programme was run by two to four professionally trained teacher–therapists who acted as conductors. It began at 6.00 a.m., and was integrated to 'maximise the interwoven reinforcement of the various activities that occurred during the day' (Heal, 1972). Goals in the following areas were sought and measured: motor development, communication, socialisation skills and educational goals. Functional movement goals were evaluated by the *Eau Claire Functional Abilities Test*, communication by the *Peabody Picture Vocabulary Test* and the *Mecham Verbal Language Scales*, socialisation by the *Wolfe-Bluel Socialization Scale* and educational development by the *Peabody Individual Achievement Test*.

Three conventional programmes were compared to the integrated programme, those at the Illinois Children's Hospital-School, the Crippled Children's Hospital and School, South Dakota and the Worthington Crippled Children's School in Minnesota. All the programmes involved an intensive therapy and education, administered by professional staff. Teaching focused on academic and vocational areas, and stressed the value of individual programmes including occupational therapy, physiotherapy and speech therapy. The majority of the children were residential and there were favourable staffing levels; class sizes of about nine to fourteen and staff–student ratios of about one to one. Both the IMCP and the conventional programmes stressed the tailoring of each child's programme to his particular needs, but the conventional programmes were segmented in their delivery. Special equipment, e.g. braces, prostheses, typewriters, book holders, etc., to facilitate the mechanics of education were encouraged for the CT group.

The results presented in Figure 3.4 indicate the overall test scores recorded in the IMCP project.

It is evident that at the start of the project, the conventional treatment group was superior to the integrated management group in all areas and that it maintained its superiority over the one-year evaluation period. Despite such a disappointing outcome, Heal (1972) concluded optimistically:

The staff ended the project as they had begun – believing firmly that the principles and procedures of Conductive Education are sound and that the effort to import them to this country should be pursued. This belief and the documented success of the procedure

Figure 3.4: Overall Test Scores Obtained in the IMCP Project

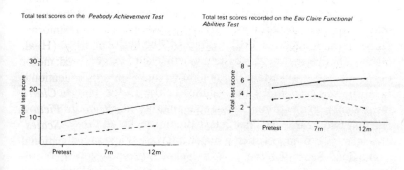

Total test scores on the *Peabody Achievement Test*

Total test scores recorded on the *Eau Claire Functional Abilities Test*

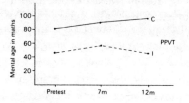

Total test scores on the *Peabody Picture Vocabulary Test*

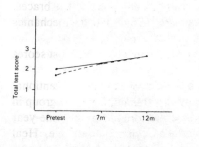

Total test scores on the *Wolfe-Bluel Socialization Inventory*

(PPVT) and the *Verbal Language Development Scales* (VLDS)

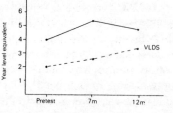

Note: ———— conventional teaching group.
- - - - - - IMCP group.

Source: Heal (1972).

in other settings must be seen as persuasive arguments for the continuation of the pursuit.

The project was not continued and, as far as can be discerned, no other attempts to employ conductive education have been made in the United States since the IMCP project. Whether or not this is the result of the project's negative findings with regard to the effectiveness of the method is uncertain. It should be pointed out, however, that Heal himself questioned the validity of the IMCP project as an instrument to evaluate conductive education (Heal, 1972). Firstly, he felt that two years was insufficient time to make all the necessary arrangements to import such a major innovation and prepare for its evaluation. Secondly, the project lacked a trained conductor or someone trained in the conventional treatment of cerebral palsy, and the high rate of staff turnover necessitated expending extra resources to train replacements. Perhaps the most debilitating factor was the incompatibility of the project with its institutional surroundings. There was a basic discrepancy between the orientation of the colony towards custodial care and that of the project to active rehabilitation of the cerebral-palsied child. This incompatibility proved a relentless drain on the energy, morale and effectiveness of the IMCP staff.

Canada

In Canada, an Integrated Treatment Unit (ITU) was set up by Dr Bruce Young in 1969, at the Ontario Crippled Children's Centre. Dr Young took his idea of an integrated treatment–teaching philosophy from a meeting with Dr Hári but, due to a major stroke in 1971, his initiative was not continued (Bate, 1984, personal communication). In 1979, with no notion of the background of the ITU classes, an occupational therapist at the centre, Mrs Elizabeth Bate, went to Ingfield Manor school in England to study with Ester Cotton. In turn, Mrs Cotton went to the Centre in Ontario to lecture for two weeks in October 1980. Between 1980 and 1981, conductive education was introduced into the kindergarten and special grade-one classes at the Ontario Crippled Children's Centre (Bate and Kucerna, 1981). Two one-hour sessions per week were led by a conductor and rhythmic intention was used as the teaching method. The purpose at this stage was solely to demonstrate the concept and to form groups for teaching purposes prior to Mrs Cotton's course in October 1980. Between 1981-2, growing interest on the part of teachers and therapists led to the inclusion of conductive education into other classrooms, i.e. a preschool class (9 children, average age 3 years) and two Bliss classes (8 severely handicapped children, aged 8-15 years) (Bate, 1982). While the time devoted to conductive education had increased to three-and-a-half hours per week, it was still used only on an episodic basis, and this continued to be the case until 1983.

As a result of the lack of therapist interest and teacher rotation, conductive education had ceased to be used at both the kindergarten and nursery levels in the summer of 1983. In September 1983, however, a detailed research project was set up at the Centre to evaluate the effectiveness of conductive education with the special grade-one class. The experimental period was the full academic year from September 1983 to June 1984. Five cerebral-palsied children, average age six-and-a-half years, were included in the conductive education group: three with spastic quadraplegia, one with bilateral hemiparesis and one with athetosis. Their intellectual functioning varied from 'mid-borderline educable to borderline normal', and all had additional perceptual deficits. There was no control group (Bate, 1983).

The approach was used five mornings a week from 9.00 a.m. to 12.00 noon, the sessions led by either a teacher or therapist acting as conductor. The basic motor pattern (Cotton, 1980) formed an important basis of the programmes, with an extended application of learned motor skills into academic activities. The children remained in the classroom as much as possible, the 'withdrawal for treatment' system being contra-indicated. In addition, the use of specific furniture, rhythmic intention as the teaching method and regularly conducted group motor sessions formed important elements of the conductive education approach (Bate, 1984, personal communication).

Detailed evaluation of conductive education at the Ontario Crippled Children's Centre was undertaken by means of formal assessment, observation and a questionnaire study. The majority of the assessments were carried out at the start of the project and at six and nine months into the school year. An extract from the results obtained at the end of the nine-month evaluation are presented in Table 3.2. As the evaluation was closely based on that of Titchener (1982) this extract is comparable to that presented in Table 4.1.

While the results indicate improvement in all task areas no child is reported to have achieved orthofunction. In their programme report Bate and Kucerna (1984) concluded that:

While Conductive Education is an enormously sensible and logical

Table 3.2: Extract from the Results after Nine Months of Conductive Education at the Ontario Crippled Children's Centre

Short-term goals	Number of children achieving criterion (out of 5)	
	September 1983	June 1984
Supine, head in midline	1/5	5/5
Prone, head in midline	3/5	5/5
Rolling	4/5	5/5
Sitting, head in midline, feet flat	2/5	5/5
Maintain grasp – pronation 2 hands	3/5	5/5
– mixed supination 2 hands	1/5	4/5
– while moving arm	0/5	4/5
Lower self onto chair	2/5	4/5
Walk pushing chair	2/5	3/5
Hold cup and drink alone	3/5	4/5
Can use knife and fork	2/5	3/5
Removes slipover garments	1/5	4/5
Fastening buttons (large)	0/5	3/5
(small)	0/5	0/5
Comb and brush hair	0/5	4/5
Use toilet alone	0/5	3/5

Source: Bate and Kucerna (1984).

approach to the learning of cerebral palsied children, it is not always easy. The therapist and teacher must be flexible and generous in mutual sharing of knowledge, time and expertise. They must spend time in consulting and planning, integrating and co-ordinating the aims of their work. The work is concentrated and intensive if we believe that any time is a good time for a child to learn. However, the time passes quickly and the children enjoy learning. It is our understanding that the Conductive Education method allows an extensive variety of interpretation to suit the specific needs of the group and the teacher–therapist team.

As a result of Mrs Bate's work, interest in the system has grown and conductive education is now being used in several other schools in Toronto.

Conductive Education in Australasia

Conductive education was first introduced in Australia in the early

1970s. Clarke and Evans (1973) reported on their use of a modified form of the method with a group of six athetoid children at the Spastics Centre, New South Wales. The children were of average intelligence and ranged in age from six-and-a-half to seven-and-a-half years. Rhythmic intention was used as the teaching method and group teaching was seen as an important pedagogic means, responsible for 'building up the self-confidence of each child and the concept of social co-operation within the group'. Work from different therapies was co-ordinated into a single programme and led by a therapist, acting as conductor. The programme ran five mornings a week from 9.00 a.m. to 12.30 p.m. Figure 3.5 illustrates the results obtained after 16 months of using conductive education at the Spastics Centre, New South Wales. No mention was made of orthofunction.

Clarke and Evans (1973) concluded that the children made great improvement in 'general body control and gross movement patterns, and little improvement in any fine hand movements, . . . probably due to the degree of handicap'. They suggested that from their experience, rhythmical intention is a suitable treatment for the severely athetoid child.

In terms of published material, the main contribution to Australian conductive education has been made by Dowrick (1978, 1979, 1982; Dowrick and Fairweather, 1979). She had worked as a teacher at Ingfield Manor school in 1974 during a working holiday in England. In 1976 she returned to Australia, greatly influenced by Ester Cotton's work, and set up the 'Petö method' at the Spastic Welfare Association of Western Australia, on a daily and full-time basis. A 'highly specialised multidisciplinary team' (Dowrick, 1979) worked with the preschool group on a shift basis. Physical, functional and educational needs were considered, and the primary aims of the unit were to promote as much independence as possible and to prepare the children for school.

In 1978, Miss Dowrick received a scholarship from the Hungarian government to study for four months in Budapest. She returned to Australia convinced that once removed from its source the method suffers through adaptation. The Australian version at that time was an adaptation of the English version of the Hungarian method (Dowrick, 1984, personal communication). She had written in 1979, 'We must realise that the political, social and economic factors involved with the application of the Petö method have important implications for its implementation into Australian society' (Dowrick and Fairweather, 1979). Despite cultural differences, however, she still considered

Figure 3.5: Results after 16 Months of Conductive Education at the Spastics Centre, New South Wales

	Aug 1970	Dec 1971
Prone:		
Lie still with arms above head	3	6
Lift and hold head up	2	6
Reach and grasp one hand	0	5
Rolling:		
Roll in both directions	2	6
Supine:		
Lie still with arms by side	2	6
Lie still with arms by side and feet against wall	2	4
Hold hands together	2	6
Extend arms with hands together	1	5
Lift rod in one hand, keeping other hand by side	2	6
Lift rod/quoit in two hands	1	5
Move legs keeping arms by side	1	5
Getting on to tables alone	0	4
Getting off tables alone	0	4
Sitting:		
Sit still in a chair with arms and keep feet on floor	1	6
Touch toes and sit up	0	5
Sit alone on a stool	0	4
Arm and hand function:		
Keep feet on floor and hand flat on table	3	6
Keep one hand supporting while other hand moves –		
(i) on the table	1	6
(ii) in the air	1	6
Spread fingers with hands flat	3	6
Maintain a fist with wrist extension	3	6
Results for dominant hand only –		
Grasp stabilised cotton reel	1	6
Maintain grasp pronation	1	6
mid supination	0	5
while moving arm	1	4
Release with wrist extension	0	5
grasp and draw – horizontal line	1	6
vertical line	0	4
circle	0	4
Sitting to standing and walking:		
Standing holding table	1	4
Standing holding table with support	0	2
Stand holding on to a chair	1	4
Walk sideways around table	0	4
Walk pushing chair	0	3
Activities:		
Feeding – Take hand to mouth	2	6
Take spoon to mouth without food	1	4
with food	1	3

	Aug 1970	Dec 1971
Eat sanwiches alone	2	4
Hold cup and take to mouth without milk	1	4
Hold cup and drink alone	0	2
Undress – Shoes and socks	0	5
Slipover garments	0	4
Pants	0	3
Toilet – Balance on pot alone	0	4
Get on to and use pot alone	0	2

Note: Numbers indicate number of children who could perform the task consistently.
Source: Clarke and Evans (1973).

certain aspects of the method to be beneficial:

(1) the unification of treatment and education;
(2) the united approach in conductive education which provides consistency in handling, and, therefore, learning;
(3) repetition and reinforcement of skills which aid learning (Dowrick, 1984, personal communication).

In 1980, Dowrick evaluated the progress of eight of the children involved in the conductive education group at the Spastics Centre. Four of the children attended on a daily basis and four were residential. The project failed to cater for many important variables, e.g. differences in diagnosis, variations in the length of time on the programme, etc., and did not involve a control group. The results are illustrated in Figure 3.6. Improvement was noted in all areas, the four residential children making more progress than the day attenders, though there were no instances of orthofunction.

Dowrick has concluded that one of the main problems encountered in the Australian work has been the resistance to the 'unity of disciplines' necessary for the conductor principle. Many therapists and teachers have felt very threatened by conductive education because it encroached on their 'territory'. In the light of such opposition the method ceased to be used in the Spastics Centre in 1982 (Dowrick, 1984, personal communication).

In contrast, interest in the method has continued at the Queensland Spastic Welfare League since it was first begun in 1976 under the guidance of Evonne Burns, who had visited England and Ingfield Manor, in 1972. Conductive education is currently being used in one class for two one-hour sessions per week, in several other classes for

Figure 3.6: Results of an Evaluation of Conductive Education at the Spastics Centre, Western Australia

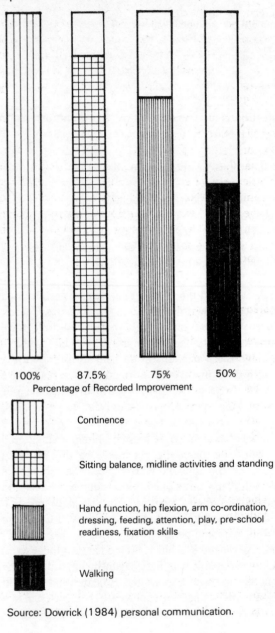

100%   87.5%   75%   50%
Percentage of Recorded Improvement

Continence

Sitting balance, midline activities and standing

Hand function, hip flexion, arm co-ordination, dressing, feeding, attention, play, pre-school readiness, fixation skills

Walking

Source: Dowrick (1984) personal communication.

one hour per week and during individual sessions held at lunch time. Several disciplines are involved including a teacher, physiotherapist, speech therapist and occupational therapist. While they admit that their involvement in the method is not extensive they are convinced that conductive education has much to offer even with such modest usage (Littler, 1984, personal communication). More recently an upsurge of interest has been reported in several other parts of Australia and a regular newsletter is now being circulated (Cooper, 1984).

Conductive education is also being used by 'a few enthusiasts' in New Zealand. Bagnall has recently described the use of the method at the Carlson School for Cerebral Palsy, Auckland. The school runs two groups: a daily, half-hour 'Peto class' teaching hand skills (such as grasp, hold and release) and another class held once a week for children who have hemiplegia. No evaluations have been made as to the effectiveness of the method but Rachael Bornsteinas, the charge physiotherapist concludes that 'the Peto therapy can work in well with other therapies, such as those taught by Dr and Mrs Bobath of England' (Bagnall, 1984).

Conductive Education in Hong Kong

In Hong Kong, interest in conductive education started about ten years ago, with a physiotherapist, Mrs Anita Tatlow, researching into approaches to the treatment of cerebral palsy. At that time the only published material on the method in English was that by Cotton (1965; 1970; Cotton and Parnwell, 1967; 1968). During her literature search, Tatlow had come by chance across the work of Luriya (1961a) *The Role of Speech in the Regulation of Normal and Abnormal Behaviour*. This provided her philosophy for rhythmic intention.

In recent personal correspondence, Tatlow has outlined in detail the developments which have occurred in Hong Kong since her first association with conductive education. Shortly after giving her first talk on the method, she started to set up groups for athetoid children at the John F. Kennedy Centre. Since then her work has expanded and the centre is now running three groups based on conductive education principles: a 'baby' group, an athetoid group and a hand class for athetoids. The group sessions are relatively short; the baby group meets for two sessions per week (one one-hour and one half-hour), the athetoid group has two half-hour sessions per week and the hand class have one half-hour session per week. All the groups consist of five children, with either one or two conductors to each group. At the John F. Kennedy Centre, only the physiotherapist and the occupational therapist take on the role of conductor, but interest in conductive education appears to be spreading to other professions. At a recent course in Hong Kong given by Ester Cotton, twenty-six professionals attended: five teachers, three nursery nurses, five physiotherapists, eleven occupational therapists, one childcare worker and one psychologist. Rather than attempting to mirror conductive education, as it might be practised in Hungary or England, workers in Hong Kong have adapted the method to their particular milieu; most equipment is specific to the Hong Kong/Chinese environment and Montessori ideas are intermingled.

Tatlow feels that many of the aspects of conductive education are particularly conducive to application in Hong Kong. It is a small, crowded territory with poor paediatric facilities where a great many physically handicapped children live in close proximity to each other. It is, therefore, relatively easy to form homogeneous groups, especially in what she regards as a group-orientated society. The method of learning which is used, 'rhythmic intention', would appear to be similar to methods already employed by teachers. As Yuan (1984) has pointed out '. . . within the Chinese culture, where there already exists a classroom tradition of "chanting" (even if now considered old-fashioned) and the emphasis is more communal than individualistic, this method may fit comfortably with patterns of teaching already established'.

Conductive education is now being used in several other centres in Hong Kong with different groups of children. At the Ko Fook In Memorial school, Shatin, and at the Wong Tai Sin Disabled Children's Centre, Kowloon, it is used at the preschool level with physically handicapped children. Recently, the method has been introduced at the Caritas Medical Centre, Kowloon. Since the course on conductive education given by Ester Cotton in April 1983, those involved with the system in Hong Kong have started their own Conductive Education Interest Group.

Conductive Education in Japan

Since 1978, conductive education has also been used with physically handicapped children and adults at the Warashibe Institute, Osaka. Initially influenced by the work of Ester Cotton in England, Dr Masanao Murai, the director of the Warashibe Institute, has done much to develop 'medico-educational treatment'. Every endeavour has been made to develop strong links with the Institute for the Motor-Disabled, in Budapest. Some of the Japanese conductors have been trained in Hungary, and all are learning the language 'in order to associate with the Petö Institute in Budapest intimately' (Murai, 1981). It seems that the Japanese attempt at conductive education may be the closest reflection of the Hungarian system so far achieved outside of Hungary.

The Warashibe Institute is a self-contained unit built specifically for the purpose of developing conductive education. There are three groups practising the method; a residential class, a mother-and-baby class and a class for school children held twice monthly on Sunday. Group teaching is employed but the groups do not appear to be homogeneous. Following Petö's example, the Japanese do not see motor handicap as primarily a physical problem but as a problem concerning the development of the whole personality. 'How to find the growing personality and how to take out his own activity for growth. This is the essence of education and is also the essence of the Petö method' (Murai, 1981).

For the 40 children in the residential class medico-educational treatment is used throughout a daily programme. Task series in lying, sitting, standing and walking have been developed based on the basic motor pattern (Cotton, 1980), and form an important part of the daily schedule. Within the Warashibe Institute 'the daily programme is organically connected with one another', as skills learnt in the task series are carried over into play, study, dressing, eating, etc. Much emphasis is placed on the children's development of inner motivation.

> We must give the handicapped children, with involuntary movement, the proper tasks in order to be able to control it. For example, we give them the tasks of upper limbs to perform the extended position symmetrically. In this way, they have valuable experiences that they try to perform their tasks themselves. Gradually, they will develop their personalities, try to find their tasks and try to perform them for themselves. (Murai, 1981, translated from the Japanese)

The mother-and-baby class, composed of six pairs of children and mothers, attend the Institute daily for two hours. During this time a programme incorporating task series in lying, standing and walking is led by a chief conductor, with a sub-conductor helping the mothers where necessary. General daily activities, e.g. toileting and feeding, are also included.

The class for school children, held twice monthly on Sundays, caters for children from 6 to 18 years who have a wide variety of motor handicaps. In view of the limited contact that this group has with the Institute, parents are encouraged to work as conductors so that the medico-educational treatment can be carried over into the home. This group also serves as a graduating step towards full integration into normal schools for children, from the residential class.

Despite this commitment to conductive education no research on the effectiveness of the method has yet been undertaken at the Warashibe Institute and information is not yet available on how many, if any, of the children from Warashibe achieve orthofunction. Nor is it known whether conductive education has spread to other centres in Japan.

Conclusion

In addition to the work outlined above, a number of other centres (in Denmark, West Germany, Poland, South America and India) are reported to be using the method. Neither published nor unpublished accounts of these attempts yet exist in English.

In Hungary, conductive education has developed in the light of particular social, political and economic opportunities and constraints. Group teaching, for example, is an important pedagogic aspect throughout all East European education, and it is, therefore, not surprising that it forms an integral part of conductive education. In contrast, the educational regimes in the English-speaking world stress the importance of the individual and have attempted to work towards smaller teaching groups, and higher staff-to-pupil ratios. Our therapists and teachers are now extensively trained in their particular specialisms and many are reluctant to move out of the boundaries of their profession to take on the conductor role. Professional jealousies appear in many cases to have been a major obstacle in the establishment of conductive education.

A number of evaluations of conductive education have now been completed in the West, yet no orthofunction has ever been documented as the outcome. This is perhaps not surprising because, despite all the effort and goodwill which have been devoted to taking up and adapting this method, no one outside of Hungary has as yet provided a convincing account of how conductive education works and how to implement it. Furthermore, all evaluations to date show major flaws in their experimental design. Many have been conducted by a member of the project's own staff and have failed to establish control groups. No consideration has been given to important variables, e.g. the effect of surrounding school milieu (Wahler and Fox, 1981), and the lack of conductor training. Heal (1972) presented the most detailed evaluation of this method but this was not exempt from both internal and external problems. Without significant evidence of its effectiveness, it is perhaps not surprising that conductive education outside Hungary is still very much an insignificant appendage to methods already employed in the treatment of cerebral palsy and is almost wholly unknown with regard to other conditions.

4 AN APPROACH FOR THE PHYSICALLY HANDICAPPED?

Jayne Titchener

As a teacher in a school for the physically handicapped, I was extremely interested to attend a local authority in-service training day in the mid-1970s, entitled 'Conductive Education'. The course tutor was Mrs Ester Cotton, consultant physiotherapist with the Spastics Society. Mrs Cotton described at some length a Hungarian method of teaching children with motor disabilities how to bring their limbs under control so that they could cope with the ordinary demands of education and enjoy a relatively normal life.

The approach seemed particularly relevant to the children that I was teaching and I consequently decided to investigate conductive education more fully. Imagine the disappointment of finding nothing published by András Pető, nothing translated from the Hungarian and only a smattering of short published articles. Certainly there was insufficient information readily available upon which to have the confidence to base any change of practice in the school where I was working. Life at the school carried on much as before but at the back of my mind was the nagging feeling that it might be possible to meet the children's needs more successfully.

In 1980 I received a year's secondment to the Faculty of Education, Birmingham University, which gave me the time to investigate conductive education in depth and the opportunity to set up a small research project which would use some of the basic principles of this method of teaching with a group of physically handicapped children. There had been a spasmodic series of reports of 'descriptions of study visits' made by people from the Spastics Society who had visited the Institute for the Motor-Disabled in Budapest. For these to move beyond simple description was difficult, because of a lack of understanding of the Hungarian language on the part of the English visitors.

Most useful was the work of Lillemor Jernqvist, an educational psychologist with the Spastics Society, who had been attempting to describe and evaluate the progress of children attending the Conductive Education Unit at the Spastics Society's Ingfield Manor school in Sussex. Unfortunately the school itself was very atypical, being residential and outside the state system (with the problems of falling rolls and an unfavourable economic climate and the new emphasis upon community placement, local education authorities are attempting wherever possible to educate their own children). The highly selective intake at Ingfield Manor school rendered it impossible to form the 'homogenous' group required by practitioners of conductive education. My review of the literature revealed no research or evaluation of conductive education in a state school for the physically handicapped in the Western world.

The Research Project

The brief agreed with the headteacher was to introduce a pilot project on conductive education into our school for the physically handi-capped, the only PH school in this particular local authority. The school was non-residential and catered for approximately 90 children aged 3 to 18 years with a wide range of physical and mental disabilities. The school was laid out in the 'open plan' and organised into three departments, nursery–infant, junior and senior. There was also a 'support service' which provided extra help for the school's most seriously handicapped pupils of all ages. This was staffed by teachers responsible for computer work, home–school liaison, further education, life skills, non-verbal communication and gross and fine motor function. The children concerned were those who did not readily fit into any group because of their particularly special needs. The majority had gross and fine motor problems, often linked with communication difficulties. It was with these eleven children that this account is concerned (see Sharron, 1983, for a brief account of the same work).

The Conductive Education Group

The ages of the children in the group ranged from 5 to 14 years; their disabilities comprised spastic tetraplegia, athetosis, dystonic tetra-plegia, right-sided spasticity, ataxia, epilepsy and extensive brain damage as a result of a road traffic accident. Two of the children came from ethnic minority groups, three were non-verbal and all but one were wheelchair-bound. The educational level of the group (taken from psychologists' assessments on record at the school) was also mixed, ranging from three children functioning at ESN(S) level to one of average ability. These children had been selected for the extra help of the support service. They had been described by their group teachers as children who could never be left to do anything on their own, who because of their motor difficulties were unable to take part in the normal academic curriculum of their peer group or to play. None of these children could:

(1) sit at a table or freely on a chair or the floor;
(2) grasp, release or keep hold;
(3) keep their arms by their sides in sitting or lying;
(4) keep their hands together in mid-line while sitting or lying;
(5) transfer between chair, toilet and floor.

All were asymetrical and took little or no active part in daily living activities such as feeding, toileting, walking, grooming or dressing. All had very poor ability for looking, listening and concentrating and did not play with other children. Ways and means had to be found, therefore, to overcome the dysfunction of these children by teaching them that they *could* learn to do something. Being 'one-off' children in their peer groups they were used to being taught and treated on a one-to-one basis. They were used to waiting for someone to come and do something either with, to or for them. They were either unsociable, demanding, preferred adults to their peers, or drifted into their own dream worlds unless receiving personal attention.

Because of the various ages of the children in the group and their different skills and abilities it was thought necessary to introduce a new and unified approach to the social and functional problems common to these children. Provided that the children had sufficient receptive language to be able to understand what was expected of them and were capable of responding in some way, it was felt that they should be able to learn by the method of conductive education.

> Professor Petö did not use intelligence tests to decide whether a child would be likely to benefit from Conductive Education. He based his judgement on the child's ability to participate in Rhythmical Intention. Providing the child understands what is expected of him and is capable of making an effort he is regarded as educable and capable of participating in the work of a group. (Cotton and Parnwell, 1968)

In order to assess this, verbal-regulation experiments developed by Sutton and Nash (1979) were carried out. The results suggested that all these children could respond to basic commands from an adult and would be able to use their speech (or the intention of speech in the case of the non-verbal children) in order to direct their own actions as suggested by the person leading the group. It was hoped that, with practice, the children's own external speech as a means of control would be internalised, to be superseded by their internal speech which would then regulate their own action with no lead from the adult. Later still the actions should become automatic and thus be ready to be generalised into different situations. Our group could be said to be homogeneous in that the problems which we were to address were common to all.

The Teaching Environment and Staff Resources

A room adjoining the nursery unit was allocated to us for the daily conductive education period. Although of good size and carpeted, it was far from distraction-free as much of the nursery unit's larger play equipment, e.g. bikes, rocking horse, trolleys etc., was stored there. This room also had to be passed through in order to enter the unit from the rest of the school. Funding was made available to buy appropriate furniture in the form of slatted tables ('plinths') and ladder-back chairs which were adjustable for height. One of our first problems was that the only suitable commercially produced furniture was designed for preschool children and had to be modified for use by our rather large children. This was done by our long-suffering woodwork teacher and a working party of boys from a local comprehensive school. The slatted surfaces of the tables and backs of the chairs made useful tools when teaching grasp and release. A variety of formations of the furniture was used depending upon the particular programme, the criterion being that the children could see both the person conducting the group and the other children at all times.

As the teacher who was researching conductive education, and who was responsible for introducing it into the school, I was to act as 'first conductor'. I had acquired a little more 'expertise' by attending a one-week residential course at Ingfield Manor school, organised and tutored by Ester Cotton, entitled 'Conductive Education'. The practical work involved in the course provided practice in the task-analysis of motor acts, in different types of facilitation and in the actual writing of programmes and transfer of skills. My role would be to use the expertise of the various therapists on the staff to enable me to prepare a series of programmes and related tasks which met the needs of the children in the areas identified. In this way, the various disciplines were represented through one person rather than through the 'multidisciplinary team' which had previously withdrawn children for individual therapy. Additional help was provided in that an extra teacher was timetabled to be with me for the daily session together with a member of the welfare staff. It was envisaged that, as part of my 'support' role, a certain amount of in-service training of staff would also occur during these sessions, which could be transferred with these particular children to other situations.

The Conductive Education Programme

During the first year the group were timetabled to spend one hour a day together. This session followed the morning break and extended into the lunch hour so that feeding and grooming skills could be practised in a meaningful context and did not need to be rushed. In the first instance, a sitting programme was developed (Figure 4.1) where the aim was to teach free sitting at the plinth. We introduced the idea of hands and feet as points of fixation. Help with the task analysis of various functions and individual facilitations was provided by a physiotherapist, an occupational therapist and a speech therapist, although none of these workers felt inclined to become involved in writing the programme.

Our long-term aims included preparing for function in the areas of eating, drinking, reading and writing, etc. The first programme, therefore, had two parts, the structured exercises followed by an activity which used the skills practised in the exercises. This was essential in order that the child might understand the purpose of the movement. This was the format that I had seen in operation at the Conductive Education Unit at Ingfield Manor school, although in contrast our groups did not stay together for the rest of the day but returned to their peer groups. Taking as the model the practice of Ingfield Manor I set out to adopt the following principles of conductive education.

1. Rhythmic intention was used to present the task to the group. The children sat at the slatted tables, the conductor spoke the command which was repeated by the children who then performed the movement as they spoke the 'dynamic word' e.g. 'I push my hands forward, push, push, push'.
2. The structured programme was written down so that the language used by the conductors was always the same, thus ensuring consistency and repetition. This was to give the children security

and confidence and a vocabulary of established terms which could elicit a specific motor response, e.g. 'forward', 'middle', 'stretch'. This constancy also made it possible for any of the conductors to conduct the lesson. Songs and rhymes were used within the structured programme to enliven the work.

This sitting programme is illustrated in Figure 4.1.

Changes

The end of the school year brought a stock-taking and forward planning time. A probationary teacher also interested in the principles of conductive education, was appointed as a member of our support department and to work in the Petö group. This released our timetable teacher who really did not feel this was the way in which she wanted to work. The welfare staff were to be rotated so that others could be initiated into the new approach and skills could be practised at toilet time, home time, etc. By so doing, we would be attempting to build consistency of approach into the school routine, to meet Petö's principle of using every situation as a situation for learning.

The hard work of the children made it possible to consider a more advanced input into our programme in the second year and to develop 'mini-projects'. For example, pre-feeding skills moved into the area of table laying and wiping, screwing up and unscrewing containers, buttering bread, stirring, tasting and pouring drinks. The children's newly acquired knowledge of left and right, top and bottom, side and middle, palmer, pincer and tripod grips and isolation of the index finger, enabled practice of classification skills linked with the fine motor skills of tearing, cutting and sticking. Following the usual structured programme, the group was presented with pictures of food items which they sorted into those eaten at breakfast, dinner or tea. Empty cartons and packets were brought to school and, following the structured plinth programme, were passed from hand to hand and looked at or smelled to identify what had been inside. Dressing skills took their place as what normally happens before going swimming or doing PE. Grooming skills became a normal activity before dinner, after painting, etc.

Reading, writing and maths were introduced into the curriculum for the conductive education hour at the beginning of our second year. The same format was maintained, the first half of the session being motor skills built upon task analysis and specific language structures, leading into a practical second half in which these skills were

Figure 4.1: Extract from the Sitting Programme

Hands *flat* on the table	1,2,3
I look at my hands	1,2,3
I look at my hands	1,2,3
I *stretch* my elbows	1,2,3
My arms are *straight*	1,2,3
I hold the table	1,2,3
I *look* at my feet	1,2,3
My feet are *flat*	1,2,3
I move my feet *apart*	1,2,3
I move my feet *together*	1,2,3
I move my feet *forward*	1,2,3
I move my feet *back*	1,2,3
My head is *up*	1,2,3
My head is in the *middle*	1,2,3

Song: Looking high, high, high

My hands are *flat* on the table	1,2,3
I *stretch* my elbows and fingers	1,2,3
I point my fingers *up*	1,2,3

Song 1 – *Fingers pointing up*
Song 2 – *I wiggle my fingers*

Feet flat, bottom back, I sit ready
Feet flat, bottom back, I sit ready

My hands are *flat* on the table	1,2,3
I turn my hands *over*	1,2,3
I *look* at my palms	1,2,3
Palms to my face *up*	1,2,3
I *rub* my face	1,2,3
I *rub* my palms together	1,2,3
I clasp my hands together	1,2,3
	(thumbs out)
I *stretch* my elbows	1,2,3
I lift my straight arms *up*	1,2,3
I bring them *down* behind my head	1,2,3
I stretch my right arm *out* to the side	1,2,3
I *wrap* my arms *around* me	1,2,3
I *squeeze* tight	1,2,3
Hands *flat* on the table	1,2,3

Rhyme
I'm as tall as a house,
Small as a mouse,
Wide as a bridge,
Thin as a pin

Feet flat, bottom back, I sit ready

My hands are *on* the table	1,2,3
I *stretch* my elbows	1,2,3
I *hold* the table	1,2,3
I lift my right hand *up*	1,2,3
I put my right hand *down*	1,2,3
I lift my right hand *up*	1,2,3
I put my left hand *down*	1,2,3
I make two fists	1,2
I look at my fists	1,2,3
I cross my fists *up and over*	1,2,3
I change over, up, down, up and over	
Fists apart	1,2,3
I hold the table	1,2,3
I let go with one hand	1,2,3
I make a fist	
I *point* my index finger	

Rhyme 1
I point at the ceiling
Song
Put your finger on your nose   5
I look at my stick
I grasp my stick in two hands
I push my stick forward
I pull my stick back
I lift my stick up
I bring my stick down
Repeat with stick in one hand
   other hand holding on.

Quoits

I *look* at my ring	1,2,3
I *hold* my ring in two hands	1,2,3
I *push* my ring forward	1,2,3
I *pull* my ring back	1,2,3
I *hold* my ring in right hand	1,2,3
I put my left hand *through* my ring	1,2,3
I push the ring up to my shoulder	1,2,3
I pull my ring down	
Repeat with other hand	

appropriately employed to achieve functional goals. Our writing programme was developed as an extension of the work with hand and sticks introduced in the original programme. The abilities of maintaining body control while moving the head, fixing and moving the eyes independently, keeping hands flat on the table while manipulating fingers, moving the hands independently, using one hand to hold and thus having the other available for function, using pincer, palmer and tripod grasp, were seen as evidence of readiness for written work to begin. Writing began when the children learnt to support themselves on the elbow of the writing hand, to make a fist and point an index finger.

At the same time the formation and sounds of letters was introduced to the children. It was decided to use 'Pictogram', a method of teaching phonics devised by Wendon (1973). It was felt that the stories behind the letters gave the abstract shapes a certain amount of realism; they were also interesting for the children and encouraged them to look and listen. At the same time, listening to the stories gave the opportunity to practise free sitting on chairs, on the floor and on the plinths: if you are taking responsiblity for your own body, it is not possible to 'switch off' – you could fall off! Reading was introduced into the curriculum in a variety of ways. As the group had such a wide age and ability range and came from different classes, there was no single reading scheme that seemed to meet everyone's needs. As the aim was to work together as a homogeneous group, the obvious answer was to write our own. Our books follow two teenagers and a dog into various real-life social situations. The story line is contained in the illustrations, as is the vocabulary which is a social sight one. Words such as 'push' or 'pull' added a further dimension to the concepts being taught in our structured motor sessions. Flash cards were used with the children free sitting, sitting at the plinth or floor sitting. Flash-card pelmanism gave further opportunity for work with hands. Various games which used the vocabulary were also included. Within the reading scheme it was also necessary to consider page turning and the scanning of lines and words from left to right. A programme to meet this need was designed with the help of the children. In all the structured programmes various rhymes, songs and jingles were used to give further reinforcement to motor skills. A selection of these were typed out, double-spaced, on our newly acquired 'jumbo-typewriter' and assembled into books with numbered pages. The children used one flat hand to hold the books steady, while use of pincer grasp enabled them to pinch up the bottom of the page, hold it and turn it over. As everyone knew the rhymes, it was quite a useful exercise to point to each word with an index finger as it was said. It was also possible to look for recurring words; to locate a word in the top or bottom line; to find the word that began with a particular sound, etc., thus linking with the pictogram characters. Maths work in the form of ordinal numbers was also incorporated within this programme, as the pages of the books were numbered. Since the children had some knowledge of shapes, back-up activities with attribute blocks were used following a structured 'hand' class. The attribute blocks reinforce the concepts of colour (red, blue and yellow), size (big and small) and shape (thick and thin; circle, square or triangle). While on the floor or sitting at the plinth, commands such as 'point to', 'touch', 'pick up', were used in a variety of situations, applied to particular children's level of fine motor function, along with the concept of negative, e.g. 'Point to a block that is not blue'.

In a similar vein, programmes were developed to link with riding, physical education, with sign and symbol systems, with use of typewriter and computer keyboard, possum etc. The original format of a structured start to the session, followed by an appropriate activity to practise the skills introduced in a meaningful context, was maintained.

Evaluation

In an attempt to monitor and measure improvements in the functioning of the group, various skill areas were identified and an assessment procedure designed which would pinpoint entering behaviour and any subsequent progress. Extracts from the results of this are summarised in Table 4.1 (a more detailed list of outcomes has been presented by Titchener, 1982).

The first column indicates the number of children who were successful on a given criterion, in March 1981, at the start of the project; the second column shows those who were successful in November 1981, seven months later. It had been intended to reassess in November 1982 but due to difficulties in getting appropriate independent observers, the pressures of the Christmas period, children's absence, and the probationary teacher's attendance at the conductive education training course at Ingfield Manor, this was not possible. Reassessment did, however, take place in July 1983. The results suggest that the conductive education programme did achieve some success. Because of the age of our particular group, the change

Table 4.1: Extract from the Results after Two Years of Conductive Education in a School for the Physically Handicapped, plus Follow up Data

Skills and short-term goals	No. of children achieving criterion (out of 11)			
	March 1981	Nov. 1981	July 1983	March 1984
Supine, head in midline	0/11	6/11	8/11	8/11
Prone, head in midline	1/11	7/11	9/11	9/11
Rolling	2/11	7/11	9/11	9/11
Sitting head in midline, feet flat	2/11	7/11	9/11	9/11
Maintain grasp				
– pronation 2 hands	3/11	6/11	7/11	7/11
– mixed supination 2 hands	3/11	6/11	7/11	7/11
– while moving arm	3/11	6/11	7/11	7/11
Lower self onto chair	3/11	6/11	7/11	6/11
Walk pushing chair	2/11	4/11	4/11	4/11
Hold cup and drink alone	4/11	6/11	7/11	7/11
Can use knife and fork	6/11	8/11	9/11	8/11
Remove slipover garments	3/11	6/11	7/11	6/11
Fastening buttons – large) small)	0/11	1/11	1/11	1/11
Comb and brush hair	2/11	7/11	9/11	9/11
Use toilet alone	1/11	1/11	1/11	0/11

Note: Activities must be maintained for ten seconds to achieve the criteria.
Source: Titchener (1982).

in behaviour cannot be said to have been simply 'developmental'. It must, however, be noted that the children's progress was somewhat uneven, better results appearing in such fine-motor areas as grooming and dressing. This could be due to the fact that these particular areas had not been previously included within the curriculum of the children in this group.

Certainly the greatest improvement, one not indicated in the final results, was in the area of motivation and physical stamina. The children were much happier and socially aware as they became active participants in the programme. For the duration of the project the length of the conductive education session was always governed by lunch in the school hall. It was felt by all at the end of the first year that the children had achieved much greater staying power and could actually go on for far longer if timetabling arrangements would allow. Whereas at the beginning of the project both staff and children were in a state of exhaustion on completion of a 40-minute programme, by the end of the academic year the children were fresh enough after a session to manage 'transfer skills', walk with an aid or self-propel their wheelchairs into the school hall and transfer yet again to the chairs or plinths where all but two fed themselves.

What is Happening to the Conductive Education Group Now?

As I knew that I would be leaving the school in January 1984 a plan of campaign had to be made to meet the needs of the conductive education group. Following discussion with the headteacher, parents and staff it was decided as follows.

(a) In the case of the two younger children it would be sensible to let them finish their stay in the infants' department, since the hourly withdrawal sessions were going to be discontinued in favour of a full-time conductive education group. One of the two children would continue with her weekly conductive education-styled riding lessons. As conductive education was not the *forte* of the infants' staff, one of the physiotherapists volunteered to prepare a daily 30-minute programme to meet the needs of all the children with gross or fine motor difficulties in the infants' department.

(b) Two of the older children would return to work full time in the senior department of the school, with individual physiotherapy as support. As they were of average and below average mental ability it was thought necessary that they should attempt to use their newly acquired skills and to put their main effort into their academic work. One of the two would keep in contact with conductive education through a weekly riding lesson.

(c) The remainder of the children would form a full-time 'special-care' group. They would be in the hands of the ex-probationary teacher who knew them and their abilities very well, having worked in the conductive education group plus a very experienced nursery nurse who was particularly interested in working in this way. These children were certainly the most handicapped of the original eleven; in addition to their being seriously physically handicapped, three were non-verbal. The emphasis in this group would be placed on a daily conductive education programme, plus the transfer of those skills in daily living activities, e.g. feeding, mobility, dressing, etc. The remainder of the time would be spent on individual work programmes with special reference to communication, verbal and non-verbal. The formation of this group was particularly popular with the rest of the staff. These would have been the 'problem children' in their groups and their being removed made life easier. There was also the feeling that there was now positive provision to meet these children's very particular needs.

How the Children Fared up to March 1984

In March 1984 all the original children were brought together and reassessed using the original measuring instruments. These results are also summarised in Table 4.1.

In the case of the two infant children, the girl who had continued with the riding programme performed at much the same standard in both gross/fine motor activities and active participation: the boy on the other hand had maintained many gross/fine motor abilities but his transfer skills, which he apparently did not often practise, were almost forgotten. He had lost the ability to use language to direct his movements and to respond in a group. His concentration span had also deteriorated badly. The results with the two older children placed in the senior department were much the same. The spastic boy – who had social and emotional problems – had lost the ability to function as a member of a group and had returned to being the attention-seeking, unhappy child who was always waiting for someone to do something for or with him. The 'average-IQ' athetoid who also continued with the riding programme and had a great sense of determination seemed to have maintained the majority of her skills – feeding, however, was rather more 'assisted' than previously. The children who remained in the full-time special-care group had improved both socially and in their use of language, particularly the ESN(S) children. They had become more aware of other children in the group, imitating their actions, recognising their names – both spoken and written – noticing eye colour, clothes, etc. and had begun to play. Animals had been introduced into the class – the group had a bird table and a pet mouse and all had learnt a lot about caring for others. In terms of responding as group members and concentration span, there was also definite improvement. There were, however, only a few gains in the areas of gross/fine motor skills. These were mainly in the fine motor areas – drawing an acceptable circle, writing name alone, etc. Two of the group had progressed to using a walking aid instead of their wheelchairs for getting to and from their classroom.

The Problems in a School for the Physically Handicapped

In many respects all had not been plain sailing with this group of children.

1. The original room was inappropriate in that it was used as an entrance to the nursery unit during the majority of sessions. Despite notices on the door, people frequently passed through, destroying concentration.

2. Some staff found it hard to maintain the 'hands-off' approach.

3. Some staff found it difficult to time sessions so that these particular children were allowed time to complete dressing, walking skills, etc.

4. Shortage of suitable furniture in the form of plinths limited the variety of programmes that could be introduced in the early days.

5. Absenteeism caused problems.

6. In attempting our own modified method of conductive education it became apparent that not all staff liked working as conductors. Certainly, finding staff willing to work within such a framework and committed to a transdisciplinary approach is a basic necessity. Such an effective and co-operative team does not evolve automatically.

7. A major obstacle to the success of the project was communication with outsiders about children's use of functional skills. Information was passed on by word of mouth, written on a card and attached to the back of wheelchairs, by sending an appropriate chair or table into the child's classroom or home or encouraging the children to show everyone, whatever the situation, what they could do for themselves. Unfortunately, however, the situation still arose where a child working to put on a coat unaided was 'helped', where the children wheeling themselves to the mini-bus were pushed, where children feeding slowly were fed and where children who had learnt free sitting were found in a wheelchair.

In September 1983 I took up a British Council scholarship to spend a two-week study period at the Institute for the Motor-Disordered in Budapest. As I had been allocated an English-speaking guide, it was hoped I would do more than observe motor acts and actually come back ready to make the school an example of real Hungarian practice. This did not happen. The work of the Institute proved far more impressive than I had expected. Observation of the mother-and-baby groups showed that on admittance the degree of motor disorder of the children was certainly comparable with that of the pupils with whom I had been working in England. Yet the spina bifida children were all in the process of being toilet trained (again the position of the lesions was comparable with the children here). All types of motor disorder were present and yet there was not a wheelchair or walking aid other than a ladder-back chair in the place.

Having seen all this, I came back to England feeling very despondent. I had thought we were doing so well, yet the Hungarians achieve orthofunction in over 70 per cent of the cases that attend the Institute. Our children had not improved enough to be independent in their peer groups in a school for the physically handicapped. The task of introducting conductive education Hungarian-style into any established PH school in the United Kingdom seemed insurmountable. Because of the nature of our schools, it just would not be possible to get the large homogeneous groups that I saw working together in Budapest. Qualified conductors are available from 7 a.m. to 7 p.m. turning the whole of daily living into a situation for learning. Grafting this type of provision into our educational system would raise more than just financial problems. Yet the message from Hungary is 'do all of it, or none of it'. To work it really does have to be intensive. Maybe it would be possible to evolve a method based on certain principles of conductive education that relate to approaches within our present educational practice – for example team teaching, group therapy, task analysis, precision teaching. But even so, not all staff would like to work as conductors – this message came across very strongly from the school in which I worked.

To pick up the threads of the group was very difficult, my original enthusiasm and energy had been sapped. We were only paying lip service to this very fine practice. It is possible for us to meet the needs of these children much more successfully than we are. The problem is that it requires a major reorganisation and upheaval to do so.

5 AN APPROACH FOR THE MENTALLY HANDICAPPED?

Philippa Cottam

In the transfer of certain aspects of conductive education to Britain and their corresponding dissemination throughout this country, there has been a progression from the use of the method primarily with the physically handicapped child of normal intelligence to other groups. These include cerebral palsied children with moderate learning difficulties, cerebral palsied children with severe learning difficulties and also, in some instances, severely mentally handicapped children without severe motor problems.

This trend was reflected in a small survey carried out by Sutton in 1982 (see Sutton, 1984b). He reported on conductive education in the Midlands, outlining the work of eight schools in the area. Of these eight, four were schools for severely mentally handicapped children, at that time classified as ESN(S). The remainder were schools for the physically handicapped, where the groups involved in conductive education were all reported to have some degree of mental handicap. The results of a further, national questionnaire study by Cottam confirm this earlier finding (see Figure 5.1). From a total of nineteen questionnaires sent to schools or units reported to be using conductive education (CEIG *Newsletter*, no 2), all nine replies received indicated that the client groups involved included children with either moderate or severe learning difficulties. This finding is reflected in several published accounts of the method (Cotton and Parnwell, 1968; Burland, 1969; Budd, 1977; Budd and Evans, 1977; Wilson, 1983; Rooke, 1983; Rooke and Opel, 1983). In view of the fact that there are many physically handicapped children in ESN(S) schools this direction of conductive education towards the least achieving in British society is not unduly surprising.

British conductive education, therefore, radically adapted from 'traditional' Hungarian conductive education has now become yet another teaching method for the severely mentally impaired in this country. Not only are many ESN(S) schools using the method but some training courses for teachers of the mentally handicapped are also incorporating lectures on conductive education into their syllabus.

Figure 5.1: General Nature of the Provision of Conductive Education in Nine Schools in Britain, Summer 1984

Schools		Age	Pupils	Conductors		Duration	
Code no.	Type		Disabilities	Numbers	Professions	How often (session/week)	Length of session (minutes)
(1)	Vol PH	5-7 10-11	Phys & Ment (ESN(M) & ESN(S))	3-4	HP T PT ST	8	60
(2)	Vol PH	3-5 5-9	Phys & Ment	3-4	T WA PT ST	4	60
(3)	LEA Hosp	5-19	Profoundly Mult	10+	T ST PT WA YOP	5	20-30
(4)	LEA ESN(S)*	3-5 8-12 12-17	1) Profoundly Mult 2) Ment & Phys	3-4	T ST PT CA	(1) 5 (2) 1	60
(5)	LEA ESN(S)	5-14	Ment	3	T PT NN	2	40
(6)	Vol PH	5-16	Profoundly Mult	6	T PT OT NN CA SRN	10	60
(7)	LEA Hosp	20+	Profoundly Mult	4	NA SEU PT	5	30
(8)	LEA PH	5-7	Ment & Phys	2-3	PT T NN	2/3	60
(9)	LEA PH	14-16	Ment & Phys	2	PT NN	3/4	30

HP   House parent
T   Teacher
PT   Physiotherapist
ST   Speech therapist
OT   Occupational therapist
WA   Welfare assistant
YOP   Youth opportunities
CA   Care assistant
SRN   State registered nurse
NN   Nursery nurse
SEU   Social education unit staff
NA   Nursery assistant

Ment   Mentally handicapped
Phy   Physically handicapped
Mult   Multiply handicapped

Vol   Voluntary
LEA   Local education authority
Hosp   Subnormality hospital
PH   Physically handicapped
ESN(S)   Severely educationally subnormal

* This school reported to be using conductive education with two groups of multiply handicapped children.

What is the Attraction of Conductive Education for Teachers of the Mentally Handicapped?

Sutton (1984b) has raised the question of whether it is 'Conductive Education, as such, that so appeals to special educators or the philosophy that it represents, which is optimistic, instructional, structured, group-orientated and unhierarchical'? With a growing need for accountability in ESN schools, teachers are being forced to look for alternatives to traditional teaching methods; conductive education appears to have provided one such alternative. At the present time:

> There can be no doubt that Conductive Education is proving an invigorating influence in special education and other forms of care for the handicapped in Britain, and that its proponents are convinced that what they are doing is bringing about effects in children in excess of those achieved by other methods. (Sutton, 1984b)

Conductive education is highly structured and provides the teacher with clearly defined objectives which can be combined to achieve functional goals. The stress in conductive education on the development of function, i.e. the ability to perform the ordinary tasks of daily living, makes the method seem entirely suited to the current special education regime, in which social education is of prime importance. Additionally, it appears to offer the sort of specific instruction, in this area of disability, required to fulfil the 'special educational needs' recently mandated by the Education Act 1981.

The lack of para-medical input, as a result of cuts in services, may be another factor in favour of teaching along conductive education lines. As Rooke and Opel (1983) have pointed out:

> (multiply handicapped children's) total developmental needs can only be met if the knowledge and expertise deriving from a number of disciplines is utilised. Very few schools are fortunate enough to have the full-time service of such relevant professionals as speech therapist and physiotherapist. It, therefore, seems sensible to seek a method of education that encompasses the aims and objectives of these various professionals into an integrated whole organised by the special care teacher.

If programmes are prepared, instigated and evaluated by all the professionals involved with the child, the animosity which often arises by encroaching on related professional territory is minimised.

Other possible reasons for the attraction of conductive education for teachers of the mentally handicapped, as revealed in my own questionnaire study, include:

(1) enjoyment at being involved in all aspects of child education;
(2) encouragement from establishing short- and long-term goals;
(3) increased morale through being involved in innovations, which in turn result in the experience of fresh progress in the children;
(4) simple language used consistently throughout;
(5) less frustration created because of the positive, useful and necessary situation provided;
(6) economy of time resulting from a short, structured group programme.

What is Conductive Education in this Context?

Many adaptations of conductive education, despite claiming to use key aspects of the method, bear little resemblance to their Hungarian counterpart. In the context of a teaching approach for the severely mentally handicapped, the substance of conductive education is altogether different from that used at the Institute for the Motor-Disabled in Budapest.

From the questionnaire study of nine special schools, within both the public and voluntary sectors (see Figure 5.1), certain general tendencies emerged. Firstly, conductive education with this population appears to mean a daily session in which a task series is performed towards 'motoric', 'self-help' or 'communication' objectives. In all the schools surveyed, conductive education programmes formed only one small part of the child's school curriculum. 'Motoric' objectives, i.e. mobility, balance, lying, hand function, perceptuo-motor and body awareness skills were of prime importance and formed the basis of most programmes. The range of objectives varied considerably from school to school, from a single specific programme to a wide range of objectives. Group teaching was another common trend to emerge from the study but there was substantial variability in age, mental level and type of physical disability occurring within one group. Finally, this enquiry revealed that 'unity of disciplines' was

being attempted both in developing conductive education programmes and in carrying them out. The number of professionals
working as conductors varied from a minimum of two to a maximum
of ten-plus. Between them they included teachers, the various
therapeutic professionals routinely found in special education and all
the variously termed welfare, ancillary and voluntary staff. Physiotherapy appears to be the main profession involved.

One Experience of Conductive Education in an ESN(S) School

Despite the upsurge of interest in conductive education in recent
years, and the increase in the numbers of teachers, physiotherapists,
etc., keen to take up the work, there have been no published accounts
of conductive education being implemented in a school for severely
mentally impaired children. It is true that there have been a few
references which have mentioned such pupils in the context of
conductive education (Cotton and Parnwell, 1968; Budd and Evans,
1977; Pepper, 1981; Wilson, 1983), but nothing on actual educational
practice. My own personal experience has been reported briefly in
other contexts (Rooke and Opel, 1983; Rooke, 1983 and Cottam,
McCartney and Cullen, 1985) but it is offered here in greater detail
because in its initiation and its outcomes it seemed fairly typical of
what happens when conductive education is tried out. It has been
unique, so far, amongst such experiences, in having been evaluated.

My first introduction to conductive education was in 1979, whilst
working as a speech therapist in the Midlands. During a chance visit
to a subnormality hospital school in Walsall I was fortunate enough to
be shown a group of severely mentally and physically handicapped
children who were being taught using certain aspects of conductive
education. Impressed by the reported improvements in the children
and the enthusiasm of the staff involved, I decided to find out more
about the method. I wrote to Ester Cotton for copies of some of her
articles, bought the Spastics Society booklet on the method (Cotton,
1975) and attended a lecture on the background by Andrew Sutton.
The more I found out about conductive education, the more
fascinating it became.

I decided, on the basis of this very scant knowledge and the help of
the staff from the Walsall hospital school, to try to introduce the
method into the special-care class of the ESN(S) school in which
I was working for two sessions a week. Visits were organised for the

class teacher, physiotherapist and paediatrician, to the group in Walsall, and also to Rutland House, a voluntary school in Nottinghamshire. Conductive education was used in both places on a full-time basis with children who were both mentally and physically handicapped. Everyone was enthusiastic about what they saw, and the headmaster was keen to introduce new ideas into the school. He agreed to buy two plinths and four ladder-back chairs (see Figure 3.1), similar to the furniture used for conductive education in Hungary. With the help of the Walsall staff and the use of their conductive education 'programmes' the method was introduced into the special-care class in 1980.

The school took up to 120 severely mentally handicapped children and was staffed by thirteen teachers and nine nursery nurses. Physiotherapy and speech therapy input was available on one day a week. The children were divided into classes according to age and not ability, with the one exception of the special-care class where children were grouped according to severity of handicap. The ages of children within the school ranged from 3 years to 19 years.

Aspects of Conductive Education Employed at the School and their Adaptation to Meet the Needs of the Mentally Handicapped

Four of the main principles of conductive education were used to develop what proved an extremely modified form of the Hungarian system. These were:

(1) the conductor;
(2) group teaching;
(3) rhythmic intention;
(4) the philosophy that motor handicap is a learning difficulty that can be overcome by teaching.

Another important principle of the method, that of teaching in homogeneous groups, could not be adhered to, due to the heterogeneous nature of the children's mental and physical disabilities.

The Conductor. In this ESN(S) school the teacher in charge of the special-care class acted as the 'main conductor'. She had no formal training and her knowlege of the subject was from articles, lectures and meetings. In view of the constraints put upon the teacher by other duties in this large special school, it was not possible for her to work as a conductor throughout the whole day. During the half-hour per day in which conductive education programmes were carried out, however, she functioned as the conductor.

From the outset we were aware that, in comparison with the intensity of the conductors' work in Budapest, this was only a token gesture at introducing the conductor principle. As Varty (1973) has pointed out, 'the conductor is a co-ordinator, an integrator and an educator'. In the ESN(S) school where conductive education forms only a very small part of the day's activities, this overall learning strategy could not be applied.

Group Teaching. Cotton (1970, 1975) had distinguished between a group and a class of children who all work at different tasks at different levels. She stated that 'in the group, children are all learning in the same way, to overcome the same difficulties in order to arrive at the solution of the same task'. Taking this definition, group teaching was used in the conductive education sessions at the school. In Hungary, however, the desired outcome of group teaching is the development of a high level of motivation in the children. Loring (1971) after visiting the Institute wrote: 'Motivation . . . springs . . . from close identification with others in the group and desire for achievement as a group.' With severely mentally impaired children this 'identification with others' and 'desire for achievement' proved invariably lacking and increased motivation could not be seen as a realistic consequence of the group approach. Nevertheless, we felt justified in using this aspect of the method as we envisaged that it might play an important role as a vehicle for modelling and imitation.

Rhythmic Intention. Rhythmic intention was used as the teaching method. The conductor stated what she wanted the children to do, this was then repeated by the helpers and, where possible, the children. The key word in the command was then repeated three times as the activity was carried out. This technique is illustrated in Figure 5.2.

The children's receptive and expressive language abilities were very limited. They were unable to use their own language to regulate behaviour, therefore, the rhythmic intention served a different purpose. It was hoped that by using the same set of commands daily, in combination with the appropriate action or object, the children's expressive and receptive language would develop to such a degree that verbal regulation could be used at a later stage.

From the start we suspected that there might be problems in using

Figure 5.2: Drinking Programme

Sing naming children
Hands *on* table; on, on, on
I *push* my hands forward; push, push, push
My arms are *straight*; straight, straight, straight
I *look* at my feet; look, look, look
My feet are *flat*; _____ flat, flat, flat
I sit up straight
My head is *up* _____ up, up, up
Look at the mat (said to each child as mats are given out)
(Give out mats – a mat for Matthew, etc.)
I *push* my arms forward
I *look* at my mat; look, look, look
I *feel* my mat; feel, feel, feel
My *feet* are flat)
) here conductor now briefly runs through a sequence
I sit up straight) of commands to remind of correct sitting balance but
) there is no repetition by helper.
My head is *up*)

Look at cup; look, look, look
(Give out cups)
I hold my cup; hold, hold, hold
I drink my orange; drink, drink, drink
Give the cup; give, give, give)
) Thank you
Give the mat; give, give, give)

Source: Rooke (1984).

conductive education with such profoundly handicapped children. Yet, like so many others, we still felt the need and the justification to carry on.

The Conductive Education Group

Fourteen children, classified by the school as 'profoundly retarded multiply handicapped', were chosen as possible candidates for either the conductive education group or the control group. There were two main reasons for selecting these severely handicapped children. Firstly, it appeared from observation that these children were not benefiting from traditional classroom teaching. With the exception of one short, individual session each day, the children would either sit for significant periods playing unconstructively with a toy or disrupt the rest of the class by wandering aimlessly around the classroom. Secondly, by introducing a new method of teaching with the most profoundly handicapped children (a group who stayed invariably for their entire school lives in a unit isolated from the rest of the school), less tension was created between the method and the wider institution of special schooling.

The children were matched according to their test scores on a specifically designed assessment schedule (Rooke, 1984), devised to measure linguistic, pre-linguistic and other skill areas for each child. Four of the children were excluded at this point for the following reasons.

Child 1:   Severe visual handicap.
Child 2:   Inability to remain seated at a table even with restraint.
Child 3: ⎫
Child 4: ⎭ Scores on the assessment were too near the test ceiling.

The ten remaining children were grouped as closely as possible, on the basis of the scores achieved on the assessment schedule at initial assessment, into five matched pairs. One of each pair was randomly assigned to the conductive education group, the other to the control group. The children in both groups exhibited a range of physical disabilities, including spastic quadraplegia, spastic diplegia and athetosis.

The Teaching Environment

The classroom used for the conductive education session was situated adjacent to the special-care classroom. The furniture employed consisted of two plinths positioned end-to-end in a line with six ladder-back chairs behind them. The criterion for the positioning of the plinths was to provide the children with a good view of the conductor's face and of the other children in the group. Positioning would vary depending on the number of plinths used (see Figure 5.3). With regard to room selection the only requirements were that:

(1) the room should be as light and distraction free as possible;
(2) there should be adequate space behind the chairs for the helpers and adequate space in front of the plinths for the conductor;
(3) furniture should be kept to a minimum.

The plinths and ladder-back chairs (see Figure 3.1), based on the design of furniture used in Hungarian conductive education, were obtained ready-made from Sherwood Industries, Nottingham. The slatted format of the table top enabled the child to grasp it in order to

Figure 5.3: Table Positions

Positioning of three tables

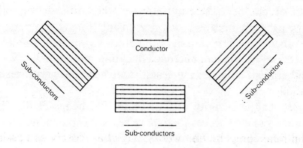

Positioning of four tables

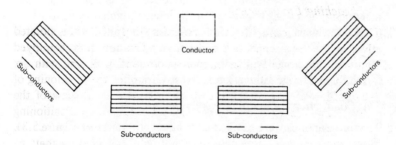

Source: Rooke (1984).

maintain balance in sitting and lying. The seat of the chair was adjustable and could be removed. The frame could be used as a standing or walking aid.

Staff Resources

The teacher worked primarily as the main conductor. As conductor, her role was to co-ordinate activities designed to fulfil the aims of various developmental areas and combine them into a single programme. Through her conductor role she created a 'unity of disciplines'. Before the method was introduced each professional had worked independently as part of a 'multi-disciplinary team', children being withdrawn for physiotherapy and speech therapy. There was little carry-over from these sessions to the general classroom teaching.

The speech therapist (myself) was the principle organiser. I instigated the method and was responsible for its evaluation. The three other key professionals involved with development and modification of the conductive education programmes were the physiotherapist, the teacher and the nursery nurse from the special-care class.

In view of the severity of the mental handicaps of the children involved it was also necessary to have several sub-conductors to help the children complete the activities during the programmes. On average there were three helpers per group for a given day. These included nursery nurses from the special-care class, parents of children from the mainstream of the school, a physiotherapist and a speech therapist. The parents and the nursery nurses helped with the programme every day, while the speech therapist and physiotherapist were available for only one day each week.

All staff involved with the conductive education group had meetings once a week to discuss any problems which may have arisen during the work, and to review progress. In June 1982, they all attended the 'swap-meet' on conductive education at Birmingham University (Sutton, 1984b) and some subsequently joined the newly formed Conductive Education Interest Group.

The Conductive Education Programme

Two programmes were devised, a drinking programme and a feeding programme, incorporating 'motoric', 'self-help' and 'communication' objectives. In part, these were based on the 'basic motor pattern' (Cotton 1980), encouraging correct sitting balance as a prerequisite for either a feeding or drinking activity. Programmes were made as concrete as possible. Real objects were used throughout, and the conductive education session was held during the morning break when the children would normally be given a drink.

For the first twelve months a drinking programme was used each day, the session lasting about half-an-hour. The aim of the programme was to develop function, the ability to perform an ordinary task of daily living. To achieve function, sitting and sitting balance are essential. Consequently the elements of these tasks, grasp and release, fixation of a limb, mid-line orientation, extension of the arms and hip flexion, were incorporated into the programme. In addition, awareness of the cup and liquid was taught, as was grasping the cup with two hands while fixing both elbows on the table.

The feeding programme was introduced after one year and was carried out during the morning break, on alternate days to the drinking programme. Developed on much the same lines, the task of feeding was broken down into grasp and release, fixation of a limb, mid-line orientation, hip flexion, arm extension, awareness of plate, spoon and food, fixation of one hand and grasp of the spoon. The same vocabulary was used in the feeding programme as had been used in the drinking programme with the exception of the nouns, plate, spoon and food and the verbs fill and eat. Rhythmic intention was used to relay the programmes to the group. The programmes were used for 22 months, the drinking programme for the complete period and the feeding programme for the last 11 months.

The language used in the programmes consisted of basic nouns (body part names and common objects), verbs, prepositions and adverbs, combined for the most part into three-element clauses (e.g. I hold my cup). Concepts, such as, straight, flat and forward were also included.

School Holidays

During the school holidays it was not possible to carry over the conductive education teaching into the children's homes. There were two reasons for this:

(1) the majority of parents of the children involved were not willing to continue the work due to other family commitments;
(2) professional back-up was difficult to provide in the holidays because the staff involved from the school were not willing to continue the conductive education group outside school time.

Evaluation

Taking into account school holidays, the experiment lasted for 22 months from September 1981 to July 1983. From discussion with the staf involved, eleven areas of development were isolated, in which changes were expected to take place as a result of the teaching:

sitting balance

attention control
co-operation
development of object permanence
development of comprehension
development of motor imitation
development of vocal imitation
development of symbolic play
development of drinking skills
development of feeding skills
development of independence

An assessment procedure was designed to measure changes in these areas.

During the first two weeks of September 1981, all the children were assessed on the schedule before starting the experimental teaching programmes. This provided a baseline measure against which the results of interim assessments could be compared. Thirteen interim assessments were then carried out at six- to eight-week intervals over a period of twenty-two months. All the children were assessed within a single week but due to work commitments it was not possible to assess them all on the same day.

From comparison of the total scores obtained by each child on the assessment schedule no significant differences between the two groups of children were evident over the 22-month experimental teaching period. Although both groups showed some improvement this could be due to maturation, incidental learning and the passage of time, rather than particular teaching methods. In essence there was no discernible benefit to the severely mentally impaired children receiving conductive education in this study. For specific details of the experiment see Rooke (1984).

In addition to assessing the children, the views of staff working with the conductive education group were obtained from a structured interview. This was given in July 1983, to four staff who had worked with the children throughout the twenty-two-month period. Due to pressure of time, a similar interview could not take place with staff working with children involved in traditional classroom teaching. The responses given to questions in the structured interview indicated that the majority of the staff felt all the children had made a certain amount of progress and that the main areas of improvement were attention control and co-operation. They felt that the method had united their approach to the children but that shorter sessions and more favourable staff ratios were needed. The attitude of the rest of the school to the introduction of conductive education was reported to be one of indifference.

Why Did the Conductive Education Programmes Fail to Achieve Accelerated Development with the Severely Mentally Impaired Children at this Particular School?

One possible explanation is that the children were not receiving sufficient exposure to conductive education. Accounts of work in Hungary stress the continuing nature of the method throughout all the child's working hours. The children at this ESN(S) school were exposed to only a short intermission during which a programme based on certain principles of conductive education was carried out, the rest of their educational input being that traditionally offered to children in the school. It may have been that there was simply too little exposure to the principles of conductive education to show any effect.

Another possible reason for the lack of difference between the experimental and control groups could be that the assessment procedure employed was not sophisticated enough. The assessment was designed to show developmentally significant changes, and it is possible that more subtle changes were being missed, and that the teachers perceptions of 'improvements', although accurate, were not reflected in the assessment procedures. The evaluation focused on substantial changes because these are what conductive education promises.

In retrospect, when one considers the cognitive level of the children involved in the conductive education group, the language used was probably inappropriate. At the time of devising the programme there was no published or unpublished material in English on this aspect of the method. Sutton and Jernqvist, however, subsequently examined the wording of teaching programmes in conductive education in conjunction with Luriya's stage theory of motor acts (Luriya, 1961a). They stated: 'There is no theoretical reason to expect that children at the preparatory stage of speech regulation are necessarily helped by saying anything aloud to accompany their acts.' They suggested that for profoundly mentally handicapped ESN(S) children the external stimulus needed may be no more than a rhythmic noise made by the conductor. This consideration could be extended to children at the first stage of verbal regulation, i.e. by having the adult alone say the regulative utterance. Jernqvist (1983) has since provided some empirical support for the model proposed by Sutton and Jernqvist

(1982) for the use of 'verbal regulation' in different ways in conductive education in relation to the child's developmental level. According to Luriya's formulations, even with the mentally handicapped child who has achieved a certain level of language development, verbal regulation could only be used in a limited and possibly confusing way. He stated that 'oligophrenics' (i.e. children mentally handicapped due to CNS damage in the pre-natal, natal or early peri-natal period), are unable to use speech in its regulatory function, and consequently are unable to reach more than the preparatory stage of verbal regulation. At this stage the adult's instructions can initiate simple action on the part of the child but the effect of the adult's speech is limited in that it has no direct inhibitory function. 'The verbal instructions are unable to alter the action already begun; on the contrary they merely intensify it' (Luriya, 1961a).

This is not to say that conductive education would be ineffective with *all* mentally retarded children. Within the conductive education group at the school, for example, one child did show slightly more improvement than the others, possibly indicating that he was potentially at a higher level. In Hungary, 'counterindicated for acceptance are only children with oligophrenia at the idiot level' (Semenova and Mastyukova, 1974), an analogous group to the most severely mentally impaired children in British ESN(S) schools, though this information has only very recently been made available in English (Sutton, 1984a, Suppl. VII). With respect to other mentally handicapped children, their suitability for conductive education is judged by their performance at the Institute over a period of time. If they prove able to 'participate in the method and become part of the group' (Kearslake, 1970) they are included in the conductive education system.

The Advantages of Introducing the Conductive Education Approach in an ESN(S) School

With severely mentally impaired children progress is exceedingly slow, objectives may take years rather than months to achieve. Long-term staff motivation is, therefore, difficult to sustain and should be an important consideration with regard to choice of teaching approach. While the conductive education programmes proved no more effective than traditional classroom teaching as far as the children were concerned, the introduction of the method played an important role in enhancing staff morale. This was reflected in answers to the structured interview held at the school in July 1983. The staff reported that teaching based on conductive education had given them 'common interest and goals', 'motivation from the children's achievements' and had 'highlighted certain problems of the children involved'. For these reasons they were keen to continue with the programmes despite lack of significant change in the children's development.

In addition, the philosophy of the conductor principle resulted in close liaison between teaching and therapy staff. Before the programmes were introduced each professional worked in isolation, being concerned only with her own particular objectives. Introduction of the method broke down professional barriers and created close co-operation and personal collaboration, not only during the conductive education session, but throughout the school day.

The Conductive Education Group after the Project

The project finished in July 1983, at the end of the summer term. This also marked the end of the conductive education group. When the school resumed in September 1983, conductive education programmes no longer formed a part of the school curriculum, and the children who had been involved returned to full-time traditional teaching. There were several reasons for this change. Firstly, the speech therapist who had instigated the method and had been the motivating force behind the work left the area. A second key professional, the teacher in charge of the special-care class, began a year's secondment and the physiotherapist took maternity leave. As Woods and Cullen (1983) have pointed out 'personal interaction, or the influence of colleagues, seem to be the strongest variables responsible for change in staff behaviour'.

How Viable is Conductive Education as a Teaching Approach for the Mentally Handicapped?

Certain aspects of conductive education, as practised at the Institute for the Motor-Disabled in Budapest, may provide a valuable teaching approach for the potentially more able mentally and physically impaired children in British ESN(S) schools. The goal for this group would not only be development of physical function but improvement in mental development and motivation, hitherto unrevealed by traditional teaching approaches.

For other mentally impaired children, however, conductive education would appear to be inappropriate in view of the cognitive-linguistic potential required. Rhythmic intention and the group as a pedagogic tool cannot be used to the same effect with profoundly handicapped children. As Pepper (1981) has pointed out with reference to the Peto Unit at Ingfield Manor school,

> we found that not all the children we received benefited from the Peto method, and we reluctantly had to reject a few children after a few months with us, as they were not making any progress. These were the children with very low IQs who were unable to respond to the group method of teaching.

Nevertheless, structured group teaching programmes with functional objectives, developed and instigated by all staff involved with the children, should provide an effective alternative to many current educational approaches. Conductive education, as such, may not be a viable alternative to traditional teaching for the mentally handicapped, but the philosophy behind the method may provide a valuable source of inspiration for future developments in special education.

PART THREE:

PROBLEMS AND PROSPECTS

6 PROBLEMS OF THEORY

Andrew Sutton

There is no blackboard on which one cannot write something.
(Jan Komensky [Comenius] 1592-1670)

What *is* conductive education? Where did it come from? How does it work? What is the essence of this approach? If we could answer these questions then we would be better placed than at present to separate out the conductive from the Hungarian in what has been observed in Budapest and to understand why we have fallen short in our own attempts to emulate what has been seen there. Perhaps a straightforward, commonsense statement of the obvious is all that is required here:

> Conductive Education is not a therapy, neither is it a magical cure. It is a method of working with handicapped children and adults constructively. The aim is simple, to equip the handicapped person to cope in the normal situation. The aim is not to make the handicapped person normal and without a handicap, but to make him a handicapped person behaving in a normal way. Its essence is simple – expect the normal. Assist only when it is really necessary, let the child or adult be himself. Give him the basic materials of assistance – slatted furniture, ladder-backed chairs, boxes and stools, to sit, stand, sleep or walk with. It is unacceptable to sweep the child off his feet at an early age into a wheelchair, only increasing his problems of spatial awareness, and his feelings of isolation. Let him appreciate that other people exist, by coming into contact with his peers, and sharing group experience.
>
> There is no set method, there are the world's theories and experience to choose from, select anything which helps the child to help himself. (Siddles, 1976)

Or perhaps just a simple statement about human adaptability and malleability: 'There is no "smell" of physiotherapy at the Institute. Conductive Education is not about programming – it is a philosophy about believing in the child's ability to learn. I would like to learn much more about this philosophy!' (Jernqvist, 1980a). Of course there is programming in Conductive Education, rigorous programming. Yet Jernqvist's central point is cardinal: we need to know much

153

more about the philosophical position from which the programming is applied to the specific task of teaching the motor-disordered to attain orthofunction.

What We Know

Theoretical statements directly from Hungary are limited in number and often confused by problems of translation or of interpretation. Even within Hungary itself there is little theoretical exposition. Petö himself wrote little and Hári ruefully admits (personal communication) that she is herself 'no theoretician'. The Institute's system of in-house training and employment and its lack of research have further restricted theoretical exposition at home. If we abroad feel puzzled about the theoretical basis of conductive education, we may be no worse placed in this respect than are many Hungarians.

András Petö

Petö made the conceptual leap of regarding motor disorder as a learning difficulty to be overcome rather than as a condition to be treated or accommodated to. This leap is perhaps analogous to that made a century-and-a-half before by the pioneers of deaf education who demonstrated that teaching deaf children to communicate opened a new way for the normal mechanisms of development, with the result that such children need no longer grow up imbeciles. Similarly, Petö set out to establish new ways of motor functioning by way of special teaching, to establish mechanisms of development that would otherwise not occur, so that motor disorder need not necessarily lead on to physical handicap.

How he arrived at this approach and how he developed the particular methods by which he and his successors have realised it remain unelucidated, even apparently in Hungary. The philosophy of Martin Buber (whose book *I and Thou* was first published in German in 1923) proved very influential in Petö's thinking, as with many other physicians and educators.[1] Yet paradoxically, whilst in general Petö had a great love of philosophising, with respect to conductive education he appears to have preferred the role of practitioner to theoretician. Accounts by those who knew him or saw him work agree that he was a gifted teacher, patient and intuitive, that he spared no effort either in himself or in others to attain his goals and that those whom he taught rose to meet this challenge. Here is the only account of Petö at work to have been published by English visitors to his Institute:

> During our first visit to The State Institute, we sat beside Professor Petö watching a group of children who had been exercising slowly and laboriously for several hours on their wooden plinths. At lunch time we rose to take our leave. Without turning his head, Professor Petö said 'The little boy in the corner is trying to stand up by himself today for the first time. No one will leave this room until he has accomplished his task'. After a further 45 minutes of effort, during which time the remainder of the group continued their standing practice, the boy succeeded in his efforts to stand. A photographer was called, and the boy said 'Come back this afternoon and I shall stand without holding on'. This incident not only demonstrated Professor Petö's appreciation of the boy's efforts and his timing of a successful situation, but also to what degree these factors and the group situation influence the child's confidence and motivation. (Cotton and Parnwell, 1968)

Writing ten years after Petö's death a Hungarian commentator epitomised the originality of Petö's approach in the following terms:

> Instead of asking, as most doctors and special educationalists do, 'how can I help the patient' Petö reversed the emphasis and posed the question 'what could the patients do to help themselves'.
>
> The specialist educationalist-therapist using the conductive method relies, of course, on the emotional relations she has developed with the child. The result is that the handicapped children usually make an all-out effort to perform on their own tasks which they could never tackle otherwise and which most specialists would consider too hard for them. Help is given by the conductor only when the child has exhausted all his resources and is only one step from success.
>
> The collective performance of the exercises by groups of children is an essential part of the Hungarian Petö method. The group gives each child an additional stimulus to keep up with the others. (Szentgyörgyi, 1977).

Szentgyögyi, like Cotton and Parnwell, emphasised the will and determination of the pupil and the vital role of the group in realising

Petö's educational goals. Perhaps Petö's notion of the group as a therapeutic force stemmed at least in part from his association long before with Jacob Moreno. The two men were close contemporaries, they were friends at medical school in Vienna before the First World War and close associates in the early twenties when Moreno was directing his *Stegreiftheater* (Impromptu Theatre) out of which sociodrama arose. Perhaps, then, one aspect of conductive education, the group, had its theoretical roots in a most improbable milieu, Vienna's red-light district in 1913, where Moreno lit upon the bases of group psychotherapy when organising a prostitutes' trade union (Moreno, 1953, pp. xxix-xxx). But Moreno left Austria for good in 1925 and, though the two men corresponded occasionally after the Second World War, they did not meet again till 1963 (Zerka Moreno, personal communication), by which time Petö's system was well established in a context where the collective or group had a meaning other than that formulated by Moreno.

There is, of course, an altogether alternative view of the relationship between the two men: might it rather not be that Moreno was influenced by Petö (Hári, personal communication)?

Mária Hári

Over the years of her directorship of the Institute Dr Hári has had to give lectures, present papers and talk to innumerable visitors who, from an enormous range of personal backgrounds, come to try and understand conductive education. To convey how conductive education works at its various levels she has read widely and borrowed models and theories from established areas of physiology, psychology and pedagogy, from sources in the United States, Western Europe and the Soviet Union. She firmly states, however, that whilst this draws in useful new insights and specific techniques, and helps her to articulate conductive education to outsiders, conductive education in its fundamentals derives solely from the work of Petö and from no other source.

It is chiefly with Dr Hári that visitors to the Institute have communicated, since few of the conductors have been able to speak English, and it is she, therefore, who has been the main interpreter of conductive education to the world. Over the course of her directorship she has visited Western Europe to make presentations of her work and has also published in English. Her works, therefore, provide our main access to the theory of conductive education. Unfortunately the material presently available is insufficient to provide a clear picture of

Mária Hári's overall theoretical position. Her presentations to conferences exist largely in the form of unpublished notes or transcripts and she would be the last to claim that her English is adequate for conveying fine points of meaning. Her essays in the collection by Akós (1975) were written in Hungarian then translated. Perhaps they have lost something in the translation. A recent collaborative exposition of the underlying principles of conductive education provides a fascinating source of insights and is available in two, slightly differing versions (Hári and Tillemans, 1984a, 1984b). It was prepared with the help of Thomas Tillemans, a Canadian professor of special education visiting the Institute, but though it provides the nearest to a detailed theoretical statement, it remains unsatisfactory. Altogether, then, only a relatively small store of theoretical statements are as yet available from Dr Hári, not enough to consolidate into a general theoretical statement of the nature of conductive education. The following examples of Dr Hári's theoretical position on a number of issues are not presented in a way to suggest an overall structure, elaboration of which must await further investigation.

Teaching not Therapy. The fundamental tenet of conductive education is surely that motor disorders may be brought under control (at least to the degree of establishing socially adequate function) by *teaching*, i.e. by educational processes aimed at generating mental development, both affective and intellective. This tenet distinguishes it from all other approaches. Hári has characterised the distinction between conductive education and what she terms the 'neurophysiological' approach as follows:

If the neurophysiological viewpoint is accepted, then the question may be raised: what neurophysiological functions or mechanisms are hidden behind the dysfunctional symptoms?

After this would be determined, we ought to provide for the activization of the missing neurophysiological function. With other words, we start here by assuming the existence of a known neurophysiological function system, a mechanism fully understood that will or, more precisely, ought to change with the development according to age, and if it does not, then the child suffers from a motor disorder. Thus the treatment should be accommodated to our neurophysiological knowledge.

On the other hand, the pedagogic question will ask what to do in order to transform the child found motor disordered here and now into an orthofunctional individual? If this question is raised by a pedagogue, then orthofunction assumes the role of an educational task, for whose achievement the pedagogue must find the conditions whereby the child (infant) can be activated and will understand, under the guidance of the pedagogue, the final objective as well as the ways and means of its accomplishment.

There is apparently just a small, but actually a tremendous difference between the two questions. Everybody knows that the neurophysiological mechanisms of the cerebral injuries or other dysfunctional cases are still far from being understood. Pedagogy is not affected by the insufficient understanding of the neurophysiological basis. In the rehabilitation of motor disorder patients the pedagogic aim is represented by the orthofunctions which mean a generally valid target readily understandable by anybody. (Hári, 1975a).

Teaching and Development. It is quite clear from the work at the Institute that Hári's view of the relationship of teaching and development accords firmly with the principle that teaching leads development. In cases of motor disorder there is a particular need for specialised teaching because the spontaneous mechanisms of the developmental process would, if left to themselves, lead to dysfunction. Once the intervention has been made, however, and the mechanisms set in motion, not only is orthofunction possible but it will be maintained by the continuing interactions and experiences that it generates: 'The primary aim of Conductive Education is to stimulate a developmental process which would not come about spontaneously, and which will continue subsequently, even when the child has been discharged from our Institute and has been integrated in a regular kindergarten or school' (Hári and Tillemans, 1984b). The precise nature of these mechanisms (which in the collection by Akós she often referred to as 'biological–social') remains as yet unexplicated. What is strongly affirmed, however, is that 'The starting point [of Conductive Education] is commonplace: that every individual has certain potentialities' (Hári, 1981b).

The Biological and the Mental. Dr Hári adopts a very practical, materialistic view of human mental development. It will be clear by now, however, that she does not adhere to a mechanistic view of the relationship of mental development to its biological base. Some idea of the understanding that is held at the Institute is apparent in the following simple analogy told by one of Dr Hári's colleagues:

> Somebody may be a highly efficient poultry breeder although there is no scientist who could explain in detail the physiological functions of a chicken. From a biological viewpoint, man can utilize the functioning of complex organisms practically almost impossible to survey, just like any other living species. The only difference is that man often is conscious of the results of these activities. (Pancsovay, 1975)

Methods. Conductive education is an educational system, the specific methods of which may vary. Particular methods employed for given purposes must not be confused with conductive education as a whole. Some who have sought to emulate conductive education in the West have seen it largely or solely a matter of techniques or (the ultimate reduction) of apparatus. It is not: 'Special equipment is a last resort and is allowable only if used temporarily, if it helps to teach skills not readily learned otherwise . . .' (Hári and Tillemans, 1984b). As an educational system conductive education can absorb a wide range of methods compatible with its overall philosophical approach: 'Neither the College nor the Institute supports a "cookbook" approach, in which conductors are expected to look up standard recipes for rapidly categorised problems' (Hári and Tillemans, 1984b). One important aspect of this overall educational philosophy is its emphasis upon the individualisation of method: 'Every person enrolled in CE, whether infant or adult, must develop his own method linking his executive and conative functions, i.e. linking what he does with what he wants to do. In order to reach this objective the programme cannot and does not depend primarily on practice and repetition' (Hári and Tillemans, 1984b). Within this highly flexible approach the pupils or patients have to discover their own methods of solving the practical tasks set them. The conductor's role is to help in this process of discovery, not to provide a pre-set solution, stepping in more directly only where the method adopted is inappropriate, self-defeating or improper. Flexible though this approach is, however, it is not empiricist, and methods which conflict with its overall philosophy are rejected. Singled out for particular opprobrium is the idea that one can build up a complex function from learning its individual motor components (its 'underlying abilities'):

In our Institute it is felt that the cortex can deal with the underlying ability only when it is subsumed under the total skill, which will make it meaningful and relevant. Specific training, as advocated by Frostig and Kephart, for example, is not used at the Institute, since it is felt that perceptual and motor skills are already embedded in more complex and complete skills which, because they are meaningful, offer much better opportunities for learning since a greater part of the cortex is involved. (Hári and Tillemans, 1984b)

Neuropsychology. The neuropsychological model of how the effects of conductive education are achieved is not yet accessible in English. The basic principle, however, is straightforward: 'Underlying this approach is the notion that for compensation or rehabilitation to take place, a creative process is needed in which the central nervous system will be permitted to restructure itself' (Hári and Tillemans, 1984b). To which may be added (in the words of another of Dr Hári's associates) an important rider: 'The pedagogue must never forget that the brain, even after a serious injury, will remain a wonderful construction, capable to learn the accomplishment of sophisticated tasks (Székély, 1975).

Conductive education is a complex blend of opposites. For example, it is highly individualised, depending as a basic prerequisite on pupils' and patients' active participation in their education: 'Conduction means that the child is guided to perform what he wants, to realise his own will ...' (Dr Hári speaking on *Newsnight*, BBC2, 5 May 1983). Yet at the same time a vital aspect of the method is its collective nature, the use of the group as a pedagogic tool.

A fundamentally new feature of the education of locomotor disorder patients is the utilization of the correlation between man and social environment, due to their inseparable unity. Education and the formation of character are appropriate tools thereof whereby the favourable habits of community life, the attraction towards community are then developed. Those suffering from disfunctions learn to live and act deliberately under community conditions. A well organized community will promote any stimulated, controlled, active learning process and, therefore, represents an essential factor in increasing the education effect. While in the rehabilitation of those suffering from disfunctions rather the individual treatment is emphasized all over the world, the development of community co-operation is one of the most important conductive pedagogy duties. (Hári, 1968)

More basically still, whilst the emphasis in all discussions about conductive education is upon the centrality of practice, it is always clear that underneath, however implicitly, there lie powerfully held ideas upon the direction that such practice should take. A proper theoretical statement of conductive education as a whole would require definitions at a variety of levels, physiological, neuro-psychological, psychological, pedagogic and social. 'Conductive Education is more than a method. This system is open to many methods; it is in its structure, the organisation of the work and the "conduction" in its teaching that its principles lie, and its result, social integration, is its fundamental characteristic (Hári, 1981c, translated from the French). Dr Hári herself delights in the practical problems, the real humane instances, far more than she cares for theoretical exposition. The following published account is endearingly characteristic.

The situation can be readily explained by an example. How can we teach to walk a patient suffering from a spinal cord lesion i.e. a paraplegic individual?

According to the general belief this problem is impossible to solve since in these cases every and each long pathway connecting the cerebral and spinal cord centres had been interrupted. But this obstacle is actually not impossible to overcome.

Let us start from a detail. How could such a patient learn to walk since he would not be able to move his legs?

But why should he not be able to do so? He has the possibility, for example, to stretch his legs while reclining. When he is lying on his back and swings himself over to his left side, this force will throw his right leg forward, over the left one, and stretch it out by its own dead weight. This, of course, is not the usual and simplest way of stretching a leg. Nevertheless, the individual himself has set this target, and accomplished it without any external assistance. All the teaching intervention was direction. Similarly, there are a number of possibilities to make the individual achieve to stretch his leg while either lying, sitting or standing.

Stretching the leg, however, is nothing but a detail of the whole problem, and was discussed here only to make the following statements easier to read.

In order to make a spinal cord injury patient walk, teaching must restore the will of the individual to do so. The patient must be taught to handle his body, including the limbs, under any conditions.

If, by deliberately creating different situations, the individual will learn to handle his limbs diversely, and if he is required but, at the same time, also assisted by creating the necessary conditions and supplying the necessary clues, to sit over from the cot to a chair, for example, or to make at least one or two little steps while clinging to his chair and sit down this way to the table, these accomplishments will surely start the learning process in the brain.

The targets thus set must be realistic biological-social requirements. Their accomplishment must be intended by the individual, while the pedagogue will have to create all the conditions under which the individual can successfully achieve the target he is to reach. Most important are the apparently simple tasks whereby the individual can learn how to stretch or bend his legs, etc. in every and any situation. Under normal conditions there is no need for the assistance of a pedagogue in setting such detail targets and to accomplish them successfully. But for the brain these are only virtually simple tasks and represent, temporarily, very important learning problems in disfunctional cases. Nothing but a systematic intention to stretch, bend, lift, etc. the legs and the exercise of doing so under the most different conditions can make the individual learn increasingly efficient solutions, and enable him to stand, walk, bend, straighten, etc. more and more safely.

After a longer period of time the brain will master how to handle the different situations, it will incorporate then various conditions into the output required for the accomplishment of the different tasks, simplify them, and finally the individual will walk rapidly and tenaciously although being 'paraplegic'. Similarly to the solution of the part problems just described, he will learn how to control his needs. His tone and trophic will change like his relation to others. At last he will be able to keep pace in his further development with the continuously increasing biological-social system of requirements in conformity with his age. He has become orthofunctional.

The organization of walking, learned as outlined above, will be ensured by the brain not through the long pathway function but, in spite of their interruption, in a by-pass manner. Nothing is known about any such by-pass, but actually we do not know the pathway details resulting in normal walking, either.

The duty of the pedagogue is to promote the discovery of the conditions which enable the spinal cord injury patient to learn how to walk, etc. and enter everyday life without any special mechanism. (Hári, 1975b)

What We Can Guess

Faced with the unfamiliar practices and processes of conductive education, with its guiding principles often expressed only in terms of specific instances, foreign visitors and commentators have been forced to make sense of the system in their own terms. Ester Cotton was the first to be faced with this daunting task. She tackled it in two ways, both of which have been influential outside Hungary in the direction of attempts to emulate and understand conductive education. At a practical level she sought to identify the central features of this system, essential for its operation. She also looked for theoreticians who might explain what was happening in the course of children's conduction, finding them in Pavlov and Luriya.

Principles of Practice

Ester Cotton's principles derived from her earliest visits, when Petö was still alive:

> Professor Petö strove for a unity of approach to the treatment, education and management of the Cerebral Palsied child and achieved this by creating a new profession – that of the '*Conductor*', by adapting a method of treatment called '*Rhythmical Intention*', and by arranging for the children to work in *groups* while adhering to a *rigid time-table* and a *long-term programme* in surroundings that are free from all distraction. (Cotton and Parnwell, 1968, emphasis in original)

In other words, 'the parts which in their aggregate amount to Conductive Education' were as follows: 'To avoid distraction – quiet surroundings. To prevent confusion – one therapist only in place of three or more now employed. To lay down and reinforce new motor problems – repetitive work and a set time-table. To establish motivation and foster stimulation – treatment in groups' (Cotton and Parnwell, 1968)

These principles subsequently proved very helpful to practitioners seeking to identify what they wished to adopt for themselves from what they had heard of conductive education in Hungary, and to distinguish the new approach from others already in use. Whether these principles themselves comprise either the necessary or sufficient bases for defining conductive education is another matter.

The Russian Connection

From her first published report, Ester Cotton emphasised the importance of rhythmical intention as a teaching method: 'Professor Petö explains that one must not touch the child. The movements are guided by the child's own speech, or attempts to speak, the cortex controlling the movements' (Cotton, 1965). Whilst it still was 'too early to understand fully the phenomenon involved in rhythmical intention' she offered Luriya's verbal-regulation experiments and ideas of the second-signal system and of cortical arousal from Pavlov. Later she added consideration of Luriya's neuropsychological work (e.g. Cotton, 1975, p. 25). During the early years of interest in conductive education in this country, however, little attention appears to have been paid to the work cited. What is perhaps surprising is that this early interest was closely associated with the Spastics Society which was simultaneously involved with the only systematic exploration carried out in this country into Luriya's ideas on the development of verbal regulation in children. A series of investigations initiated by Joseph Schubert included studies of the use of verbal regulation by cerebral-palsied children (Schubert, 1964; Burland, 1969, 1971; Schubert and Burland, 1972), yet the two lines of work within the same organisation do not appear to have come together. Indeed, it seemed possible to dismiss the likely value of such a theoretical formulation altogether in favour of a more pragmatic approach:

> Being developed in Hungary by Professor Petö – based on Russian neuropsychology (some theory quite doubtful) – this seems to me unimportant. Interesting but not worth many arguments! Luria or no Luria it is clear to me that the family with a handicapped child in its midst needs a commonsense, all-round education for that child. (Jernqvist, 1977)

There the possible Russian connection seems to have rested, an interesting, supportive theoretical background but of little further heuristic or practical value. Anita Tatlow in Hong Kong, however, had been struck by the possible relevance of Luriya's ideas on verbal regulation to the problems of cerebral-palsied children, only subsequently learning of the existence of conductive education through Ester Cotton and Ingfield Manor school (see Chapter 3). And in 1980 Ann Mintram in Birmingham was struck by the close similarities between her own study of the mental control of motor acts, conducted within the Vygotskian paradigm (Mintram, 1981) and reports that she had heard through the professional grapevine of the work at Ingfield Manor school.

Mintram's 'discovery' of conductive education from such a viewpoint sparked off a series of theoretical investigations. From what information was then available it seemed reasonable to expect that Hungarian pedagogy, psychology and physiology would have been strongly influenced by powerful Soviet models in the years following the Second World War and that conductive education might be an offshoot of Soviet defectology. Particularly, it seemed reasonable to see affinities between Pető's rhythmical intention and verbal regulation, and between the conductive group and the Makarenkoist tradition of collective upbringing (Sutton, 1982). The literature available on these and associated topics was influential in interpreting the two practical studies into conductive education then under way in the Birmingham area (see Chapter 4 and Chapter 5) and, given the dearth of other relevant material, Soviet theory proved a useful basis to examine the whole field (Sutton, 1983a; da Silva, 1984).

It is indeed convenient to understand what is happening in conductive education from within the wider Vygotskian metatheory: social interaction is creating new mental structures, the biological in development is being subordinated to the psychological (see Sutton, 1983b). Within this wider framework two strands of A.R. Luriya's work are of immediate relevance. Firstly, his experimental exposition of the role of speech in the regulation of motor acts, as an illustration of Vygotskii's wider views on the role of speech in human mental development, provides a suggestive pointer to certain aspects of rhythmical intention as the child develops new functions. The Institute's own account of this process contains a section which seems almost pure Luriya:

> Rhythmic intentionality is the combination of intentionality and rhythm, with which one can regulate the rhythm of the activity. For example, in the example of paraplegics and athetoids who must carry out their exercise through verbal intentionality followed by a movement, counting ensures that the result will be reached. As this regulating becomes firm, first counting is left out and *then the activity takes place simultaneously with the verbal intentionality . . . later still, internal silent intentionality becomes sufficient and finally even this becomes unnoticeable: it becomes merely the*

motivation towards the activity, which is common to the orthofunctional. (Hári and Akós, 1971, p. 176, translated from the Hungarian, present author's emphasis)

Secondly, Luriya's work on the restoration of cortical function in brain-injured adults, well known and widely respected in the West since the 1960s, has a clear bearing on conductive education, most obviously in the case of adult patients. 'The basic principle of restoration of the functions through a restructuring of the functional system and specially through an incorporation of the system of semantic connections (connections formed on the basis of the second signal system) remains identical for all lesions, regardless of their concrete forms' (Luriya, 1969). Again, it is perhaps surprising that Luriya's work has not attracted more widespread attention generally to the possible role of speech in establishing alternative cortical systems in cases of motor disorder – and, through this, to conductive education in a way such as is outlined in Chapter 7.

Also springing directly from the Vygotskian tradition, though until recently far less well known to English-language readers, is A.N. Leont'ev's Activity Theory on the creation of new mental structures through internalisation of socially meaningful practical activity to create new mental structures (Leont'ev, 1981) and P.Ya Gal'perin's instructional theory on the use of externalisation as part of the progressive transfer of generalisable skills from teacher to pupil, from without to within (Gal'perin, 1957). Outside of psychology, the 'cognitive phsyiology' of N.A. Bernshtein (1967), who had close personal and philosophical links with Vygoyskii and his heirs, insists upon the purposive nature of movements, their objective to change some aspect of the organism's outside world, and, therefore, the need to understand them in the light of their intention. In the field of handicap the defectology established by Vygotskii (Sutton, 1980) makes qualitative distinctions amongst the retarded and raises questions of aetiology, intervention and outcome, that shed considerable light upon aspects of conductive education. Luriya was involved in this latter work and, through his writings (e.g. Luriya, 1961b) these formulations became available in the West in the 1960s.

Following the renewed interest in the relevance of Russian psychological theory to conductive education, Jernqvist has conducted some interesting experiments on the stage-development of verbal regulation amongst children in the Petö Unit at Ingfield Manor school, based upon a Luriyan model proposed by Sutton and

Jernqvist (1982). Preliminary results (Jernqvist, 1984a) suggest that consideration of pupils' stages of verbal regulation results in their participating to a higher degree in their teaching programmes. A more extensive account of this work is in preparation.

A somewhat separate Russian tradition, which has appeared to shed considerable light on conductive education, is the pedagogic tradition stemming from the work and writings of A.S. Makarenko (see Bowen, 1962). The methods of 'collective upbringing' deriving from Makarenko became widely known in the West in the 1970s, from Bronfenbrenner's (1974) book comparing American and Soviet child-rearing practices. The following extracts from an account by a visitor to Fót Children's Town for orphans and for deprived and ill-treated children, run on explicitly Makarenkoist lines, provides an interesting parallel to the accounts of visitors to the Institute for the Motor-Disordered:

> Mere facts and figures can give no idea of its heart-warming atmosphere. The whole place radiates happiness ... it is one of those utopian communities that one reads about but never expects to see because they sound too good to be true. Therapy to restore self-confidence is attempted not so much by clinical treatment as by the creation of a genuinely family atmosphere ... The stress on group organisation, as the principal was at some pains to emphasise, does not mean that individuality is in any way suppressed ... No one paid me the slightest notice. Everyone was intent on minding his own business ... With so much going on it was impossible for an outsider to fathom the careful organisation that lay behind it all. Enough to say that from start to finish I never saw a glum face. (Special Correspondent, 1964)

One might also see parallels between aspects of conductive education and the work of more recent Soviet workers and writers in the Makarenkoist tradition, e.g. V.A. Sukhomlinskii (1977). In the West, however, discussion of the group as an aspect of conductive education, has not involved the developed pedagogic approaches elaborated by such authors.

It is hardly surprising, however, that two visitors to the Institute in Budapest from the Institute of Defectology in Moscow found it very easy to identify what they observed in their own terms:

> In working out the system of conductive upbringing, Prof. A. Petö

took into account the basic theories of learning of I.P. Pavlov, according to which the word is the predominant stimulus for man – the 'signal of signals'. The whole method of work with children suffering from cerebral palsies, in correspondence with this theory, is constructed on the base of the mastery of movements, skills and knowledge through the word: each movement and action which the child has to fulfil is first spoken through by the conductor, then he does it through together with the child and speaks through each movement, each action. As a result the child spontaneously tries to accompany his movements, his actions, his intentions, with a verbal framework.

In so far as the intentional-melodic [i.e. rhythmical-intentional – *Trans.*] aspect of language is manifest early on in the child's speech activity, then children of an earlier age accompany their movements, actions and intentions with a song, a verse, a recitation.

All activities over the course of the day are in practice activities concerned with the mastery of new movements, skills and knowledge, and are directed to the development of the mental, speech and motor functions, i.e. in this system speech, movement and other mental processes develop through day-by-day, active, practical activity. This corresponds to contemporary physiological and psychological research on the role of activity in the development of the mind. (Semenova and Mastyukova, 1974, translated from the Russian)

Nor perhaps is it surprising that Dr Hári, when talking or writing in Russian, has found it easy to express the theories of conductive education concisely within the Soviet theoretical framework (see Sutton, 1984a, Suppl. VI). Even to an English audience she has found it convenient to state herself in somewhat Pavlovian terms:

The conductor (the qualified conductive education instructor) will increase the individual's spontaneous activity by prompting the patient's discovery of how to arrive at a solution by setting appreciable and controllable objectives and guiding tasks. The motion thus brought about on the basis of the first-signal system is connected by the conductor to the second-signal system, speech, and thereby made conscious ... With the rhythm and motion elements engaged, the method promotes the conscious control of motion itself: the stability of speech exceeds that of the motion sequence and the connection of the motor details is ensured by the speech. (Hári, 1970)

Yet, as Hári herself frequently states, if she uses foreign theories, models and terms to articulate conductive education, this does not mean that conductive education derived from any of the theoretical systems cited. She readily acknowledges similarities with the works of Pavlov, Bernshtein, Vygotskii, Luriya, Leont'ev, Makarenko and other Soviet authors but is quite ready to take issue with them over particular points:

Thus, from a pedagogic viewpoint, every method is good which activates to orthofunctional manifestations and leads to the target set. At the same time, adherence to a schematic idea or selecting the method to be used not so much according to the given situation but rather as an idolised fetish, is a pedagogic error, like the principle represented by Luriya et al. in the 3rd volume of the Handbook of Clinical Neurology (a section on 'Restoration of motor functions by reorganization of functional systems') where they claim that '. . . During the process of rehabilitation, the whole complex motor act must be programmed. The patient is taught to restore each individual link of his movement; only then can he be taught to make the smooth and continuous transition from one motor link to another, i.e. the necessary motor connection or continuity between the individual consecutive links is established. Only then can the patient start to learn to reproduce the "pattern" of this whole complex motor act.' (Hári, 1975a)

The system at the Institute was founded firmly on the work of Pető and all that his colleagues and successors have done is continue and elaborate his work. But was Pető himself influenced by Soviet models in his creation and development of conductive education? Certainly he was aware of Soviet provision, for one of his few published articles during his time as director of the Institute was a review of special education for the motor-disordered in the Soviet Union. But the peculiar history of Soviet psychology makes it unlikely that there was the direct influence on Pető's work that has been implied (Sutton, 1983c). For example, Luriya did not do his work on verbal regulation till the early 1950s, by which time conductive education appears to have been well under way, and Vygotskii's writings did not begin the long process of rehabilitation and republication till 1956. The neo-Pavlovian movement in Soviet psychology, which began to retreat in the Soviet Union in the late fifties, seems also to have been influential in most of Eastern Europe during the 1950s but even the encyclopaedic

Razran (1958) was unable to shed any light on what was happening in Hungarian psychology at that time.

It is tempting to think that Petö was indeed an original thinker and that the fundaments of conductive education were quite indigenous. Then, in the Rakósi period; it would be advantageous or legitimating to express the work publicly in Pavlovian terms. Later, when Luriya's work won wide recognition, this was used in a similar way. (When Luriya himself visited Budapest Petö interrupted his official programme to take him to the Institute to point out the similarities.) Furthermore, since conductive education was developing in a socialist state, it probably assimilated many of the pedagogic practices of that state, and Petö's 'group' (whatever its origin) came to have much in common with groups in general in Hungarian education. Over the 40 years of its development conductive education may have been enriched by the fertile field of Soviet developmental psychology, especially following the defeat of neo-Pavlovianism, but like so much else to do with conductive education this issue awaits more extensive inquiry at source.

Other Ways of Seeing

If one is looking to explain or understand conductive education from outside then of course the view taken will depend very much upon one's previous background, experience or ideology. One visitor to the Institute, for example, was able to see what was going on in a way quite opposed to the views of the Vygotskian school, in terms of operant conditioning (Haskell, 1977). Skinnerian interpretations of educational or therapeutic processes are now familiar in the English-speaking world and behavioural or related approaches to conductive education and the problems of the motor-disordered are to be expected. Indeed, it is surprising that the area has not attracted far wider behavioural interpretation and involvement.

Most of the interest in conductive education outside Hungary has been from the English-speaking world or from areas under its cultural influence. In contrast, da Silva (1984) has addressed the issue from the perspective of a special educator from Portugal. Whilst his prime consideration was the possible explanatory force of Soviet work in this area, he could not help but be attracted by the analogies of much in conductive education with French *psychomotricité* which, though almost unknown in the English-speaking world, comprised a central part of his own socialisation as a special educator. For example, the importance of rhythm is something emphasised by all authorities in psychometricity, thus:

> It is commonly observed that a rhythmic succession of movements is far easier to execute and causes less fatigue than a non-rhythmic succession of the same movements. This ease of execution and decrease of fatigue are further enhanced when a succession of rhythmic sounds are heard at a constant rate. By discarding parasitical movements rhythmic activity regulates the flow of nervous energy and undoubtedly provides pleasant sensations ... Indeed, if rhythmic movement is easier to execute this is because it requires less 'intellectual' effort than non-rhythmic movement since fatigue increases with the complexity of neuromuscular effort and with the increase of attention upon the gestures. (Picq and Vayer, 1976, p. 35, translated from the French)

As yet there has been little awareness of conductive education in the French-speaking world (though Piaget was another visitor to Budapest whom Petö took to show the work of the Institute). Had there been, rather different aspects of the work in Budapest might have been considered worthy of note, whilst others (the children's apparent lack of fatigue, for example) might have excited rather less comment. There may also have been quite different speculations about the theoretical bases. One of the major inspirations for psychometricity was Henri Wallon whose name and work are probably even less widely known in the English-speaking world than are those of Petö. Wallon's theory of child development paid great account to the contribution of motoric and emotional factors in the formation of human personality. Thus, with respect to conductive education, the prime importance of establishing an appropriate 'contact' between conductor and pupil would be immediately recognised as a familiar principle. 'The role of the emotions is undoubtedly a system which precedes articulated language, a system that is necessary in order that powerful collective reactions may be released through a kind of contagion' (Wallon, 1959). Wallon, like Vygotskii, Luriya and Leont'ev, was a Marxist, and his psychology like theirs was profoundly influenced by his philosophical background. A psychometrician can, therefore, find ready parallels between the two psychological systems (da Fonseca, 1981). Wallon himself spent the years 1950 to 1952 as professor of psychology in Cracow in Poland. The first Hungarian account of his theory of development was published in 1947, other reviews followed over the next 20 years and an anthology of his work was published in Hungarian in 1971 (Zazzo, 1975, pp. 208-19). But did Wallon's thinking influence Petö and his successors, either directly or via the *Zeitgeist*? Again, we do not know.

Whether a given theoretical position has been directly influential in conductive education or not, it should be clear that any theory of the transformability of human beings might have explanatory value, whilst those that are philosophically compatible might potentially interact with conductive education to mutual benefit. An obvious example of a compatible theory which, though developing contemporaneously with conductive education, has so far had no contacts with it at all, is Feuerstein's notion of cognitive modifiability. This derived from work with children and young people whose problems of development are superficially quite different from those of the motor-disordered (Feuerstein, 1980), yet some at least of conductive education can be readily stated in Feuerstein's terms. For example, conductive education appears to produce unexpected departures from an otherwise expected course of development, despite present levels of functioning and aetiologies from which our present experience predicts very limited outcomes. It can be seen as generating changes in the learning process that generalise across many areas, the new rate of change itself providing conditions for further development, with the emphasis throughout upon volitional and conscious activity. Its underlying basis is a belief in plasticity as the most characteristic feature of humanity, ensured by learning experiences that are socially mediated, reciprocal, semantic, motivational. It would be interesting indeed to follow developments, both theoretical and practical, if conductive education were taken up by Youth Aliyah.

No attention has been given here to orthopaedic or neurological issues. There is nothing yet available from the Institute on such matters and, at the time of writing, no orthopaedic specialists or neurologists from the English-speaking world appear to have directed their attention to conductive education. Such attention is urgently required. And though attempts to understand the workings of conductive education have so far concentrated largely on children's mental development and on teaching methods, little account has been given to wider dimensions of the pedagogic process, involving questions of the organisation and provision of conductive education. Despite clear pointers from visitors' accounts and the continuous insistence of Dr Hári herself, important lines of inquiry do not appear to have been followed up by western emulators – even though considerable theoretical support for the Institute has emerged from our own practical experience. Firstly, there is the question of the institutional structure within the Institute and the degree of personal autonomy and discretion that the conductors enjoy within the collective framework. Increasingly, practitioners in this country have become aware of the futility of trying to achieve change in pupils or patients if one fails to pay account to the organisational structures through which their provision is made (McPherson and Sutton, 1981). How this matter is arranged at the Institute, the way in which provision at the personal level is facilitated by its wider organisational framework, may prove a fruitful line for further inquiry. Certainly, it is clear that the optimism, technical skill and consistency of the conductors are maintained at a high level by the way that their work is organised and that this closely integrated system must itself constitute an important factor in any superiority that conductive education might possess over systems of provision less favourably organised to generate and maintain such vital factors. Secondly, there is the matter of the conductors themselves. Despite a tendency in this country for conductive education to be regarded as a therapy, its operation appears never to have been related to the one fairly sure piece of knowledge to have emerged from generations of research into *psycho*therapy here in the West, including 'educational therapies'. It has long been widely known that, regardless of the specific methods used, a certain personality, a certain kind of relationship with the client, can have major effects upon the outcome of an intervention:

> These findings suggest that the person (whether a counsellor, therapist or teacher) who is better able to communicate warmth, genuineness and accurate empathy is more effective in inter-personal relationships, no matter what the goal of the interaction (better grades for college students, better interpersonal relations for the counseling center, adequate personality functioning for the seriously disturbed mental patient, socially acceptable behaviour for the juvenile delinquent or greater reading ability for third grade teaching instruction students. (Truax and Carkhuff, 1967, pp. 116-17)

Further accumulating evidence in the same direction has raised the difficult issue of how far 'warmth, empathy and genuineness' might be not only necessary factors in an effective intervention but also, in certain circumstances, sufficient:

What about client problems that involve lack of information or knowledge, lack of skills of various kinds: are these deficiencies of a cognitive or a motor nature? Surely where these are lacking or inadequate the providing of a relationship is not sufficient. Although it might appear to be a resort to specious reasoning, dealing with such problems would appear to be education (or re-education) or teaching rather than [psycho-] therapy. While it might be difficult to draw a line between therapy and (remedial) teaching, there would seem to be some value in doing so. One difference might be that therapy is concerned with persons who are not lacking in knowledge or skills but who are unable for some reason to use their knowledge or skills. Their problem, in the distinction made by many learning theorists, is not one of learning but one of performance. Therapy as a relationship is sufficient for enabling them to do those things that they are capable of doing. On the other hand, the relationship may not be sufficient where there is a lack or deficit. . . However, even here, two comments are in order. First it is becoming increasingly recognised that learning is not simply a cognitive process. . . Second, the teacher–student interaction involves a personal relationship, and evidence is accumulating that the same factors that lead to therapeutic personality change also facilitate cognitive learning. In fact, in some teaching – perhaps in the best teaching – creating a suitable relationship may be sufficient for some kinds of learning by learners. (Patterson, 1980, pp. 661–2)

Consideration of conductive education in such a light justifies Dr Hári's insistence that would-be conductors are taken into the Institute only on a trial basis, to demonstrate whether they can indeed make the 'contact', and opens an important area of further inquiry which ought not to be neglected by workers in this field.

Theoretical Contrasts

From a viewpoint outside of Hungary we can, therefore, guess fairly confidently that much in conductive education is compatible with theories of child development within the three major divisions of psychology in the developed world, the Anglophone, the Francophone and the Russophone. We can also see much that is *in*compatible with many notions that are widely and dearly held here in the West. And whilst we can be sure than much in conductive education is typically Hungarian, we have also to be aware that the overall theoretical basis of conductive education is not necessarily shared by Hungarian education as a whole, or even by Hungarian special education, and be alert for conflicts over important aspects between the approach of the Institute and influential views in its surrounding system. The acrimony of such conflict (see Hári, 1975a, pp. 44-5 and 48-9) reflects major differences of philosophy, theory and practice. The Institute for Motor Disorders, for example, insists upon generic training carried out alongside full-time professional practice. The Gustav Barczi College of Special Education trains specialists; and its students do not undertake simultaneous full-time employment. The Institute deplores standardised tests; the special-education college advocates their use (and also Frostig's programme of sensori-motor diagnosis and training). Hungary is a country of startling contradictions and contrasts in all fields of social life. One of its 'major achievements in the science of education' over the past 30 years has been proclaimed as follows:

It is only natural that Hungarian educationalists chiefly rely on the findings of, and methods used in the socialist countries and on those of Western research workers of Marxist orientation. However, Hungarian pedagogues maintain connections with bourgeoise educationalists from capitalist countries, often attend international meetings and participate in international organisations, as long as this can be done without the violation of these convictions. (Szarka, 1976)

A difficult tightrope to walk. A series of English-language articles on the Budapest Study of Mental Retardation that was conducted over 1971-2 indicates something of the ambiguous theoretical context with which the Institute must co-exist. The first report of the Budapest Study (Lányi-Engelmayer, 1973) pointed out the 'very strict instructions' within official Hungarian regulations that only the 'truly mentally deficient' should be directed to special school: 'Children who become retarded because of underprivileged social and cultural conditions, or those facing temporary difficulties in their learning ability, should not be considered as mentally defective.' This distinction is directly analogous to that made within Soviet defect-ology (Sutton, 1980). In the Budapest Study this differential diagnosis appears to have been made on the basis of clinical judgement, though considerable psychometric data were also collected. Later analyses concentrated upon these psychometric data.

Czeizel and Métneki-Bajomi (1978) invoked 'the English school of genetics' and 'the normal distribution of intelligence' to account for 'familial-cultural mental subnormality'. The chief means of preventing such retardation was stated as more birth control for families of low socio-economic and intelligence level. This position is made hardly more compatible with the ideals of a Marxist state by the further suggestion that 'the socio-economic conditions of these families should be improved in order to help the children to fully evolve . . . their weak inherited capacities'. Two further papers here reiterated his analysis (Czeizel, Lányi-Engelmayer, Kluber, Métneki and Tusnády, 1980; Lányi-Engelmayer, Katona and Czeizel, 1983), though still maintaining what appears to be a foot in the dialectual camp, for example: 'In addition to the psychometric evaluation, the capacity to learn and the skill ability of the child are examined in a situation in which the performance-improvement is monitored as a function of the pedagogical assistance given to the child' (Lányi-Engelmayer, Katona and Czeizel, 1983). This surely refers to Vygotskii's zone of next development. It does not, however, suggest that a satisfactory synthesis has been achieved between East and West. These four papers indicate the insoluble theoretical and methodological problems that the authors have posed themselves, by trying simultaneously to follow the ultimately incompatible models of, on the one hand, Soviet defectology and, on the other, *passé* British theory and out-of-date American technique. It may be that Petö's Institute, in its insistence on the unity of theory with practice and its strict adherence to a dynamic, interactive view of development, is following a theoretical course more in tune with the ideological foundations of the Hungarian state than is necessarily the case in every area of the wider education system.

At the moment, then, it remains impossible from outside the Institute to specify precisely what is conductive education, to trace the origin of the approach or to identify its essence. For some, the commonsense view will certainly suffice: anyone who has learned to march or to dance may regard verbal instructions, counting, rhythm, music, the influence of fellow learners, etc. as obvious aids to the mastery of movement patterns that do not 'come naturally'. Yet if conductive education is to be a communicable expertise, generalisable and modifiable to different social conditions and subject to the normal processes of scientific investigation, then finer and more robust understandings than simple commonsense are required. Despite

Cotton's (1965) pointers made right at the start of public discussion of conductive education in this country, professional attention has been directed chiefly to methodological specifics. Until relatively recently theory has gone largely ignored. This has impoverished not just the work of the protagonists of conductive education but also misled its critics (e.g. Rosenbloom, Reynell and Horton, 1970), denying us the opportunity of informed national or international debate.

Margaret Peter (personal communication) first visited the Institute in the mid-sixties, when Petö was still alive. She did not much like what she saw. She visited again only in 1984 and was somewhat surprised that she now liked what she saw. In part, she reports, there had been a change in the atmosphere in the Institute itself, it was somehow warmer, mellower than it had been two decades before. But she was also very aware of two important changes in herself as an English educationalist over the same period. In the mid-sixties there had been a very powerful ideology afoot in our state education system, that formality, structure and discipline were contrary to children's best interests and acted against the learning process. It was also confidently thought that the massive professional expansion then under way in the West would offer children far more benefit than apparently Spartan provision of the sort observed at Villány út ever would. How things have changed in 20 years! Formality, structure and discipline are now being eagerly re-examined and the new emphasis on effectiveness and evaluation has evoked serious interest in approaches that promise to be economical and cost-effective. Perhaps now, therefore, we as a society are more ready to address and perhaps even embrace the theoretical issues raised by conductive education at all its levels. In doing so we might not only better serve conductive education but also shed useful light in return on wider issues than the habilitation and rehabilitation of the motor-disordered.

7 PARKINSON'S DISEASE

Veronica Nanton

The muscles themselves are normal, the nerves supplying the muscles are normal, the spinal cord and local mechanisms for controlling muscles are entirely normal and even the more sophisticated motor mechanisms coming from the brain itself are capable of functioning normally. Somebody with Parkinson's Disease, given a big enough stimulus, can leap into action in an amazing way. (Professor David Marsden)

Sometimes I don't sleep very well, and when I wake up I get a piece of chocolate and I have to go through a door from my bedroom to the kitchen where the chocolate is. One night, coming to the door, I couldn't get through it and I had to force my way through. It was as if one's feet were glued to the ground. I've tried tricks like dancing through and sometimes it's worked. (Terry Thomas)

That the motor system of immobile incapacitated patients can be suddenly switched to useful activity provides one of the most challenging yet encouraging problems for all those engaged in the field of extrapyramidal disorders. (Dr Gerald Stern)

An Essay on the Shaking Palsy published in 1817 by Dr James Parkinson gave the first clinical account of the condition which was later to become known as Parkinson's disease. He described six patients who demonstrated 'involuntary tremulous motion with lessened muscular power in parts not in action even when supported with a propensity to bend the trunk forward and to pass from a walking to a running pace' (Parkinson, 1817). With the development of the understanding of Parkinson's disease, distinctions have been made between idiopathic and post-encephalitic Parkinson's disease and symptomatic Parkinsonism or Parkinsonian syndromes (Parkes, 1982). Idiopathic Parkinson's disease is the present focus of concern because it is with this condition that conductive education in Hungary has been undertaken effectively.

Symptoms

It is unwise to be categoric regarding any particular symptom of Parkinson's disease as its manifestation varies markedly between patients. The major features of the idiopathic condition are, however, characteristic. The best known of these is tremor, although this may be absent in a quarter of patients. Tremor usually starts in one limb, from which it may spread. At first it is most evident at rest, diminishing on voluntary movement. Over time, even during movement the tremor may still be apparent. The frequency range is generally between 4 and 8Hz and the amplitude may vary greatly within as well as between individuals. The second major characteristic of the disease, though one which Parkinson did not describe, is muscular rigidity. This refers to the resistance that can be felt when patients' joints are passively moved and the affected muscles stretched. When this resistance is uniform and equal it is described as 'lead pipe rigidity'. Frequently, however, there may be a regular, rhythmical, variable or jerking quality which is known as 'cog-wheel' rigidity. Rigidity usually appears first in axial and shoulder muscles and progresses to the limbs of one or both sides of the body. The last and perhaps most disabling of the primary features of the disease are akinesia and bradykinesia. These terms refer to the poverty and slowness of movement which render normally spontaneous motor acts so difficult for the sufferer. Akinesia and bradykinesia may give rise to functional problems such as getting out of a chair or turning over in bed. They are responsible for patients' difficulties in dressing and shaving. Akinesia and bradykinesia also underlie the characteristic facial immobility of sufferers ('the Parkinsonian mask'), infrequent blinking and the loss of arm swing and gesture.

Bradykinesia, rigidity and an abnormal centre of gravity are responsible for the characteristic flexed posture of the Parkinsonian patient. The head tends to bend towards the chest and the shoulders become rounded. Gait disturbance also occurs, as James Parkinson had recognised. Steps become shorter and there is a tendency towards festination, the *'marche à petits pas'* where the patients totter forwards, bent over as if to stop themselves from falling. As the disease progresses many patients develop difficulty in initiating movements and the problem of 'freezing' before the movement has been completed. This is most apparent with respect to walking but may occur with any action the patient tries to perform.

Sufferers of Parkinson's disease frequently develop micrographia.

Indeed, this often appears amongst the first symptoms. The handwriting disturbance parallels the characteristic disturbance of gait. The first word of a sentence may start relatively well formed and controlled. Size will then diminish, with the sufferer apparently unable to control speed until the individual letters become indecipherable. Estimates of the proportion of patients whose speech is affected by the condition range between 33 per cent and 64 per cent (Marmot *et al.*, 1982; Oxtoby, 1982). The extent to which this disturbance occurs varies greatly. Speech may become hesitant and lose inflection. It may also become mumbled and lose volume. Numerous autonomic disturbances may also add to the discomfort and difficulty of the Parkinsonian patient. Urinary problems, constipation, seborrhea and sweating are amongst the most common.

James Parkinson stated that the senses and intellect remained unimpaired by the disease. Early in the course of the condition this appears to be the case but it is now considered by many commentators that this is untrue of the later stages of the disease. As Parkes (1982, p. 13) has said, however, 'the problem lies in separating the effects of severe Parkinsonism – gross motor retardation, the advance of senility and changes in mood from the effects of drug toxicity. Difficulties in differential diagnosis with the definite occurrence of dementia in some forms of Parkinsonism as compared with idiopathic Parkinson's disease, add to the problem of assessment.'

Lees and Smith (1983) have claimed that even in the first few years of the disease, subtle changes may be noticed by some patients, or by their relatives. Patients may show a slight lack of spontaneity, loss of imagination and a tendency to repetition. They may become a little forgetful and occasionally lose their way in unfamiliar surroundings.

Numerous studies of specific cognitive deficits amongst patients with varying degrees of physical disability have been undertaken. Amongst these, investigations have shown impairment of reaction time (Evarts, 1981), reduction in tracking ability (Flowers, 1976) and difficulties in judgement of the visual vertical and horizontal (Danta and Hilton, 1975). Lees and Smith (1983) have recently demonstrated amongst a group of mildly disabled patients slight difficulties in shifting conceptual set and the commission of perseverative errors in tests of card sorting and word fluency. Many psychological studies have reported negative results, however, and no impairment of general intellectual function, directly attributable to Parkinson's disease has been found (Marsden, 1980). Depression amongst patients is common. The incidence has recently been estimated as high as 90 per cent (Parkes, 1982). There is nevertheless little agreement on the relative proportions of primary and reactive depression.

Pathology

The pathology of Parkinson's disease lies within the basal ganglia, part of the extrapyramidal motor system. The component bodies of the basal ganglia and its main connections are illustrated in Figure 7.1. Figure 7.2 shows the principle connections between the basal ganglia and the cerebral cortex.

Figure 7.1: The Main Fibre Connections between the Basal Ganglia (schematic representation)

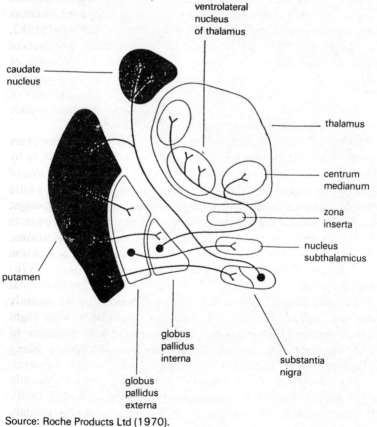

Source: Roche Products Ltd (1970).

Figure 7.2: Principal Circuits Linking Cerebral Cortex and Basal Ganglia (schematic representation)

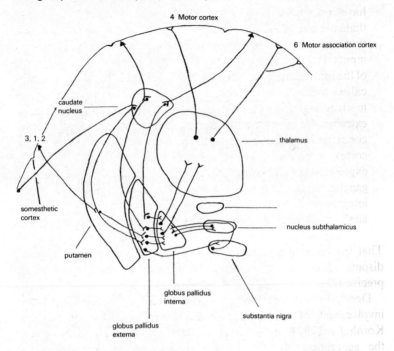

Source: Adapted from Eccles (1977).

The principal change which occurs in Parkinson's disease (though not the only one) is that dopaminergic neurones of the zona compacta of the substantia nigra degenerate thus producing a deficiency of dopamine in the corpus striatum (the caudate nucleus and putamen). At post-mortem, as well as depigmentation of the substantia nigra, cytoplasmic inclusion bodies known as Lewy bodies may be seen within its cells.

The deficiency of dopamine interferes with the normal function of the basal ganglia. The precise nature of this function is still not fully understood and the views of commentators are wide ranging. The difficulty appears to be, in part at least, one of perspective. As Marsden (1980) has said:

Motor physiologists have attempted to attribute a specific aspect of motor organisation to the basal ganglia, but have tended to ignore the massive afferent inputs into this structure, and its possible role in cognitive and motivational processes. Sensory physiologists have concentrated on the striking polysensory input from midline thalamic nuclei to the striatum which has led them to suggest that the basal ganglia are instrumental in orienting to a range of sensory inputs. Psychologists have found their niche in examining the role of the basal ganglia in complex behaviours which cannot strictly be called motor or sensory and to which the term cognitive or motivational is applied. Of course, each of these views must be an extreme, for no part of the nervous system can be considered as concerned solely with one aspect of brain function. Even the motor cortex receives a sensory input and is involved in the motor expressions of higher mental functions. Yet to assert that the basal ganglia are concerned with some mystical form of sensory motor integration is to take an equally extreme view for in the last analysis all parts of the nervous system undertake such a process.

That the basal ganglia are involved in motor function is beyond dispute. There is, however, little consensus with regard to its precise role.

Denny-Brown (1962) and Purdon Martin (1967) emphasised the involvement of the basal ganglia in maintenance of posture. Kornhuber (1974) agreed that the basal ganglia are concerned with the generation of slow 'ramp' movements, in contrast to the cerebellum with its involvement in fast 'ballistic' movements. More recent evidence, however, indicates that a view of the basal ganglia as associated with only one class of movement is inadequate. Hallet (1980) has suggested that the basal ganglia are involved in muscle control. He includes both the selection and inhibition of appropriate and inappropriate muscles for a particular action. Elliot *et al.* (1981) have favoured a more general view of the basal ganglia as implicated in the provocation of rest through a capacity to suppress unwanted muscle contraction. It may be, they argue, that the basal ganglia prevent muscular responses that might interfere with or prevent an immediately important act, in the same way that other parts of the brain suppress a mass of sensory information from invading an experience on which one is concentrating. In Parkinson's disease this mechanism may be seen as operating too efficiently without cause, thus producing akinesia.

Marsden is critical of studies claiming a role for the basal ganglia in higher mental processes. He emphasises the difficulties involved in extrapolation from studies of animal behaviour to human beings. From his clinical experience he also emphasises the lack of cognitive impairment that Parkinson's disease patients show. As he points out, it is only in the later stages of the disease when the damage has become more widespread that significant changes appear. Lees and Smith (1983) taking up this criticism, have attempted to clarify the issue by their examination of minor cognitive changes in early stages of the disease. They maintain that these changes are similar to those seen in patients with various forms of frontal lobe damage. This similarity and the connections which exist between the frontal lobes and the basal ganglia assist the frontal lobes in mediating and monitoring behaviour. They did not, however, discuss the form or manner of this assistance. Marsden's position is that a consideration of the anatomy of the basal ganglia must lead to a rejection of the notion of a unitary function. The basal ganglia include a receiving area, the striatum which projects to an executive motor area – the globus pallidus[1] from which the output of the system to other brain areas arises. The function of the receiving and executive areas is likely to differ.

Other commentators have ascribed a role to the basal ganglia in processing and programming movement information and the planning and execution of movement (Stern and Lees, 1982; Parkes, 1982). Marsden through this attention to structure attempts to be more specific. He considers that the striatum may be involved in motor planning both at the level of where and when as well as how. The pallidum, he argues, receiving input from the striatum is concerned with which muscles to activate and in what sequence. Despite this tentative conclusion Marsden emphasises that current understanding of the basal ganglia continues to be largely speculative.

For present purposes, therefore, it must remain sufficient to accept that in Parkinson's disease the loss of dopamine in the basal ganglia through the degeneration of the nigro-striatal pathway, brings about postural abnormalities and deficiencies in the smooth execution of voluntary movement, the precise mechanisms of which remain a matter of debate.

Epidemiology

Similar figures for Parkinson's disease have been reported around the world. Black populations in America and South Africa are slightly less commonly affected than the white populations: worldwide, however, there is a lack of data confirming racial differences. In the United Kingdom there are an estimated one hundred thousand sufferers. In the population over sixty, one in one hundred individuals is affected. Yet Parkinson's disease is not solely a disease of old age as one sufferer in seven is under fifty at the time of diagnosis (Stern and Lees, 1982). Slightly more men than women are affected. Considerable investigation of possible hereditary factors in Parkinson's disease have taken place and the conclusion has recently been reached that the disease is largely non-genetic (Ward, 1983).

Treatment

Medication

Medical treatment of some sort for Parkinson's disease has existed since the turn of the century. The first of such treatments comprised extracts from herbs and plants, such as black henbane and thorn apple. Later a Bulgarian elixir containing belladonna became popular. During the 1940s similar, synthetically prepared medications with fewer side effects were introduced and these remain in use today (Stern and Lees, 1982). This group of drugs are known as anticholinergics. They reduce the symptoms of Parkinson's disease by reducing the action of the neurotransmitter acetylcholine which acts in opposition to dopamine. The anticholinergics have significant effects on the reduction of stiffness and rigidity. They may produce side effects, amongst the most serious of which are glaucoma, where a predisposition to this condition exists and mental confusion.

The discovery by Cotzias in 1967 that oral doses of the dopamine precursor levodopa could dramatically reduce Parkinsonian symptoms, heralded a major advance in treatment. It was hardly surprising that levodopa (or L-dopa) was greeted as a wonder drug. On taking levodopa, certain patients with advanced post-encephalitic Parkinson's disease who had existed for years in almost catatonic states, were suddenly able to move and speak, though in the majority of cases this dramatic improvement was not sustained (Sacks, 1982). The early forms of levodopa required large dosages and gave rise to numerous side effects. Refinements have since been made through the addition of decarboxylase inhibitors which through reducing the peripheral decarboxylisation of levodopa in the gut, liver and kidney and blood vessels, help to reduce these effects and the need for such large dosages. Nevertheless, although there is no doubt that levodopa has remarkedly improved the quality of life for countless patients, it continues to have its limitations and disadvantages. Even with the addition of decarboxylase inhibitors, levodopa is not without side effects. Many patients suffer various degrees of dyskinesia which may worsen over time, and mental disturbance in some patients has been recognised as a problem in the long term. In addition, the effectiveness of the drug may be considerably reduced as the disease progresses. Patients may suffer extreme variation between 'on' and 'off' periods with the on periods becoming shorter and less frequent.

Todes, a psychiatrist diagnosed as suffering from Parkinson's disease at the age of 39 has stated 'The on/off syndrome is without doubt central to patients with chronic Parkinsonism.' After twelve years' experience of the condition he said of himself: 'Flexibility, both internal and external, is at a premium by this stage of the illness, there are only 3 or 4 really good hours a day and hopefully another 6 mediocre ones with mobility. On/off plays havoc with life and hence erodes continuity and confidence' (Todes, 1983). Also in common use is the drug amantadine. This is an anti-viral agent. Its usefulness in Parkinson's disease was discovered by chance in 1968. Amantadine reduces tremor, rigidity and bradykinesia. Its effect is slightly greater than the anti-cholinergics but not as long lasting.

More recent drugs are the ergot derivatives, bromocriptine, lisuride and pergolide. The latter two are still only in experimental use. These act by stimulating dopamine receptors (mimicking the effects of levodopa). In general these drugs are used in combination with levodopa and can help maintain a good response through smoothing out its action.

The last drug currently used in the management of Parkinson's disease is deprenyl, first synthesised in Hungary. Deprenyl is a monoamine oxidase inhibitor.[2] Unlike other drugs in this category, however, it acts selectively blocking only the action of the enzyme which destroys dopamine, allowing the continuation of normal degradation of other monoamines. It thus increases brain dopamine by preventing its breakdown within nerve cells and in the gaps between nerve fibres. It is, therefore, used to enhance the effectiveness of levodopa.

Surgery. Between the 1930s and late 1960s stereotactic surgery (primarily thalamotomy) was carried out for the relief of tremor with relative frequency. The benefits were short lived and undesirable consequences such as speech problems, memory loss and weakness were common. Since the advent of levodopa, surgery has been used less often and is now, in Britain at least, comparatively rare.

Adjunctive Therapies

Physiotherapy

Following the advent of levodopa, physiotherapy fell out of vogue in the treatment of Parkinson's disease. More recently, a resurgence of interest has taken place. Physiotherapists are becoming, it appears, increasingly concerned to develop their skills with this group of patients and to evaluate their intervention. The evaluations which have appeared to date have not, however, shown physiotherapy to have lasting benefit with respect to motor activity (Gibberd *et al.*, 1981). It is nevertheless felt by many therapists and doctors that the active involvement of the patient in the management of his condition through participation in physiotherapy is of considerable psychological importance.

Speech Therapy

A somewhat similar situation exists with respect to speech therapy. Though various evaluations have shown short-term improvements, it appears that benefit is fairly rapidly lost once intervention ceases (Perry and Das, 1981). A recent study by Robertson and Thompson (1984) has however shown that intensive short-term therapy for Parkinson's disease patients may be effective. The short supply of speech therapists generally renders long-term intervention impractical though the innovation of group work is occurring in at least one area.[3] (See also Scott *et al.*, 1985).

Occupational Therapy

Focusing on adjustment rather than remediation, the services of the occupational therapist may of course be invaluable in assisting patients and their families to cope with the practical difficulties of everyday life. To be effective, in a progressive condition such as Parkinson's disease, contact with the occupational therapist must continue from the onset of functional difficulties throughout the course of the illness.

The Tips

The pathology of Parkinson's disease and many aspects of its biochemistry are, therefore, now well understood and there is a considerable *armamentarium* of medications and adjunctive therapies. Some of its manifestations and inconsistencies nevertheless remain mysterious and puzzling.

In many patients, as has already been noted, with the progress of the disease, the problem of initiating movements and in sustaining regular action over a period of time becomes a major restriction. Both patients and professionals refer to this phenomenon as 'freezing'. There has emerged spontaneously amongst patients a folk psychology which offers methods of overcoming this problem. This folk psychology comprises a number of 'tips'. Many of these are widely known amongst sufferers and are accepted as useful ways of getting going. The most common of these are listed in Figure 7.3. Some involve the sufferer's own imagination, some verbal instructions by the sufferer or someone else and some visible objects or sounds. The usefulness of these tips has been widely acknowledged by the medical profession and they are mentioned in much of the literature. Sacks (1982) in his account of the early effects of levodopa on post-encephalitic Parkinsonian patients describes a number of such individual strategies. Purdon Martin (1967) working with similar patients at the Highlands hospital has also described the use of such cues or devices. In professional folklore it is a standing joke that at the call of 'Fire!' Parkinsonian patients will be the first out of the hospital.

Despite the intriguing nature of this phenomenon and its theoretical and clinical potential it has been the subject of only one systematic account (Stern *et al.*, 1982). This involved a postal questionnaire and interviews aimed at discovering the extent and nature of freezing and the kind of action taken to overcome it. Out of 61 patients suffering episodic freezing only 14 had discovered no strategem to override the symptom. As the disease progressed respondents reported freezing became more frequent and individual strategies for getting going less effective.

References to these strategies or tips frequently, however, appear in books written specifically for sufferers and families where they are generally referred to as 'tricks'. Such discussion as there has been about the possible mechanisms underlying this phenomenon is usually in terms of 'sensory reinforcement', the tips or tricks

Figure 7.3: Some of the Strategies Used by Patients to Overcome Freezing

Nails on shoes
Railway lines
Walking over cards on the floor
Instructions to self (inner)
Instructions to self (out loud)
'Heel down'
'One, two'
'Left, right'
Tapping a stick
Instructions from others
Cassette with music
Imagine a brick
Following partner's footsteps
Partner tapping foot
Cracks in pavement
Pools of light
Metronome
White handkerchief
Imagine a white line

being tacitly accepted as physiological rather than psychological phenomena (Duvoisin, 1981). Thus responsibility for encouraging their use has been assigned along with other exercises to the province of physiotherapy (Stern and Lees, 1982).

The chief and common feature of all these tips, however, is a mental element and their serious investigation and discussion has arisen in psychology. The first investigations of sufferers' tips were undertaken before the start of modern drug treatment. Starting in 1926 two Russian psychologists, A.R. Luriya and L.S. Vygotskii, carried out a series of observations and experiments with Parkinsonian patients at the Moscow Institute of Psychology (Luriya, 1932). Luriya's name has been closely associated with conductive education. Thus his analysis of methods of overcoming the deficits produced by Parkinson's disease are of considerable interest here. The broad theoretical context within which the experiments were undertaken, generally unfamiliar in the West, has been described by Sutton (1983). It is nevertheless necessary to give some attention to three important principles originally formulated by Vygotskii and later developed by Luriya and related to his clinical practice. These principles may also be considered for their wider reference to conductive education. They are the relationship between speech and thinking, dynamic functional localisation and the notion of stage.

Speech and Thinking

A central tenet of the position of Vygotskii and Luriya is that human consciousness cannot be reduced to its physiological base. The physiological substrate is a necessary but not a sufficient condition for its development. Mental functions are viewed not as simply functions of structure but as processes that are externally formed, systemically developed and hierarchically organised in the course of the developing child's interactions with the world, especially the social world. Vygotskii regarded the development of speech as crucial in the formation of all human mental complex cognitive processes. Speech, developed initially for communication between people, had more profound consequences. Unlike all other species man organises mental processes and directs his activity through signals, words which have been socially created (Luriya, 1966).

The physiologist, I.P. Pavlov, also in the 1920s, described speech as a second signalling system of reality, a system which is crucial to the establishment of human consciousness and to man's capacity for intentional, planned activity. According to Vygotskii, human mental development occurs as a product of interaction between children and their social world, the world of adults, in which they acquire and internalise human experience to create qualitatively new mental structures. Speech is a most important means by which this occurs (though not the only one). The adult names objects for the child. In time the child learns to name the object out loud himself. Eventually he knows its name. The external communication has become an internal sign. In Vygotskii's view, therefore, all mental functions make their appearance *twice* in the course of development. First as social activity between individuals or inter-mental functions. Then as internal properties of the child's thinking or intra-mental functions (Luriya, 1966).

Dynamic Functional Localisation

Out of Vygotskii's analyses emerged a complex concept central to Luriya's subsequent neuropsychology. This was the conceptualisation of the brain as a functional system, a view countering both the narrow localisation theory and the holistic model of brain activity which existed in mutual opposition at the time. Luriya's 'system' refers to highly differentiated zones and levels of the brain working in concert. This is functional because of its inherent ability to allow the

formation of new relations between areas according to the requirements of particular tasks. New skills and activities are not, therefore,
dependent on morphological modifications of the brain. Dynamic
functional localisation (Luriya, 1976) was an extension of this
conceptualisation of the brain as a functional system, the dynamism
being manifest at two levels, the immediate and the long term. In the
short term, as new forms of activity are acquired and mastered so both
the psychological structure of that activity is altered and its cortical
organisation is modified.

Luriya illustrated this with the example of writing. In the child,
learning to write is a conscious 'expanded' activity, depending upon
memorising the visual form of every letter. It takes place through a
chain of isolated motor impulses each of which is responsible for only
one element of the graphic structure. With practice the structure of the
process is altered and writing converted to what Luriya termed a
'single kinetic melody' or automatic skill which no longer requires the
memorising of the visual form of each isolated letter and individual
motor impulses for the making of every stroke. The participation of
primary areas of the auditory and visual zones of the cortex, essential
in the early stages of formation of any activity, are no longer
necessary in its later stages. In the longer term dynamism refers to the
way in which as the structure of cognitive activity becomes more
complex over the course of psychological ontogenesis so the
functional relationship between areas of the brain alters. The
establishment of higher cognitive processes is dependent on the
unimpaired development of elementary sensory ones. Concepts
cannot be formed without initial percepts. During development,
however, their relationship changes. Higher processes obtain
independence from and then dominance over the elementary ones.
From the concept of dynamic functional localisation, Vygotskii
predicted damage to the same area of the brain would have different
consequences in adults from those which would occur in children. A
view which has been endorsed by later western workers such as Hebb
(1942) and Geschwind (1974). Both aspects of dynamic functional
localisation, the short- and the long-term, were crucial to Luriya's
later work in the restitution of cortical function and are important
considerations in the interpretation of the working of the sufferer's tips.

Stages

Vygotskii like the many investigators of mental development better
known in the West, described the emergence of adult cognitive

activity as occurring through a series of discrete, invariant stages. Within each stage growth is quantitative. The child increases his repertoire and mastery of skills to a certain level of complexity until the change in amount leads to a change in kind and there is a sudden qualitative transformation in the structure of the child's thinking. Luriya subscribed to Vygotskii's stage theory and undertook a series of experiments to exemplify stage change in children with respect to one particular aspect; the verbal regulation of motor acts (e.g. Luriya, 1959a).

He also described the dissolution of verbal regulation in adulthood as a result of pathological states of the brain though here he made only fleeting reference to Parkinson's desease (Luriya, 1959b).

Luriya and Parkinson's Disease

In Parkinson's disease the damage to the basal ganglia impedes what Luriya described as the 'kinetic melody' of automatic movement. Concentration and effort help the sufferer to an extent. At a certain stage in the course of the disease, however, these are no longer sufficient for the initiation of movement or its smooth execution.

Luriya had started his early experiments as a result of observing that certain patients who had difficulty in walking across a floor were easily able to climb stairs. He hypothesised that, when climbing stairs, each step follows a signal to which patients' motor impulses respond: the successive, automatic flow of movements that occurs when walking along a level surface is thus replaced by a chain of separate motor reactions. A conscious response to each link in a chain of isolated signals replaces the subcortically organised, involuntary system of ordinary walking. In his first experiment (Luriya, 1932), patients were asked to walk over a series of cards which had been placed on the floor to form a track. The patients were able to do this without difficulty. By making the task analogous to the act of walking upstairs, the mental process involved in walking had been reorganised. *Because the brain is a functional system* he concluded *it allows different means to the achievement of the same result.*

In his next experiment patients were asked to squeeze a rubber bulb in a steady sequence. Certain subjects found it impossible to squeeze regularly and with a constant pressure. Luriya then asked them to wink and squeeze the bulb at the same time. He thought that the patients would be able to use a system which was still intact to produce their own cues to act as stimuli for actions. The wink would become a conditional signal. This method of eliciting the response was indeed effective with these patients. When speech is intact, subjects may be able to initiate an action upon their own verbal instruction. When this is not possible, however, the internalised verbal system may still be used to bring the initiation of movements under cortical control. Luriya demonstrated this in his last set of experiments. Some patients were not able to squeeze the bulb repeatedly when asked 'Squeeze five times.' Yet when told to squeeze in answer to a question such as 'How many points on the star in the Kremlin flag?' or 'How many wheels on a wagon?', they were able to squeeze the correct number of times. *The motor action had become dependent on a cognitive act, thus altering its underlying structure and creating a new functional system.*

Luriya's account raises many questions of experimental design and method. Although he referred to these experiments in subsequent discussions he never gave any more detail. The focus of his later clinical practice was the restitution of function after cerebral trauma, thus, he did not return to the investigation of Parkinson's disease, a progressive condition. Despite the limitations the experiments were important in that they demonstrated, like the sufferers' own tips, the capacity of the intact second signalling system to override or circumvent a lower order deficit.

Conductive Education

The fact that sufferers can in certain circumstances overcome the effects of their motor disorder demonstrates that the potential for movement remains. In addition to present understanding of the neuropathology of the condition, Parkinson's disease may be described neuropsychologically as causing a break in a functional system in which higher order mental functions usually remain intact. From this starting point, the results of Luriya's early investigations and the extensive empirical evidence of the sufferers' tips, it was hypothesised that the creation of new functional systems by verbal means might open up a much needed and useful additional approach to rehabilitation. Information about conductive education with children, limited as it was, suggested that analogous processes might be operating in that system. Enquiries were, therefore, made to discover whether work had ever been carried out at the Institute in Budapest with Parkinson's disease sufferers. It was discovered that such work was indeed taking place and appeared to achieve remarkable results. This suggested that structural intervention and practice could bring about a neuropsychological reorganisation with a significant rehabilitative outcome.

Since its beginnings, the Institute for the Motor Disabled has provided teaching for Parkinson's disease patients. The extent to which this has occurred appears to have varied. In the mid-sixties Cotton (1965) visited the Institute and reported that Parkinson's disease patients were amongst the adults attending as outpatients. Their presence was again noted by a visiting physiotherapist in 1973 (Carrington, 1973). No further attention appears to have been paid to this group by foreign commentators until the early 1980s. At this time several physiotherapists working with Parkinson's disease in Britain, having learnt of conductive education through Ester Cotton, reported using 'Petö methods'. Little detail regarding the methods used has been made available and short-term evaluations have not been encouraging (Gibberd *et al.*, 1981; Franklyn *et al.*, 1981)

One physiotherapist, Rowena Kinsman, who had visited the Institute for the Motor Disabled in 1982 to look specifically at the work with adult hemiplegic patients came across a fairly recently established group of Parkinson's disease patients. The impression that this made on her was such that she started her own group amongst hospital outpatients, based on what she had seen.

Kinsman has not as yet evaluated the effectiveness of her group though she reported (personal correspondence) that while patients perform the routines successfully during the sessions the carry over to the home and to everyday situations is limited. Kinsman does, however, advocate her approach for Parkinson's disease (1983a, 1983b).

The Practice in Budapest

In May 1984 I had the opportunity to go to Hungary for ten days to look at the work of the Institute with special reference to Parkinson's disease. I returned to Budapest in October 1984 and saw many of the same patients again. There follows an account of the practice of conductive education as I observed it and of the patients' experience of it. The aim of conductive education for the patients, as in the case of children, is the achievement of orthofunction. Three elements stand out as of particular importance in this approach, as the account will illustrate. First, the establishment of a positive emotional state amongst the group members; second, the development and use of verbal regulation; finally the creation of rhythmical intention.

Because of lack of space at the Villányi út site the Parkinson's disease group was being held some distance away, in a gymnasium in a school basement. Two sessions of almost two hours each were held from Monday to Friday and twice weekly half-hour speech sessions also took place. There are about 15 'students' in each group, most of whom were in their sixties and seventies, though they included both somewhat older and younger sufferers. Most students had been diagnosed as having Parkinson's disease between five and ten years ago, a few, however, were diagnosed more than ten years ago and some less than five years ago. Members attended the group twice or three times weekly. Sufferers living in the counry came in monthly with their relatives for instruction and advice. Two conductors took it in turns to lead the group through the sessions. One or two student conductors were usually also present and gave particular attention to newer group members and to sequences with which any particular individual had difficulty.

The 'Warm Up'. At the beginning of each session the group members were seated at tables. First, attention was given to the control of tremor by the fixation and extension of the arms in various positions. Hands were clasped over the head and on the table, turned palm up and then palm down. Then fine movements were practised with each hand in turn. During these sequences, students were concentrating not on the tremor but on the smooth execution of the movement. To establish rhythm and flow of movement the group were led through a rapid sequence of standing up, sitting down, bending over, etc. As soon as the activity began the students began to concentrate and became alert and attentive. This is in itself a goal of the teaching for the achievement of the ability to observe and attend is an important step towards the capacity for self-awareness and self-control.

The style of the conductor was vigorous, firm and encouraging. She gave an instruction for a particular action and followed this with a brisk count up to five, which the group members joined in. This style is necessary, as the conductors explain, because of the nature of the problems experienced by Parkinson's disease sufferers. As the disease is characterised by difficulties with the initiation, smooth execution and termination of movement, it is important for each sequence of movements practised in the class to begin smartly and with momentum, to be carried out with a rapid regular rhythm and to finish cleanly. In other conditions affecting adults such as multiple sclerosis and hemiplegia, as well as with the children, group members may repeat the instruction, given by the conductor in the first person (I raise my arm) before they start counting. Within the Parkinson's disease group the instructions themselves are often brief and although the students will sometimes repeat a one-word instruction, in general, movement and counting commence simultaneously, immediately following the conductor's command. The instruction creates the intention. Whereas a hemiplegic or a multiple sclerosis sufferer needs time to co-ordinate intention and movement, in Parkinson's disease a delay will cause this co-ordination to break down.

Once these sequences have been completed, every set of routines is directed towards a specific function. An accomplished achievement of the function is the goal and end product of the routine and the various sequences are thus regarded as *preparations* for function.

Hand-writing. Newly sharpened pencils were given out to each class member. Instructions are then called out by the conductor for a series of specific fine hand movements. The pencils were twiddled between the fingers and then passed from thumb to first finger, first with one hand and then the other, always with the same rapid but measured pace.

Exercise books were then handed out. Each class member has his own book to provide a continuous record of progress. On each page the conductors had ruled double spaced red lines to serve as guidelines for writing. Within one set of lines the conductor had written a looped series of writing patterns and within the other a phrase. The task to be performed was to copy both pattern and phrase into the exercise book, first with one hand then the other. This was carried out with obvious enjoyment and considerable pride. The degree of control shown in the scripts varies somewhat but all the class members succeeded in producing large rounded letters. All the exercise books I saw had begun with characteristic Parkinsonian micrographia. All showed improvement over time in size, control and fluency and in the majority this improvement was very marked (see Figure 7.4). Later on in the session a similar routine took place with group members writing on two blackboards at the front of the class. This time the group members had to draw the guidelines themselves and again had to use each hand. The conductor emphasised the importance of keeping the free hand in contact with a firm surface to help maintain balance and control.

Daily Routine. In an adjoining room, chairs had been set out in rows. Here a variety of sequences were practised aimed at enabling the

Figure 7.4: Writing Patterns and Phrases

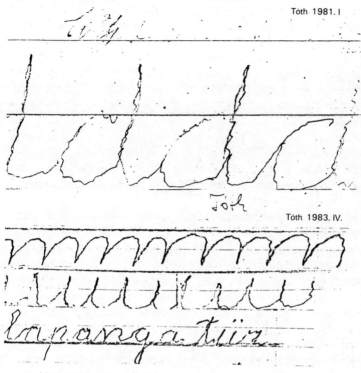

Tóth 1981. I

Tóth 1983. IV.

(a) Improvement in control

Sárkány 1981. December

Sárkány 1983. XII.

(b) Maintenance of size

Figure 7.5: Free Writing. Increase in Size and Clarity over 22 Months

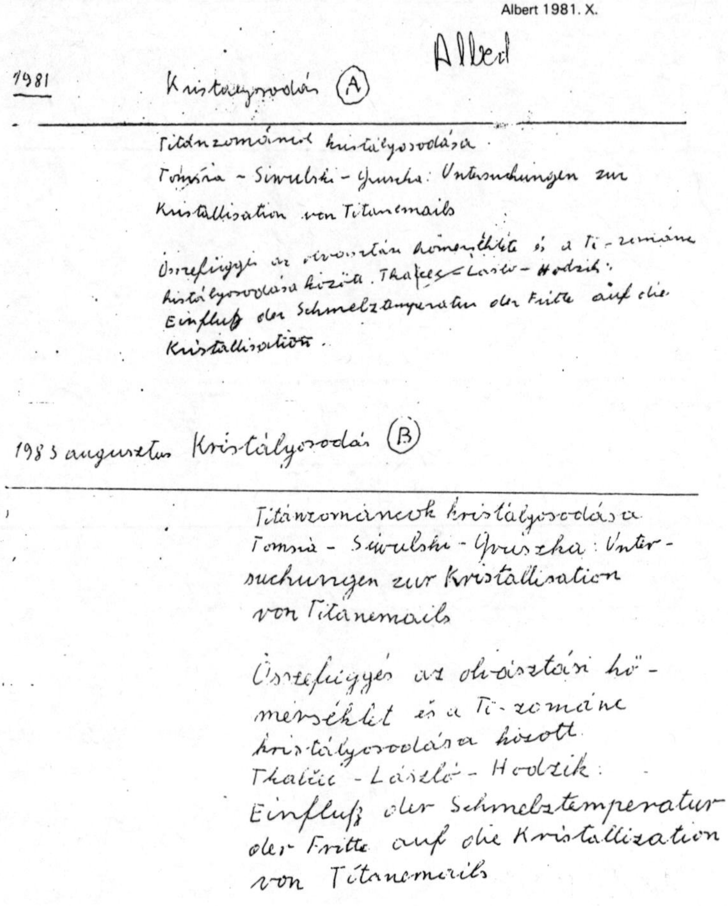

performance of ordinary day-to-day activities, e.g. dressing, washing, getting up out of a chair, getting on and off buses, etc. Some of the actions are accompanied by poems and songs, the words of which all the group members know by heart. Their strong rhythm served to facilitate the action. While one conductor led the group, the other and the student conductors joined in with the counting, recitation and singing, correcting anyone whose action was not quite right.

Figure 7.6: Free Writing. Increase in Size and Clarity over
11 Months

Vadas
1982. I.

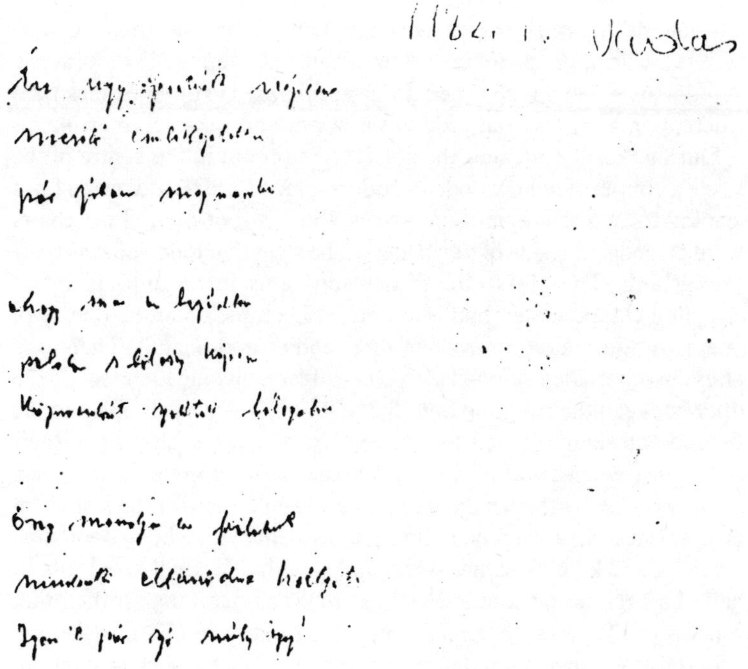

Vadas
1982. XI.

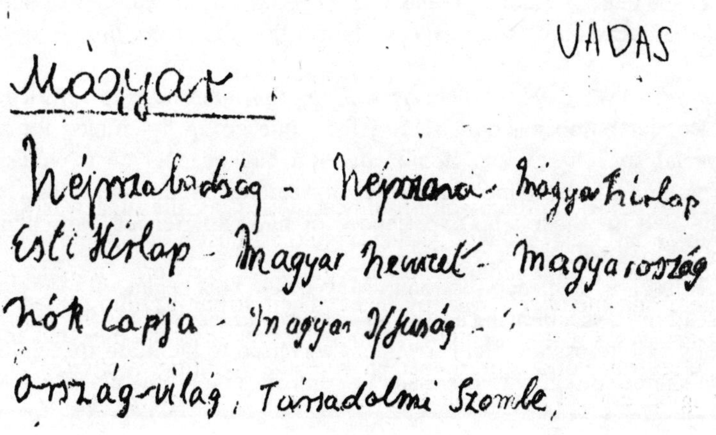

Coping with Obstacles. The chairs were put away and the class members moved into a large circle. To everyone's obvious delight a sequence then began which involved walking, walking backwards, high stepping and then marching around the gym. The students swung their arms purposefully and all join in counting 'one, two, one, two' and singing vigorous, marching songs. The rhythm was then changed to a slow march to extend the length of step and to practise maintenance of balance. Then it was accelerated to double quick time whereupon the class ran around the room amidst much merriment.

During these sequences the conductors set out in the centre of the circle a couple of light, wooden 'ladders' placed end to end on the floor leading to two low gymnastic boxes about a foot high. Two chairs were placed at the side of the ladders. The sight that followed was quite astonishing. The class circled the apparatus in an anti-clockwise direction clapping their hands in time with a rapid count of 'one, two, one, two' alternately in front of their bodies and behind. Then, one after the other, they stepped along the ladders, placing their feet on the floor between the rungs up onto the first box, down, then up on to the second and then rejoined the circle. There was no faltering in their pace, no freezing and no loss of balance. The apparatus was then whisked away by the conductors and class members for the last event of the session, a hugely enjoyable sequence in which bouncing, catching and kicking games were played with a football-sized rubber ball. To become orthofunctional, as well as relearning all the other aspects of life which become a problem in Parkinson's disease, the sufferer must once again learn to react rapidly and appropriately to the unexpected and unpredictable.

Two hours of concentrated activity had taken place – tiring enough for even healthy elderly people. No one, however, appeared tired and all the participants were eager to affirm that they were not.

Speech. Two days a week, as soon as the main session finished, a smaller number (about six) of the same group assembled for a special speech session. Some attention had been given to voice, breathing and facial mobility in the main session but this small class is intended for those who experienced or had experienced particular difficulties with speech.

I observed a speech session in May 1984. This began with simple breathing tasks, blowing a straw in a glass of water and blowing a ping pong ball across a table. Movement was used to facilitate speech in the same indirect way it is used to control tremor. The class began chanting consonant and vowel combinations beating out the rhythm with a pencil on the table top to help maintain regularity. This was carried out first by the group as a whole, and then individually. The class then went on to tackle tongue twisters, using strong arm action to help increase the volume of their speech.

The sequence of exercises served as a reminder of the close relationship between speech, mental and motor acts. The conductor wrote a series of words upon the blackboard from which the class members had to make anagrams. This was followed by the appearance of a huge word on the board, the task being to make as many anagrams as possible from each syllable. Next, each member of the group was given a die with a letter on each side. The conductor counted to five and rolled the die, whereupon the individual concerned had to say the name of a town. One gentleman turned up an N. He looked straight at me and shouted out 'Nottingham!' Lastly the class were given photographs of various places in Hungary which they had to point out on a map. They then had to speak to the rest of the class for a few minutes about the place. One man in his fifties, a schoolteacher, who had only joined the group three weeks earlier and who had considerable speech problems was shown how and encouraged to use his arms and body movements while speaking.

Six months later when I returned to Budapest, this gentleman no longer experienced difficulties with speech. Whereas in May he was considering taking early retirement because of ill health, by October he felt confident of his ability to continue. The latest improvement that he had noticed was that, about three weeks earlier, he had regained the ability to put slides into a projector.

Sufferers' Experiences

On each occasion that I was present, several members came over to talk to me after the group dispersed. All were enthusiastic about conductive education and were full of praise for the conductors. One woman, herself a teacher, stated quite firmly that the conductors were the best teachers she had ever seen. A smartly dressed gentleman, a former chemical engineer in his early sixties, was eager to tell his story. He had been diagnosed six years previously. He had stopped working and eighteen months ago his condition was so bad that he was taking up to two hours to dress and was having difficulty in making himself understood in shops. He then joined the Conductive Education Group at the suggestion of his neurologist. His improvement had been such that now he was able to dress in ten minutes, his speech was perfectly clear and he had even returned part time to work. To show how mobile he was and how well he felt he stood up from a chair without holding on, ran around the room, sang a song and demonstrated a complicated Hungarian folk dance! A lady in her sixties had also been attending for 18 months. When she first came she had trouble walking and was very rigid. Proudly she told me that she now came to the class on foot – a 50-minute walk – and that she was once again able to play the harmonium. She was still a little stiff, she said, but this was improving. One of the older frail women had been housebound and hardly able to move across the room. Now she regularly travelled across Budapest on three trams to attend the sessions.

The Conductors' View

The conductors are evidently extremely enthusiastic and committed to their work. They firmly stress that their role is a general educational one and should not be seen as restricted to leading a routine of physical exercises. Every aspect of their interaction with the group and its individual members is part of the teaching and learning process. While working with and through the group structure, the concern of the conductors is with every individual member and his functioning within the group. The conductors recognise that, significant as the physical disability arising from Parkinson's disease is, the withdrawal from life which is highly likely to accompany it unless motivation can be maintained is an even greater disability. The creation of motivation is thus an essential part of conduction. The conductor must help each individual build up his self-awareness, confidence and thereby his capacity for and facility in social relations. Participation in the group is thus in itself practice for participation in ordinary social life. Through the group the patients should lose their sense of social isolation.

Conductors also stress the particular importance of rhythmic intention in Parkinson's disease. The group members are taught to perform movements precisely and correctly. Practice, however, is not viewed as a mechanistic repetition of meaningless motor acts but as a conscious process of learning optimal motor solutions to particular problems. It is the achievement of the functional goal which is of major importance.

The Status of Conductive Education for Parkinson's Disease Patients in Hungary

Most of the Parkinson's disease group members had been referred by one neurologist, Dr K. Baraczka of the Neurology Clinic of the Semmelweiss Medical School. She had been approached by the conductors at the time that this group was established. Initially sceptical, she had agreed to try out conductive education. She has followed up thirty patients in the group over two-and-a-half years. The results of this evaluation are shortly to be published in English. They suggest an overall decrease in drug dosage, improvement in motor and social skills, in psychological state and in sex life. Age and severity of the disease do not preclude the patient deriving benefit from the method. Conductive education can have little effect with Parkinsonian symptoms arising from other conditions, such as arteriosclerosis, or with pre-existing dementia. Social problems such as lack of family co-operation also limit its usefulness.

Clinical and personal evidence of the effectiveness of conductive education is such that the question must be asked as to why it has aroused such little interest amongst Hungarian neurologists. Until recently, little had been done to publicise this aspect of the work of the Institute. In 1983, however, the group's senior conductor had presented a paper at a rehabilitation conference in Szeged. In November 1984, Dr Baraczka presented her results to the Hungarian Neurological Congress where, it seems, much interest as well as incredulity was expressed. She considered that the lack of previous interest has been in part due to a narrowness of vision amongst the medical profession and a bias towards drug therapy and more accepted practices. Pharmacological and pharmaceutical research is well established in Hungary, indeed one of the newer drugs used in the treatment of Parkinson's disease, selegeline hydrochloride (deprenyl) was first synthesised there. All the drugs prescribed in the West are in use in Hungary though supplies of some are more readily available than others. Stereotactic surgery for the relief of tremor appears to be carried out more frequently than is current practice in Britain.[4]

Organisational factors may also have played a part in the lack of general awareness within Hungary of conductive education for adult groups. While conductive education forms the official provision for motor-disordered children, with respect to adults it has no such status. Although the Institute was originally under the control of the Ministry of Health, in 1963 this control was transferred to the Ministry of Education. It appears that much of the adult work which had been undertaken until this time, fell into temporary abeyance. Now that conductive education with adults has received some attention both abroad (following the Institute's international seminar in October

1984) and at home (following the Hungarian Neurological Congress in November 1984), and the Institute is about to move to new prestigious premises, it will be of interest to see whether the work itself will achieve greater recognition and status.

Importing Conductive Education for Parkinson's Disease Patients to Britain

The practical problems of importing conductive education *en bloc* to Britain are of course enormous. Apart from these considerations the question must be asked whether the method can be successfully transplanted into a different cultural context. Group work, for example, is a feature of the Hungarian educational system. Collective achievement rather than competition is a norm which does not have to be taught to group members. Apart from initial shyness there is no resistance to participation.

In Britain the prevailing model of treatment is essentially passive. To a great extent it is something which is 'done to' the patients. In general Parkinson's disease patients are not young and will have already had experience of such treatment. How would they respond to the considerable demands made by an *educational* approach to the problems of overcoming their deficits? How would the relatives react? How would the doctors and para-medicals?

These questions cannot be answered before the attempt to introduce conductive education has been made. Conductive education is not a method of treatment. It makes no claims as a *cure* for Parkinson's disease or any other condition. The improvement in the quality of life which this method of teaching and learning seem to offer, however, is such that every effort to overcome the difficulties of its establishment, both practical and cultural must be worthwhile.

The apparent effectiveness of conductive education in Parkinson's disease is to a certain extent not surprising, for many of its features accord with common experience of the condition. It is widely acknowledged that concentration or willpower and the exhortation of others can help the patient, at least early on, to overcome both his motor and his intermittent minor cognitive difficulties (Lees and Smith, 1983). The use of tips, too, provides an indirect method of achieving motor acts, demonstrating that the capacity for action still remains, though it becomes increasingly difficult to elicit.

Drug therapy is of course of tremendous value in Parkinson's disease. Physiotherapy and speech therapy have not as yet demonstrated direct long-term benefit. Conductive education may be seen as bridging the gap between the physiological and the psychological. It consolidates through carefully structured practice what the tips may achieve spontaneously.

Apart from its possible clinical value, conductive education is of great theoretical interest and gives rise to many questions. For example, how does the recovery of function which it brings about accord with present views and assumptions regarding the role of the basal ganglia? What are its implications regarding plasticity of function in the brain? Could there be any difference in the rate of progression of the underlying disease in patients receiving conductive education? How far may the reduction in medication be taken and how might the response to medication change over time? It is only by careful monitoring of patients at various stages of the disease and of the precise details of their improvements in performance, that answers to some of these questions could be suggested. Undoubtedly, too, the establishment of conductive education in Britain for Parkinson's disease patients would generate many more questions, questions which, as yet, cannot even be posed.

Notes

1. Although it is not the primary area affected by Parkinson's disease, damage to the globus pallidus does frequently occur in the condition.

2. These are the drugs which inhibit the action of an enzyme, monoamine oxidase, present in various parts of the body including the brain, blood vessels and liver, which destroys excessive amounts of monoamines such as adrenaline, noradrenaline and dopamine.

3. One Midland branch of the Parkinson's Disease Society has the services of a speech therapist who works monthly with several small groups of patients.

4. This is an impression conveyed to me by Hungarian neurologists critical of neuro-surgery although they did not have comparative data. Toth, S. and Vajda, J. (1980) illustrate the optimism regarding stereotactic surgery in Parkinson's disease described to me.

8 FURTHER DEVELOPMENTS

Philippa Cottam and Andrew Sutton

In the earlier chapters we have contrasted conductive education in Hungary, with attempts at the system in Britain. Brief consideration has also been given to its application in other countries. The time has now come to raise two fundamental questions:

(1) What has gone wrong in establishing conductive education outside Hungary?
(2) What is to be done?

What Has Gone Wrong?

It is now 20 years since conductive education was first described by Ester Cotton, and as a result of her enthusiasm, knowledge of the method has spread throughout the world. Interested professionals, teachers, doctors, physiotherapists, psychologists, from a host of countries have visited the Institute in Budapest and many reports have been written. All these profess to the outstanding nature of the approach. The method has 'an almost hypnotic effect on the visitor' (Wilson, 1970). Despite these positive reports interest in conductive education has remained limited to a very small and select group of professionals. Several textbooks have given brief mention to the method (e.g. Finnie, 1981; Woods, 1975; Gordon, 1976; Cruikshank, 1976; Levitt, 1982) but these have done little to stimulate further investigation. Small wonder in some cases. The ultimate reduction of the method was made by Finnie (1981) who only gave an illustration of the 'Peto chair', with no description of the method whatsoever. Woods (1975), on the other hand, wrote a brief but positive account of conductive education. Under the title 'Further Educational Policy' she recognised a certain dissatisfaction with existing approaches and looked forward to a shift in emphasis: 'A method originating in Hungary, the Peto method, which demands active co-operation and concentration is coming to the fore.' Unfortunately this shift has been slow and ten years later the establishment of conductive education in Britain is still only at a very rudimentary stage.

In the late 1960s and early 1970s there was substantial interest created in the method particularly within the Spastics Society. In their newsletter *Spastics News* they published many features on the method with such titles as : 'The Peto Method is more than a Transitory Idea', 'Peto Experiment is Working well here', 'Experts Confer on the Peto Work'. (Knowles, 1968, 1970) Nevertheless, it was not until the 1980s that interest in conductive education flourished – at least as indexed by written reports. Figure 8.1 summarises trends in the output of English-language materials relating to conductive education and derivatives of the method in the West from the first, in 1965, up to the end of 1984.

Throughout the 1970s conductive education had not, however, been dormant. Despite the lack of written materials a small body of professionals, primarily influenced by Ester Cotton, were using conductive education-based approaches in their schools and other centres. Some of these came under the auspices of the Spastics Society, but in recent years professionals in state schools have also tried to introduce the method. These attempts have been extremely enthusiastic and many have gained positive results but, in contrast to the achievements gained in Hungary, these are minimal. In many instances the work bears little resemblance to conductive education as practised in Budapest and often reflects only certain palpable aspects (i.e. rhythmic intention, plinths, etc.) rather than the overall system which seems the key to the method's success. It is fair to say that conductive education as practised at the Institute for the Motor-Disabled in Budapest has never been successfully achieved in Britain, or perhaps even anywhere outside Hungary.

What are the Main Contrasts between Hungarian Conductive Education and Attempts at the Method outside Hungary?

Orthofunction. As Dr Hári pointed out during her visit to Britain in 1968, when consideration was first being given to bringing conductive education to this country: 'the object of conductive education is not to accommodate the severe dysfunctional in an Institute, or to send them to a special school, but to accomplish a basic task to render possible a normal education, travelling in the streets, self-supporting and work' (Hári, 1968). This is what is meant by orthofunction. Yet, while many people are aware that this is the desired outcome of the method no one (except perhaps in Osaka) appears to have succeeded in achieving it. Improvements have been noted in all those experiencing conductive education but these represented only relatively small *quantitative*

Figure 8.1: Trends in Output of English-language Materials on Conductive Education and its Derivatives from 1965 to 1984

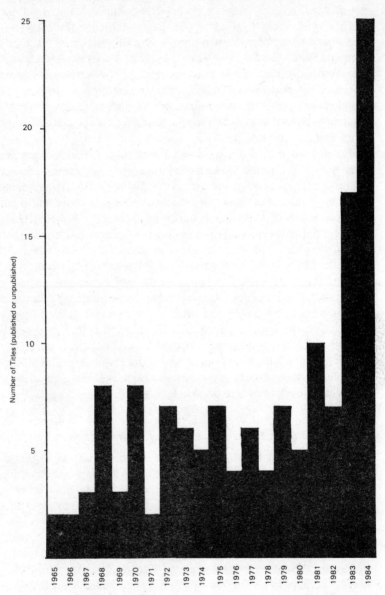

Source: Cottam (1985b).

changes. As a result of using the method, the handicapped child or adult is much more able but can still only function within a 'special' environment. In contrast the majority of cases involved in conductive education in Hungary seem to achieve *qualitative* changes. The motor dysfunction is mastered and the person is able to lead a normal life within society. It is the Institute's philosophy that: 'In order to bring about an equilibrium between child and environment we do not change the environment, but the adaptation of the child's constitution' (Hári, 1968). Without the goal of orthofunction are we really attempting conductive education?

The Group. In Hungary the group is a powerful pedagogic tool. The groups are large, 15 to 20 or more in each group, and are directed towards common educational goals. Outside Hungary the groups tend to be very small, on average six to ten individuals to a group, and the children within them exhibit a wide range of physical and mental handicaps. More importantly 'group' in Britain tends to mean a collection of individuals working together; at the Institute it refers to a particular educational method.

Teaching Method. In Hungary the teaching method is a very complex process, hundreds of programmes are used to teach children or adults to overcome their motor disabilities. 'The conductor is able to monitor the unfolding of the programme and to combine, change, or modify parts of it as she sees fit. She will also see to it that a proper balance between the introduction of new skills and the application of already established ones is maintained and that they mutually reinforce each other' (Hári and Tillemans, 1984a). The conductor does not draw on a range of set programmes but programmes are devised as they are required to meet individual needs. Above all the method is *flexible*, it caters for each individual within the group and reflects any changes that occur.

In contrast the method which is being used in most countries outside Hungary is a much more restricted approach. In developing the 'basic motor pattern' Ester Cotton has drawn out certain aspects of conductive education to develop a range of short programmes which can easily be employed within existing special education systems (Cotton, 1980). While the value of these programmes is not disputed it is important to remember that: 'Conductive Education is a much wider subject dealing with all facets of pre-school training for the cerebral palsied child' (Cotton, 1980). Introduction of the conductive education *system*, however, could mean catastrophic changes in the current special-education regime.

Conductor Training. With the exception of a small number of Japanese conductors (three to date) no one outside Hungary has been willing or able to embark on a four-year training in Budapest. The importance of conductor training to the method's success has, however, been affirmed and re-affirmed: 'Conductive Education stands and falls with the conductor' (Hári, 1974, as reported by Cotton, 1983). It has also been well recognised by English visitors: 'The selection and training of conductors is paramount and is possibly where our systems differ most' (Barker, 1981).

Training outside Hungary is exceedingly limited. Most professionals who are attempting to use conductive education are doing so on the basis of one-week introductory courses run by the Spastics Society, supplemented in a few cases by short observational visits to Budapest. In Britain there is a widespread assumption that conductive education is a physiotherapeutic technique. Possibly physiotherapists feel their training to be most appropriate in view of the physical handicaps of the children and adults involved. Others have stressed Cotton's principle that the 'unity of disciplines is the key to Conductive Education' but 'this is an English notion . . . the trade and training of conductors represents a highly advanced pedagogy. The conductor is above all else a *teacher*' (Sutton, 1984a).

The inadequacy of conductor training at the present time has not gone unnoticed. Cotton (1983) devoted a complete paper to this issue, bringing up many important questions and outlining the Ingfield Manor Training Scheme, which has recently been developed into the suggestion of a two-year course open to the various professionals now trying conductive education in Britain. This would involve a first year in this country to establish a common knowledge base followed by a year of training in Budapest. At the International Seminar on Conductive Education held in October 1984, the problem of conductor training was a central theme in papers by Cotton and Keil. In a review of the seminar Jernqvist (1984b) stated that: 'Training was discussed on several occasions and at some length. We hope that the sense of unity which the seminar has brought into being will encourage future training and exchanges between Ingfield School and the Institute'. Proper conductor training, appears the decisive factor in the successful establishment of conductive education outside Hungary: 'On this solution depends the future of Conductive Education in the West' (Cotton, 1983).

What is to Be Done?

A range of conclusions is possible from the preceding chapters of this book. Perhaps Petö and his followers in Budapest have made a quantum leap in the understanding of physical handicap, by separating out the motor disorders in which, with proper teaching, physical disorder need not result in functional disability. Conversely, perhaps a host of visitors to an exciting and exotic land have been over-eager to interpret what they have observed there as the panacea for terrible human problems that cry out for better solutions than medical science can presently offer. Or perhaps the Institute in Budapest, through the enormous and unquestionable devotion of its staff and its system of total and consistent care, does indeed provide a far better outcome for most of its clients than do our own often sparse, spasmodic and unco-ordinated services – with results which, though correspondingly superior to our own, are not of a revolutionarily different order. One may debate such possibilities endlessly on the basis of presently available information but, at our present state of knowledge, any final conclusions drawn must be recognised as deriving, in part at least, from faith (or prejudice) and not simply from the facts alone. The authors of this book all incline to the view that Petö initiated a quantum leap. They also, however, strongly assert that the issue can only be settled properly by subjecting conductive education to a fair and careful test.

Certainly, the evidence to support the claims made for conductive education have not yet been supported by 'hard' scientific evidence. But hard scientific evidence is not the only basis for human decision-making – and certainly not the basis traditionally relied upon for major innovative change in our education system, far from it. (Nor is it, incidentally, a feature of the physiotherapies currently offered to the motor-disordered in this country.) Meanwhile, those who have actually seen the work of the Institute in Budapest offer the 'soft' evidence of what they have seen there with their own eyes. They may of course have been gullible and over-optimistic in this, their judgement clouded by expectation, language and culture. Nevertheless, on the basis of the accounts brought back from Budapest, great energy has already been devoted and considerable resources diverted to attempting something like conductive education in many contexts and countries outside Hungary. As often happens, therefore, soft evidence is already affecting what we do in this country, whatever the hard scientific justification.

Despite the traditionally low status of careful evaluation in the choice of educational method in this country, the spirit of the times and the current situation with respect to conductive education around the world join to urge that this apparent breakthrough from Budapest should be given a proper trial. For if it is indeed a quantum leap then its implications for established practices and for future policies demand the firmest possible corroboration of its effectiveness. On the other hand, should the apparent promise of this approach prove unfulfilled, then very firm evidence indeed will be required to displace the enormous hope and enthusiasm already directed into conductive education into possibly more productive courses.

The experience of the Birmingham group of researchers in conductive education has suggested six principles that need to be followed to reveal the real worth of conductive education:

(1) conductive education can successfully be transferred out of Hungary only with the Institute's active collaboration in passing on its knowledge and experience;
(2) the system must be established, initially at least, in an institution set up specially to receive it;
(3) the work must be carried out at first in as Hungarian a way as possible;
(4) the outcome of the work must be evaluated;
(5) then, and only then, should conductive education be adapted to our indigenous ways, with the effects of any modifications very carefully monitored; and finally . . .
(6) an account of the essence of conductive education, the active factors in its success, may be offered tentatively for generalisation to new contexts.

1. Collaboration. Visitors to the Institute have repeatedly affirmed the supreme importance of conductor training. In Hungary it takes four gruelling years to train highly selected young people to be conductors. Somewhere in this complex process of socialisation, indoctrination, academic study and daily hard practical experience, the would-be conductors absorb the essence of the work and, however implicitly, begin to 'know' how to do conductive education. At a recent Belgian symposium on the Petö method Dr Hári stressed this point to emulators and would-be emulators abroad:

A method can be learned on a course but *the system of Conductive*

Education cannot be applied by conductors who have received a training in Conductive Education of less than four years. Gaining results from Conductive Education is a function of the training of the conductors. . . One must understand what it is that one is calling Conductive Education or the Petö method at this symposium. (Hári, 1981b, translated from the French, emphasis in original)

Or, more succinctly: 'One can come to the Institute for eight days and know that one wants to do it: in more visits of eight days one can never learn how to do it' (Hári, personal communication). Certain features of conductor training at the Institute, however, present enormous difficulties for foreigners who would like to train there:

- the training is closely integrated with practical work;
- conductive education demands a high level of personal communication between teacher and taught (most basically trainee conductors have to speak the same language as their pupils!);
- conductive education is a developmental system of intervention in which those who receive it change, and training must cover the whole of this process;
- conductive education is a group method and it is a lengthy and skilful job to form an effective group.

It is hard to see how access to knowledge and experience of the Institute in Budapest is possible unless the staff there feel that it might be as important for them to overcome such difficulties as it is for those who wish to learn from them. That it *is* possible to overcome some of these difficulties has been demonstrated by the Institute in Osaka, Japan.

2. A Special Institution. Conductive education is radically different from established practices outside Hungary. It is not simply that certain of its aspects clash with aspects of other systems of education and therapy but that conductive education might potentially render obsolete our present special-education or physiotherapeutic services for the motor-disordered. There is, therefore, something intrinsically implausible about seeking to introduce conductive education into the nursery and infants' department of schools for the physically handicapped where, if it were successful, it would deny the primary and senior departments most of their non-orthopaedic pupils. The effect of this would be to lower school rolls below viability level and disrupt the whole system. Subsections of institutions such as schools cannot successfully operate according to goals quite different, even quite contrary to the goals of the institution as a whole. The importation of conductive education requires more than just new methods to be slotted into existing curricula or programmes of treatment, more even than the provision of an establishment where this highly unfamiliar pedagogy can be implemented to the full. At the very least it requires the active goodwill of education authorities willing to accommodate this alien organism within their wider system of identification, assessment, placement and integration of handicapped pupils – and correspondingly sympathetic medical services. Again, the Japanese have indicated that this can be done.

3. The Hungarian Way. Petö's Institute has accumulated 40 years' experience. Its way of working is of course a Hungarian way, every single aspect of which may be neither necessary, appropriate, nor even possible in Britain or other countries outside Hungary. We do not yet know, however, which aspects of the system are essential and conductive and which merely superficial and Hungarian – or even, whether certain aspects are both Hungarian and essential. Take, for example, the roles of music and the group in conductive education. Following the work and inspiration of Kodály, music occupies an important place in Hungarian education and, since the end of the Second World War, the principles of collective upbringing have been far more influential in Hungary than in Britain. But in conductive education, do music and the group fulfil essential roles or are they merely local peculiarities? If we wish to import conductive education into an educational system that is not very musical and far from collective, then initially our conductive education will have to incorporate such factors – even if this demands an artificial and protected environment – at least until it demonstrates the same order of results as in Hungary. Conductive education is a complex mechanism . . . we should not tinker with it until we are sure that we have it working satisfactorily.

4. Evaluation. To demonstrate conductive education one must define the physical and mental status of those who receive this intervention. Outcomes must be compared with those of existing systems of provision. Such research would face problems such as the inevitably limited numbers involved in a first successful transfer of conductive education out of Hungary, the question of what constitutes a legitimate 'match' for control group purposes and the need to create new measurements in an as yet uncharted field. Yet there exists a huge comparison population receiving other provisions and, if conductive education does indeed prove a quantum leap, then its effects should stand out despite methodological problems.

5. *Modification.* If British people do conductive education in Britain with British children then the system would inevitably adapt to British ways. Such a process of naturalisation is very clear (to British eyes) in accounts and films of the Institute in Osaka where, however conductive the regime and the practice, they are certainly also very Japanese. This naturalisation process is not only inevitable, it is also desirable. The relationship between educational practice and the wider life of a country is no accident: they are mutually dependent. Whilst an altogether alien system of education might be maintained artificially for experimental purposes in a protected environment, it will not survive intact in the outside world if it proves incompatible in important respects with our own way of doing things – however valued its product. If conductive education in the Hungarian fashion is successfully transplanted for evaluation in a demonstration project outside Hungary, it is still not necessarily ready for wider promulgation. Modifications may have been made from the outset (these will have to be carefully monitored) but the wider society will almost certainly expect further changes to suit local conditions (the emphasis on music or the group, for example). Adaptations may embrace not just specifics of method, however, but even the criterion of orthofunction, since our own notion of integrating handicapped children into normal schools would deny us the clear-cut statement of success or failure available in the Hungarian education system. Major adaptations at this stage would have to be very carefully monitored indeed, in case the essence of conductive education were to be dissolved and lost in the process. If conductive education is successfully demonstrated outside Hungary then it must be recognised that its further incorporation into a national system of prevention will have to be one of natural accommodation.

6. *Explication.* Adaptation of conductive education in the transition to a new host culture enhances the possibility of deriving some of its underlying mechanisms, pedagogic, psychological and neuro-psychological and separates out which aspects are superficially

Hungarian and which essentially conductive. This process of theory-building is important if the experience of conductive education is to offer wider, more generalised benefits.

It seems essential to follow these principles, in the order presented if we are to gain any potential benefit from the skill and experience of the Institute in Budapest, verify the effectiveness of its approach and generate communicable knowledge of how it works. It is counter-productive, for example, to carry out comparative evaluation of schemes implemented without a sufficient knowledge base and already adapted to the demands of existing institutions. The latter course is not only wasteful of the efforts of those involved in specific schemes but also puts at risk the wider general endeavour to establish whether or not Petö and his followers have indeed made a qualitative leap in the understanding of motor disorder. A principled and ordered approach allows not only for the establishment of formal bodies of practical and theoretical knowledge but also the possibility to exit from the system at the evaluation stage should this appear appropriate. It also holds out reciprocal benefits for conductive education in Hungary, through close exposure to other ways of thinking and working and through the development of research methodologies, which could have important effects on the further development of conductive education in its native land.

A Political Question

Conductive education implies radical change in the way that society provides for the motor-disordered. With respect to children, for example, it denies special schools for the physically handicapped and straightforward integration alike:

> If we are aiming at total happiness and fulfilment for the whole child, then we could perhaps accept that a relatively short space of time on such a specific programme of rehabilitation suitably adapted to our own culture, might indeed be a short cut towards the personal independence so necessary for future life. Academic achievement without physical independence has not produced much happiness for some of the cerebral palsied of past years. (Kearslake, 1970)

For 20 years now the development of conductive education in this country has been in the hands of the professionals and their employing institutions. Despite the hard work and high hopes of individuals, these 20 years have not seen a substantial effect upon our wider national understandings or services, and conductive education has remained largely unknown, misunderstood or ignored. Most importantly, it has not been brought to the attention of those who are the most entitled to know of it and judge it, the families of young motor-disordered children and adults suffering from motor disorders. Indeed, the argument may be heard that parents and patients ought to be actively 'protected against false hopes'. Yet unless the people with the most powerful imperative of all to get something done about conductive education apply individual and corporate pressure, there seems little chance that the next 20 years will see substantial changes either. Services and provisions depend upon political forces. Politicians allocate resources, 'cut the cake', in response to many influences amongst which a system's worth or effectiveness may be a relatively minor consideration. Conductive education *could* be taken seriously in this country – but probably only in a response to a national demand. The importation of conductive education is, therefore, ultimately a political issue. The chief technical aspect is that the job be done properly. Professionals on their own can neither create an appropriate political climate nor ensure an adequate programme of work. It is also a long-term matter involving far more than simply new methods, treatments or programmes. Should it prove possible to extract, evaluate and explicate conductive education (a lengthy process in itself) then many years would pass before its possible benefits were available to all the motor-disordered. In the meantime existing professionals need not see conductive education as a threat: there is already more than enough unmet need in other areas for their generic skills.

Britain had a head start over most other countries in the 'discovery' and further exploration of conductive education and there is probably a greater interest in this approach in this country than in any other outside Hungary. Britain has even acted as a mediator or interpreter of conductive education to the rest of the world. But if consideration of conductive education does now shift to a higher level, then our earlier experience confers no interest advantage. All countries start the new stage at an equal footing. If we in Britain do not urgently devote serious consideration to conductive education then some other country, with greater political motivation to overcome the effects of motor disorder, most certainly will.

Some Useful Addresses

Birmingham Conductive Education Project

Correspondent: Andrew Sutton
Department of Psychology
University of Birmingham
Birmingham B15 2TT
England

Conductive Education Group of Australia

Correspondent: Lynne Cooper
O'Dea Road
Koyuga 3622
Australia

Conductive Education Interest Group

Correspondent: Lillemor Jernqvist
Ingfield Manor School
Five Oaks
Billingshurst RH14 9AX
England

Mozgássérültek Petö András Intézete

Correspondent: Dr Mária Hári
Budapest XII
Kútvölgyi út 6
Hungary H-1125

BIBLIOGRAPHY

Akós, K. *Scientific Studies in Conductive Pedagogy* (Institute of Conductive Education of the Motor Disabled, Budapest, 1975)

Antalffy, G. *A Short Geography of Hungary* (Corvina, Budapest, 1977)

Aubrey, C., Sutton, A. '"Budapest" – a Brief Sample of the Copy-writing of School-age pupils at the Institute for Motor Disorders, Budapest', unpublished manuscript, 1985

Bachmann, W., Gordos-Szabó, A. and Lányi-Engelmayer, A. *Biographies of Hungarian Educators* (Schindele, Rheinstetten, 1977)

Bagnall, D. 'Learning Skills the Peto Way', *New Zealand Herald*, 2 July (1984)

Barker, M. 'Conductive Education Unit Staff Visit to the Institute', unpublished manuscript, 1981

Bate, E. 'Classroom Reports on Consultation in Conductive Education, September 1981–June 1982', unpublished manuscript, 1982

───── 'An Experiment in Conductive Education, Special Grade One', unpublished manuscript, 1983

───── and Kucerna, E. 'Adapted Conductive Education (Peto Method) in Special Grade One', unpublished manuscript, 1981

───── and Kucerna, E. 'Conductive Education Program Report, Special Grade One Class, 1983–1984', unpublished manuscript, 1984

Bencédy, J. *Public Education in Hungary* (Corvina, Budapest, 1982)

Bernshtein, N.A. *The Co-ordination and Regulation Movements* (Pergamon, Oxford, 1967)

Bowen, J. *Soviet Education: Anton Makarenko and the Years of Experiment* (University of Wisconsin Press, Madison, 1962)

Bronfenbrenner, U. *Two Worlds of Childhood: USSR and USA* (Penguin, Harmondsworth, 1974)

Budd, B. 'Report of a Visit to the Institute of Conductive Education', unpublished manuscript, 1975

───── 'Refusing to Believe: "You Can't Do Anything With Subnormals"', *Spastics News*, September (1977), pp. 3–4

───── and Evans, E. 'What is their Future? An Experimental Project in Conductive Education with the Multiply Handicapped', *Apex*, vol. 4, no. 2 (1977), pp. 18–22

Burland, R. 'The Development of Verbal Regulation of Behaviour in Cerebral Palsied Multiply Handicapped Children', *Journal of Mental Subnormality*, vol. 15 (1969), pp. 85–9

───── 'The Implications for Speech Therapy of a Study of the Verbal Regulation of Behaviour in Multiply Handicapped Children', *British Journal of Disorders of Communication*, vol. 6 (1971) pp. 120–6

Carrington, E. 'An Appraisal of Assessment and Treatment Techniques of Handi-capped Children in Europe', unpublished manuscript, 1973

───── 'Handicapped Children in Europe', *Physiotherapy*, vol. 60, no. 10 (1974), pp. 315–16

Caspar, C. 'A View of Conductive Education from a Parent Who Went to Budapest', *Disability Now*, August (1984), p. 5

Choksy, L. *The Kodály Method: Comprehensive Music Education from Infant to Adult* (Prentice-Hall, Englewood Cliffs, 1974)

Clarke, J. and Evans, E. 'Rhythmic Intention as a Method of Teaching for the Cerebral Palsied', *Australian Journal of Physiotherapy*, vol. 34, no. 2 (1973), pp. 57–64

Clarke, P. 'An Evaluation of the Efficacy of Conductive Education', unpublished MSc dissertation, University of London, 1973

Conochie, E. 'Examination of an Assessment Schedule for Conductive Education', unpublished MSc dissertation, University of London, 1979

Cooper, L. *Conductive Education Newsletter* (Australian), no. 1 (1984)

Cope, C. 'An Evaluation of a Schedule for Assessment of Functional Ability in Cerebral Palsy', unpublished MSc dissertation, University of London, 1973

Cottam, P. 'Seminar on Conductive Education, Budapest, October 1984', unpublished manuscript, 1984
—— 'Evaluation of a Teaching Approach for Profoundly Multiply Handicapped Children Based on Aspects of the Conductive Education System', *Mental Handicap*, in press (1985a)
—— 'Conductive Education Bibliography', 2nd edn, unpublished manuscript, 1985b

Cottam, P., McCartney, E. and Cullen, C. 'The Effectiveness of Conductive Education Principles with Profoundly Retarded Multiply Handicapped Children', *British Journal of Disorders of Communication*, vol. 20, no. 1 (1985), pp. 45-60

Cotton, E. 'The Institute for Movement Therapy and School for Conductors, Budapest, Hungary', *Developmental Medicine and Child Neurology*, vol. 7, no. 4 (1965), pp. 437-46
—— 'Integration of Treatment and Education in Cerebral Palsy', *Physiotherapy* (April 1970), pp. 1-5
—— 'Improvement in Motor Function with the Use of Conductive Education', *Developmental Medicine and Child Neurology*, vol. 16, no. 5 (1974), pp. 637-43
—— *Conductive Education and Cerebral Palsy* (The Spastics Society, London, 1975)
—— *The Basic Motor Pattern* (The Spastics Society, London, 1980)
—— 'Conductor Training in England', *Conductive Education Interest Group Newsletter-3-Supplement* (1983)
—— and Kinsman, R. *Conductive Education and Adult Hemiplegia* (Churchhill Livingstone, London, 1983)
—— and Parnwell, M. 'From Hungary the Peto Method', *Special Education*, vol. 56, no. 1 (1967), pp. 7-11
—— and Parnwell, M. 'Conductive Education with Special Reference to Severe Athetoids in a Residential Setting', *Journal of Mental Subnormality*, vol. 14, no. 1, (1968), pp. 50-6

Cruikshank, W. *Cerebral Palsy, a Developmental Disability*, 3rd edn (Syracuse University Press, New York, 1976)

Czeizel, A., Métneki-Bajomi, J. 'Present Possibilities for the Prevention of Hereditary Mental Subnormality', *International Journal of Rehabilitation Research*, vol. 1 (1978) pp. 301-8

Czeizel, A., Lányi-Engelmayer, A., Kluber, L., Métneki, J., Tusnády, G. 'Etiological Study of Mental Retardation in Budapest, Hungary', *American Journal of Mental Deficiency*, vol. 85 (1980), pp. 120-8

da Fonseca, V. *Factores Psicomotores à luz de A.R. Luria* (Instituto de Investigaçao em Educaçao Especial, 1981)

da Silva, J. 'Conductive Education Practice and Theory', unpublished MEd dissertation, University of Birmingham, 1984

Danta, G. and Hilton, R.C. 'Judgement of the Visual Vertical and Horizontal in Patients with Parkinsonism', *Neurology* (Mineapolis), vol. 25 (1975), pp. 43-7

Denny-Brown, D. *The Basal Ganglia and their Relation to Disorders of Movement* (Oxford University Press, Oxford, 1962) de Parrel, G. *Traité de Reéducation* (Les Ordres de Chevalerie, Paris, 1946)

Dévény, A. 'A gyógyito mozgás megközelitése esztetikai uton, *Balneologia Rehabilitácio Gyógyfürdöügy*, vol. 1, no. 2 (1980), pp. 51–60

Dowrick, M. 'Conductive Education', *Special Education Bulletin* (Australia), vol. 20, no. 2 (1978), pp. 4–6

——— 'Peto Treatment Programmes', *Proceedings 10th Medical and Educational Conference of the Australian National Cerebral Palsy Association, Melbourne,* November (1979), pp. 16–20

——— 'Education and Habilitation – Rehabilitation Needs for Children. A Hungarian Approach', Address – Australian College of Rehabilitation Medicine, Second Scientific Meeting, Sydney, Australia (1982)

——— and Fairweather, L. 'The Peto Method', *Special Links (Australia)*, vol. 56, no. 1 (1979), p. 11

Duvoisin, R.L. *Parkinson's Disease – a Guide for Patient and Family* (Raven Press, New York, 1981)

Eccles, J.C. *The Understanding of the Brain* (McGraw Hill, New York, 1977)

Elliott, P.N.C. *et al.* 'Akinesia, Physiological Rest Mechanisms and the Basal Ganglia' in Rose, C.F. and Capildeo, R., *Research Progress in Parkinson's Disease* (Pitman Medical Publications, London, 1981)

Eöry, E. 'Conductive Education', *Hungarian Digest*, nos. 4–5 (1984), pp. 41–6

Evarts, E.V. *et al.* 'Reaction Time in Parkinson's Disease', *Brain*, March, vol. 104 (1981), pp. 167–86

Feuerstein, R. *Instrumental Enrichment: An Intervention Programme for Cognitive Modifiability* (University Park Press, Baltimore, 1980)

Finnie, N. *Handling the Young Cerebral Palsied Child at Home*, 2nd edn (Heinemann Medical Publications Ltd, London, 1981)

Flowers, K.A. 'Visual Closed Loop and Open Loop Characteristics of Voluntary Movement in Patients with Parkinsonism and Intention Tremor', *Brain*, vol. 99 (1976), pp. 269–310

Franklyn, S., Kohout, W., Stern, G.M. and Dunning, M. 'Physiotherapy in Parkinson's Disease' in Rose, C.F. and Coapildeo, R., *Research Progress in Parkinson's Disease* (Pitman Medical Publications, London, 1981)

Gal'perin, P. Ya. 'An Experimental Study in the Formation of Mental Actions' in Simon, B. and Simon, J., *Psychology in the Soviet Union* (Routlege & Kegan Paul, London, 1957), pp. 214–25

Gardner, L. and Price, A. 'Some Psychological Measures and Comments', *Special Education*, vol. 56, no. 1 (1967), p. 11

Geschwind, N. 'Disorders of Higher Cortical Functions in Children' in *Selected Papers on Languages and the Brain* (D. Reidel Publishing Co., Boston, Mass., 1974)

Gibberd, F.B. *et al.* 'Controlled Trial of Physiotherapy and Occupational Therapy for Parkinson's Disease', *British Medical Journal* 11 April (1981)

Goldberg, I.I. 'Comparative Special Education for the Mentally Retarded', *Proceedings of the 1st International Conference for the Scientific Study of Mental Deficiency* (Jackson, Reigate, 1968), pp. 147–54

Gordon, N. *Paediatric Neurology for the Clinician* (Heinemann Medical Books Ltd, London, 1976)

Halász, Z. 'Home Thoughts from Across the Channel (travel notes)' *New Hungarian Quarterly*, November (1965), pp. 100–13

Hallet, M. and Koshbin, S. 'A Physiological Mechanism of Bradykinesia', *Brain*, vol. 103 (1980), pp. 301–14

Hare, N. 'Group Treatment of Cerebral Palsy', *Physiotherapy*, vol. 65, no. 12 (1979), pp. 377–8

Hári, M. Address Given on Conductive Education, Conference on the 'Petö' Method,

Castle Priory College, Wallingford, Oxford, 1968
———— 'Lecture on Conductive Education', presented at Castle Priory College, Wallingford, Oxford, 1970
———— 'Conductive Education', presented in Oxford, 1972
———— 'Therapy or Teaching: A Discussion on Rehabilitation' in K. Akós (ed.) *Scientific Studies on Conductive Pedagogy* (Institute for Motor Disorders, Budapest, 1975a), pp. 41–55
———— 'The Idea of Learning in Conductive Pedagogy' in K. Akós (ed.) *Scientific Studies on Conductive Pedagogy* (Institute for Motor Disorders, Budapest, 1975b), pp. 10–17
———— 'Conductive Education and the Preparation of Children for Entry into Normal Schools', unpublished paper presented in Dublin, 1981a
———— 'Journées d'Étude sur la Méthode Petö', *Motricité Cérébrale*, vol. 2, no. 2 (1981b), pp. 92–5
———— 'L'Education Conductive', unpublished materials presented to the Brussels Conference, 1981c
———— and Akós, K. *Kónduktiv Pedagógia* (Tankönyvkiadó, Budapest, 1971)
———— and Tillemans, T. *Conductive Education* (Institute for Motor Disorders, Budapest, 1984a)
———— and Tillemans, T. 'Conductive Education' in D. Scrutton, *Management of the Motor Disorders of Children with Cerebral Palsy* (Spastics International Medical Publications, London, 1984b), pp. 19–35
Haskell, S. 'Visit to the State Institute for Conductive Education of the Motor Disabled and College for Conductors', unpublished manuscript, 1971
———— 'Conductive Education' in S. Haskell *et al. The Education of Motor and Neurologically Handicapped Children* (Croom Helm, London, 1977), pp. 168–74
Heal, L.W. *Evaluating an Integrated Approach to the Management of Cerebral Palsy* (Bureau of Education for the Handicapped, Washington DC, 1972)
———— 'Summary of 1972 Evaluation', *Exceptional Children*, vol. 46, no. 6 (1974), pp. 452–3
———— 'The Comparison of Intact Groups Using the Analysis of Covariance', *Journal of Special Education*, vol. 10, no. 4 (1976), pp. 427–36
Hebb, D.O. 'The Effect of Early and Late Brain Injury upon Test Scores and the Nature of Normal Adult Intelligence', *Proc. Amer. Phil. Soc.*, vol. 85 (1942), pp. 275–92
Holt, K. 'A Single Nurse, Teacher, Therapist', *Child: Care, Health and Development*, vol. 1, no. 1 (1975), pp. 45–50
Horváth, M. 'Education in Hungary between 1945 and 1972' in F. Arató *et al.*, *Hungarian Education* (Tankönyvkiado, Budapest, 1976), pp. 31–54
House, J. 'Breakthrough in Budapest. An Interview with Professor J. House about a Method for Helping Severely Disabled Children', *Ideas of Today*, vol. 16 (1968), pp. 110–14
Ignotus, P. *Hungary* (Ernest Bevin, London, 1972)
Jernqvist, L. 'My Head is in the Middle – 1', *International Cerebral Palsy Society Bulletin*, Winter (1977), pp. 2–3
———— 'My Head is in the Middle – 2', *International Cerebral Palsy Society Bulletin*, Summer (1978b), pp. 2–3
———— 'Preliminary Evaluation of Conductive Education. The Progress of 11 Children with Twelve Months Attendance at the Petö Unit at Ingfield Manor School', unpublished manuscript, 1978a
———— 'Visit to the Institute of Conductive Pedagogy, Budapest', unpublished manuscript, 1980a
———— 'Preliminary Evaluation of Conductive Education: The Progress of Twelve

Children with Two Years Attendance at the Conductive Education Unit at Ingfield Manor School', unpublished manuscript, 1980b

————— 'Rhythmic Intention – the Use of Speech in a Regulative Function', *Conductive Education Interest Group Newsletter*, no. 5, supplement (1984a)

————— 'New Sense of Unity in Budapest', *Disability Now*, December (1984b), p. 4

Kátona, F. 'An Orienting Diagnostic System in Neonatal and Infantile Neurology', *Acta Paediatrica Hungarica*, vol. 24, no. 4 (1983), pp. 299–314

Kearslake, C. 'Visit to the Institute for Conductive Pedagogy in Budapest', unpublished manuscript, 1970

Kelmer-Pringle, M.L. 'A Training College for Teachers of the Handicapped in Hungary', *Special Schools Journal*, vol. 44, no. 3 (1955), pp. 26, 29

Kinsman, R. 'Conductive Education Helps Adults too', *Therapy Weekly*, vol. 10, no. 8 (1983a), p. 4

————— 'Workshop on Parkinson's Disease', *Physiotherapy*, vol. 69, no. 1 (1983b), pp. 20–1

Knowles, J. 'The Peto Method is still more than a Transitory Idea', *Spastics News*, December (1968), p. 7

————— 'Experts Confer on the Peto Work', *Spastics News*, November (1970), p. 5

Kovács, C. (ed.) *Disabled Persons: Some Data about their Situation in Hungary* (National Association of the Blind and the Partially Sighted/Department of Public Education of the Ministry for Cultural Affairs, Budapest, 1981)

Kornhuber, H.H. 'Cerebral Cortex, Cerebellum and Basal Ganglia. An Introduction to their Motor Functions' in F.O. Schmitt and F.G. Worden, *Neurosciences Third Study Programme* (MIT Press, Cambridge, Mass., 1974)

Lányi-Engelmayer, A. 'Budapest Study on Mental Retardation (psychological aspects)', *Proceedings of the 3rd Congress of the International Association for the Scientific Study of Mental Retardation* (Polish Medical Publishers, The Hague, 1973) pp. 276–80

Lányi-Engelmayer, A., Katona, I. and Czeizel, A. 'Current Issues in Mental Retardation in Hungary', *Applied Research in Mental Retardation*, vol. 4 (1983), pp. 123–38

Laurance, J. 'A Miracle for Cripples?', *New Society*, 11 Oct. (1984), pp. 69–70

Lees, A.J. and Smith, E. 'Cognitive Deficits in the Early Stages of Parkinson's Disease', *Brain*, vol. 106 (1983), pp. 257–70

Leont'ev, A.N. *Problems of the Development of the Mind* (Progress, Moscow, 1981)

Levitt, S. *Treatment of Cerebral Palsy and Motor Delay*, (Blackwell Scientific Publications, Oxford, 1982)

Lomax, B. (ed.) *Eye-witness in Hungary: The Soviet Invasion of 1956* (Spokesman, Nottingham, 1980)

Loring, J. 'A Visit to the Petó Institute for Spastic Children in Budapest', *New Hungarian Quarterly*, Summer (1971), pp. 140–3

Luriya, A.R. *The Nature of Human Conflicts* (Liverwright, New York, 1932, paperback 1976)

————— 'The Directive Function of Speech in Development and Dissolution. – I Development of the Directive Function of Speech in Early Childhood', *Word*, vol. 15, no. 2 (1959a), pp. 341–52

————— 'The Directive Function of Speech in Development and Dissolution. – II. Dissolution of the Regulative Function of Speech in Pathological States of the Brain', *Word*, vol. 15, no. 3 (1959b), pp. 435–63

—————*The Role of Speech in The Regulation of Normal and Abnormal Behaviour* (Pergamon Press, New York, 1961a)

————— 'An Objective Approach to the Study of the Abnormal Child', *American*

Journal of Orthopsychiatry, vol. 31 (1961b), pp. 1–16
——— 'Brain and Mind', *Soviet Psychology and Psychiatry*, vol. 4, nos. 3–4 (1966), pp. 62–9
——— 'The Neuropsychological Study of Brain Lesions and Restoration of Damaged Brain Functions' in M. Cole and I. Maltzman (eds.), *A Handbook of Soviet Psychology* (Basic Books, New York, 1969), pp. 277–301
——— *The Working Brain* (Penguin Books, Harmondsworth, 1976)
Marmot, M. *et al. Epidemiology of Parkinson's Disease*. (Funded jointly by the Parkinson's Disease Society and the Tobacco Advisory Council, 1982)
Martin, J.P. *The Basal Ganglia and Posture* (Pitman Medical Publications, London, 1967)
Marsden, C.D. 'The Enigma of the Basal Ganglia and Movement', *Trends in the Neurosciences*, vol. 3 (1980), pp. 284–7
McCormack, A. 'Conductive Education Re-assessed', unpublished MSc dissertation, University of London, 1974
McPherson, I. and Sutton, A. (eds.) *Reconstructing Psychological Practice* (Croom Helm, London, 1981)
Mesterházi, L. *Budapest Anno . . .*, 2nd edn (Corvina, Budapest, 1984)
Mészáros, I. 'Kodály and Pedagogics', *Pedagogical Review: A Selection from the 1982 Issues of 'Pedagogiai Szemle'* (National Institute for Education, Budapest, 1983), pp. 177–80
Miller, C. 'The Speech Therapist and Group Treatment of Young Cerebral Palsied Children', *British Journal of Disorders of Communication*, vol. 7, no. 2 (1972), pp. 176–83
Mintram, A. 'Mental-Motor Acts as a Means of Differentiating Special Educational Need', unpublished MEd dissertation, University of Birmingham, 1981
Moreno, J. *Who Shall Survive? Foundations of Sociometry, Group Psychotherapy and Sociodrama*, 2nd edn, (Beacon House, Beacon, New York, 1953)
Morley, P 'Evaluating the Effectiveness of Conductive Education: An Investigation of a New Schedule', unpublished dissertation for the Diploma of Education of Physically Handicapped Children, University of London, 1979
Murai, M. *Guide to Warashibe-En.* (Warashibe Institute, Osaka, 1981) in Japanese
Norman, J.B. 'The Process of Implementing Educational Policy in Hungarian Policy and Practice', *Comparative Education*, vol. 16 (1980), pp. 121–7
Oxtoby, M. *Parkinson's Disease Patients and their Social Needs* (Parkinson's Disease Society, 1982)
Pancsovay, J. 'Relation of Learning to Teaching in Conductive Pedagogy' in K. Akós (ed.), *Scientific Studies on Conductive Pedagogy* (Institute for Motor Disorders, Budapest, 1975), pp. 24–30
Parkes, P. *Parkinson's Disease* (Update Postgraduate Centre Series, Roche, 1982)
Parkinson, J. *An Essay on the Shaking Palsy* (Sherwood, Neely and Jones, London, 1817)
Parnwell, M. 'Report of a Study Tour', unpublished manuscript, 1966
Patterson, C.H. *Theories of Counselling and Psychotherapy*, 3rd edn (Harper and Row, New York, 1980)
Pearson, L. 'General Education in Hungary and its Interface with Special Education', unpublished manuscript, 1984a
——— 'Tables of Information and Statistics', unpublished manuscript, 1984b
Pepper, D. 'A Comparison of the Philosophies and Rationales of the Petö and Doman Delacato Treatment of Brain Damaged Children', unpublished manuscript, 1981
Perry, A.R. and Das, D.K. 'Speech Assessment of Patients with Parkinson's Disease'

in C.F. Rose and R. Capildeo, *Research Progress in Parkinson's Disease* (Pitman Medical Publications, London, 1981)

Picq, L. and Vayer, P. *Education, Psycho-motricé et Arriération Mentale* (DOIN, Paris, 1976)

Purser, A. 'Peto Experiment is Working Well Here' *Spastics News*, October (1970), p. 2

Razran, C. 'Psychology in Communist Countries other than the USSR', *American Psychologist*, vol. 13 (1958), pp. 177–9

Richmond, W.E. 'Educational Planning in Hungary', *Comparative Education*, vol. 2, no. 4 (1966), pp. 93–105

Robertson, S. and Thompson, F. 'Speech Therapy in Parkinson's Disease: A Study of the Efficacy and Long Term Effects of Intensive Treatment', *British Journal of Disorders of Communication*, vol. 19 (1984), pp. 213–24

Roche Products Ltd. 'Parkinson's Disease and the Parkinsonian Syndrome' (1970)

Rodker, J. 'Remarkable Trials with Spastics', *The Times*, 7 June (1967)

Rooke, P. 'A Cross Disciplinary Approach to Teaching the Profoundly Retarded Multiply Handicapped Using Speech as a Regulator of Behaviour', paper presented at the *14th International Congress of Logopedics and Phoniatrics*, Edinburgh, Scotland (1983)

———— 'A Structured Teaching Programme for the Profoundly Retarded Multiply Handicapped Based on Certain Principles of Conductive Education', unpublished MEd thesis, University of Manchester, 1984

———— and Opel, P. 'An Approach To Teaching Profoundly Multiply Handicapped Children Based on Certain Principles of Conductive Education', *Mental Handicap*, vol. 11 (1983), pp. 73–4

Rosenbloom, L., Reynell, J., Horton, M.E. 'Conductive Education', *Physiotherapy*, July (1970), p. 315

Sacks, O. *Awakenings* (Picador, London, 1982)

Schubert, J. 'Verbal Regulation of Behaviour and Intellectual Development', *Learning Problems of the Cerebral Palsied*, Report of a Study Group, Pembroke College, Oxford (Spastics Society, London, 1964), p. 90-101

———— and Burland, R. 'The Performance of Cerebrally Palsied Children in the VRB Test', *British Journal of Social and Clinical Psychology*, vol. 12 (1972), pp. 96–7

Scott, S., Caird, F.I. and Williams, B.O. *Communication in Parkinson's Disease* (Croom Helm, London, 1985)

Seglow, D. 'A Report on a Study Tour to the Institute for Movement Therapy in Budapest', unpublished manuscript, 1966

———— 'Mother and Baby Groups', unpublished paper presented on course – Introduction to Conductive Education, Ingfield Manor School, Sussex, 1981

Semenova, K., Mastyukova, E. 'O konduktivnom vospitanii detei s tserebral'nymi paralichami v Vengerskoi Narodnoi Respublike', *Defektologiya* (1974/2), pp. 93–5

Sharron, H. 'Communal Road to Recovery', *Guardian*, 9 March (1983), p. 12

Siddles, R. 'Conductive Education, October–November', unpublished manuscript, 1976

Special Correspondent 'Fót Children's Town: The Makarenko Approach', *The Times Educational Supplement*, 27 November (1964), p. 974

Stern, G. *et al.* Akinetic Freezing and Trick Movement in Parkinson's Disease, *Journal of Neural Transmission*, suppl. 16 (1982), pp. 137–41

Stern, G. and Lees, A. *Parkinson's Disease – The Facts* (Oxford University Press, Oxford, 1982)

Sukhomlinskii, V.A. *On Education* (Progress, Moscow, 1977)

Sutton, A. 'Backward children in the USSR', in J. Brine, M. Perrie and A. Sutton

(eds.), *Home, School and Leisure in the Soviet Union* (Allen & Unwin, London, 1980), pp. 161–91
—— 'Conductive Education: An Annotated Guide', unpublished manuscript, 1982
——'The Problem of Conductive Education', unpublished manuscript, 1983a
—— 'A Theory of Speech Regulation: Some Problems of Utilising it in the Field of Conductive Education and a Possible Way Forward', *Conductive Education Interest Group Newsletter – 6 – Supplement*, 1983c
—— 'An Introduction to Soviet Developmental Psychology' in S. Meadows (ed.), *Developing Thinking* (Methuen, London and New York, 1983b), pp. 188–205
—— 'Conductive Education and the Birmingham Project', unpublished manuscript, 1984a
—— 'Conductive Education in the Midlands, Summer 1982: Progress and Problems in the Importation of an Educational Method', *Educational Studies*, vol. 10, no. 2 (1984b), pp. 121–30
—— and Nash, S. 'Experimenting with the Development of the Young Child's Verbal Regulation of his own Actions', unpublished manuscript, 1979
—— and Jernqvist, L. 'Some Preliminary Notes on a More Formalised Approach to the Speech Regulation of Motor Acts in Conductive Education', unpublished manuscript, 1982
Szàrka, J. 'The Science of Education, its Present Status, Goals and Institutions in Hungary', in *Hungarian Education* (Tankönyvkiadó, Budapest, 1976), pp. 101–10
Szekély, F. 'Didactics in Conductive Pedagogy' in K. Akós (ed.), *Scientific Studies on Conductive Pedagogy* (Institute for Motor Disorders, Budapest, 1975), pp. 18–23
Szentgyörgyi, T. 'Success of the Conductive Education Method: Outstanding Hungarian Achievements in Rehabilitation of the Handicapped' (*Buda Press*, release no. 27/77, 1977)
Tillemans, T. 'Co-ordination and Integration of Services in Selected Countries in Western and Eastern Europe', paper presented at the *3rd National Conference of the Canadian Association for Children with Learning Disabilities*, Moncton, NB, October 15–17, 1981
Titchener, J. 'The Peto Method, Conductive Education. An Investigation of a Method for Teaching Motor Disabled Children', unpublished BPhil(Ed) dissertation, University of Birmingham, 1982
—— 'A Preliminary Evaluation of Conductive Education', *Physiotherapy*, vol. 69, no. 6 (1983)
Todes, C. 'Disabilities and How to Live with them inside Parkinsonism . . . A Psychiatrist's Personal Experience', *The Lancet*, April 30 (1983), pp. 977–8
Toth, S. and Vajda, J. 'Multi-target Technique in Parkinson's Surgery. Meeting of the Amer. Soc. Stereotactic and Functional Neurosurgery', *Applied Neurophysiology*, vol. 43 (1980), pp. 109–13
Truax, C.B. and Carkhuff, R.R. *Toward Effective Counselling and Psychotherapy* (Aldine, Chicago, 1967)
Varnai, I. 'They are Taught Determination and Readiness to Act', *Hungarian Trade Union News*, vol. 11 (1984), pp. 14–18
Varty, E. 'The Petö Institute', unpublished manuscript, 1970a
—— 'Conductive Education', *Physiotherapy*, vol. 56 (1970b), pp. 414–15
—— 'What about the Integrated Child?' *Special Education*, vol. 62, no. 1 (1973), pp. 24–6
Vincze, E. 'Special Education in Hungary', *Proceedings of the International Conference on the Education of the Retarded, Goldsmiths College, London, April 1962* (*Forward Trends*, Summer/Autumn 1962), pp. 28–30
Wahler, R.G. and Fox, J. 'Setting Events in Applied Behavioural Analysis: Toward a

Conceptual and Methodological Expansion', *Journal of Applied Behavioural Analysis*, vol. 14, no. 3, Fall (1981), pp. 327–38

Wallace, M. 'What Kinds of Treatment Do Brain Damaged Children Need?' *The Sunday Times*, 23 Nov. (1975)

Wallon, H. 'L'Étude Psychologique et Sociologique de l'Infant', *Enfance*, vol. 3 (1959), pp. 297–308

Ward, L. 'What is the Damage in Parkinson's Disease?' *Practical Medicine, GP*, 21 January (1983)

Wendon, L. *The Pictogram System* (Pictogram Supplies, Cambridge, 1973)

Wilson, M. 'The Institute for the Treatment and Education of Patients with Motor Disability', unpublished manuscript, 1970

Wilson, M. 'Therapy at School for the Physically Handicapped', *Remedial Therapist*, 8 April (1983), pp. 4–5

Woods, G. *The Handicapped Child* (Blackwell Scientific Publications, 1975), pp. 106, 169–70

Woods, P. and Cullen, C. 'Determinants of Staff Behaviour in Long-term Care', *Behavioural Psychotherapy*, vol. 11, (1983), pp. 14–17

Young, P.M. 'Kodály as Educationalist', *Tempo: Quarterly Review of Modern Music*, special issue: Zoltán Kodály, Winter (1962–3), pp. 37–40

Yuan, S. *Humanistic Possibilities in Education for the Mentally Handicapped Child* (_____, 1984)

Zazzo, R. *Psychologie et Marxisme: la Vie et l'Oeuvre de Henri Wallon* (Denoël Gonthier, Paris, 1975)

Zibolen, E. 'On the Past of our Public Education', in *Hungarian Education* (Tankönyvkiadó, Budapest, 1976), pp. 11–30

Zöldi, L. 'Constant Reform: An Educational Debate', *Hungarian Review*, no. 9 (1978), pp. 5–6

INDEX